W. J. Corrigan Oct 191

BRAINS ON TUESDAY

NO BRAINS ON TUESDAY

THE COLLECTED WIT & WISDOM OF

KEITH DUNSTAN

SCHWARTZ & WILKINSON

Schwartz & Wilkinson
is an imprint of

Information Australia
45 Flinders Lane
Melbourne VIC 3000
Telephone: (03) 654 2800
Fax: (03) 650 5261

ISBN 1 86337 067 6

The National Library of Australia
Cataloguing-in-Publication entry

Dunstan, Keith.
No brains on Tuesday.
ISBN 1 86337 067 6.

I. Title.

082

Cover design Graphic Connection
Printed in Australia by Australian Print Group.

For Marie Rose.
Without her help on Monday
there would have been nothing on Tuesday

About the Author

Keith Dunstan is a veteran newspaper columnist. He has written for most of Australia's newspapers and magazines. He has specialised in exploding public myths, irritating politicians and putting in print the unexpected. It was surprising that he was not expelled from Melbourne for starting the Anti Football League while working for the nation's most football besotted newspaper, the *Sun News Pictorial*. He has been the curse of architects and builders while running the National Distrust, an organisation which gave awards for the least lovable buildings. This is his 24th book following his autobiography "No Brains At All". For the past six years he has written columns for the *Sunday Age* and the *Age* which features him on Tuesdays.

About the Illustrator

Jeff Hook is a national institution. It would be an understatement to say that more than a million people look for his cartoons every day in Melbourne's *Herald-Sun*. When he forgets to toss in his little hook there is an eruption the equivalent of a rail strike. Not only is he a good cartoonist he is an exceptional black and white artist. He started with the *Hobart Mercury*, and moved to the *Sun News Pictorial* in 1964. He has won fame by winning international awards for his cartoons in Belgium in 1987 and 1991.

Foreword

I discovered Keith Dunstan's journalism when I was a 13-year-old paper boy. At first light, halfway through my round, I would rendezvous with the milkman, swap a bottle of milk for a newspaper and together we would take a two-minute break mainlining on the fresh milk, fresh ink, the snorting of the cart horse and the crowing of the roosters. Our brief reading ritual focussed on the front pages of three papers, the sports pages and 'A Place In The Sun.' We felt we had started the day well.

I remember the *Sun News-Pictorial* published extracts from one of Keith's first books, *Supporting a Column*, about how the haunted crew of daily columnists went about filling the white space every day. The first paragraph of the first extract told how writing a daily column was like walking a tightrope across Niagara Falls; a little scary until you get used to it. It helped nudge my resolve to walk the path into the uncertain and perilous, but exciting world of journalism.

In the same piece, Dunstan described Herb Caen of the *San Francisco Chronicle* as perhaps the best columnist of them all. Fifteen years later, I met Dunstan for the first time in Caen's home town. Dunstan was the US West coast correspondent for the *Sun*; I was posted there for the *Age*.

By then, it had become clear why Dunstan admired Caen so much. Both are almost unbelievably prolific, having written six columns a week for more than 20 years. They share a love of their own cities as the best place in the world to live; they both have a marvellous ability to make the ordinary sound riveting, to identify and describe the ironies and idiocies of life. Above all, they enjoy nothing more than mocking themselves and their own struggles to come to terms with life's charms and silliness. In a profession not short on egos, Caen and Dunstan stand as mountains of humility. Readers repond to this. When I left San Francisco, I wrote a farewell piece to California that tried to describe the paradoxes of Lotus Land. Keith sent me a letter saying that he enjoyed the piece. It was one of the nicest letters that I have ever received, the journalistic equivalent of Paul Keating congratulating John Hewson on an economic policy initiative.

None of this is to under-estimate the power of Dunstan's journalism. He has been Melbourne's best-read columnist for more than 30 years and when he campaigns he usually wins. He has done more for causes like bicycling and historic building preservation than herds of thundering editorial writers.

He does it gently and has a lot of fun along the way. Few appointments have pleased me more than Dunstan coming to the *Age*, a place he described as his natural home at that stage in his career. In 200 years' time, Dunstan's columns and books will be used as a primary source by scholars trying to understand Melbourne's culture in the second half of the twentieth century. No journalist could wish for more.This book is part of it.

Michael Smith
Editor, The Age

Contents

Introduction

Sometimes in my blackest moments I compare my perfidy with that of Ron Barassi. After 34 years with Melbourne's *Sun News Pictorial* I ratted, I left to write a column for the *Age*.

Yet I was just a tiny figure in the town so my perfidy could never be compared with that of Ron Barassi. In 1964 Ron Barassi was captain of Melbourne, generally described as the greatest Demon of them all. He was Mr Football, and Melbourne, of course, was the most distinguished club, it invented the game of Australia Rules.

In 1964 Ron Barassi defected to become captain and coach of Carlton. It is generally agreed everywhere that the defection of Ron Barassi was the greatest news story of any kind in 1964. Every little kid in Melbourne as soon as he can walk is given a football sweater, offering curious allegiance to some club. In 1964 three out of four of those sweaters were exact replicas of official Melbourne sweaters and they all sported 31 on the back, Mr Barassi's number. Can you begin to imagine the impact of Mr Barassi's defection when he went to Carlton?

At the time I received an avalanche of letters of complaint. It is a mystery why they came to me. However if you write a daily column in a large city then you become a sort of public wailing wall. I had a remarkable number of letters from budgie owners. One lady at Lilydale reported how patiently she taught her budgie to say, "Come on, the Demons", "Kick a goal, Barassi", and "Good kick, Barassi". My advice was that budgies could be taught only at an early age. It would have been impossible for those budgies to understand Barassi's switch of allegiance. One can only presume all those budgies had to be strangled.

I repeat I was only a minuscule figure in town compared with Mr Barassi, but it was tricky nevertheless. I virtually grew up in the *Sun News Pictorial*. My father was the

General Manager, and I wrote the column "A Place in the Sun" from 1958 to 1984. There were several interruptions, but let me say I battled there for six days a week.

It was late 1985 when I received calls from Max Suich, chief editorial executive of the James Fairfax & Son and Creighton Burns, editor of the *Age*. Would I write columns for the *Sydney Morning Herald* and the *Age*? It seemed that I had written everything I could possibly write for the dear old *Sun News Pictorial*. The same stories, the same situations kept returning. I needed a change badly and this seemed a wonderful change of course, a new spur. I was now working for the *Sun* just as a contributor and besides, the enemy, Fairfax, were offering double the money.

So I committed the act of perfidy. I did a Barassi and defected. The first column for the *Age* and *Sydney Morning Herald* was in September and I was overcome with terrible guilt. What would my late departed father have thought? Would my mother have been ashamed? After all these years I had spurned the *alma mater*. Right in the depth of my miseries there was a telephone call. "Mr Carlyon wants to speak to you," said the voice. Les Carlyon was editor in chief of the Herald & Weekly Times Ltd. I waited for the caning.

He said: "Keith, hey, I wanted to offer my congratulations. I think you have done the right thing. So this is a call to wish you well. You will find them marvellous people at the *Sydney Morning Herald* and the *Age*."

It was one of the most timely telephone calls I ever received. But not all former colleagues were so kindly. I met a former chairman of the Herald & Weekly Times several weeks later. It was at a reception in the Arts Centre and Prince Charles was about to make a speech. The chairman looked at me sourly and said simply: "I used to like you but I don't any more."

So much for my perfidy. *No Brains on Tuesday* is a collection of articles most of them written for the *Age* on Tuesday. Many of them appeared in the *Sydney Morning Herald* and some appeared in the *Sunday Age*. The book is meant to be a small sequel to an autobiography, *No Brains At All* published by Viking O'Neil in November 1990. The title was a remark made to me by a kindly science teacher at Geelong Grammar, Charlie Cameron. He tried as hard as any man could, to teach me the mysteries of chemistry. Finally he gave up in desperation and said: "Dunstan you're stupid. You've no brains at all."

It is a problem I have battled with ever since.

Writing a column is a tricky business. Inevitably you find you are always running on empty. In a way it is like being a dairy farmer, no matter how you feel, no matter where you are, no matter if you have a pain in your back, or a hangover from yesterday, those cows still have to be milked. Ah, but the difference between being a columnist and a dairy farmer is this: the dairy farmer usually can find his cows. Mostly they will even walk up to be milked. The columnist has many days when he has no idea where he will find his cows.

I thought that writing a weekly or bi-weekly column would be easier. It did not turn out that way. Instead of having crises six days a week there were two crises a week. Yet it is a very curious thing and I am sure other columnists have had the same experience. You go away on holidays and you think, "Marvellous, I will have a whole bank of ideas when I return."

It does not work out that way. A great deal of nonsense has been written about writer's block. It is the deadline, the fear of the axe, that gets rid of the block. The deadline forces the dull brain cells into action and makes one think up new angles. It is odd indeed but often the best columns are written in times of greatest desperation.

After leaving the *Sun News Pictorial* we settled on the Mornington Peninsular. My office is a little bungalow out in the garden with a window overlooking a small vineyard. Once upon a time I invented an organisation called the Society Against Progress, which had the premise that nothing ever gets better, things only get worse. However, the invention of the microchip and the personal computer is an incredible exception. I have always been a gadget lover and even as early as 1979 I fell in love with the computer word processor. The computer made it possible to live permanently 90 kilometres from the office. I had only to hook up the modem to the telephone, my computer went into an embrace with big brother computer in Spencer Street, press a button, and by extraordinary black magic my column went on its way at 1200 words a minute.

So here are the columns which have been delivered that way. They have a certain emphasis on eating, drinking, domestic life, cricket and the agonies of creating a vineyard. One only hopes they have remained readable.

COLUMNS WHICH DRIP WITH NOSTALGIA...

1

Columns Which Drip With Nostalgia

Who Smashes the Beethoven, Bach and Brahms LPs?

Looking back on it my audio life has been a mess.

We heard this week that Polygram Records are not making any more LP discs. It's all tape or CD from now on. You will notice I am not saying compact disc. If you don't slip into the vernacular with CD you are nowhere.

All right, Polygram is one of the big ones. They produce Phillips, Deutsche and I don't know what else. Maybe other companies are still producing LPs, but like the wind up clock, and the 26 ounce beer bottle, it's practically all over.

All the new releases now come on CD or tape. They don't even think of LP. So there it is, all your lovely LPs, hundreds of them maybe, beautifully arranged in their specially designed LP sized cabinets, obsolete. To say nothing of that wonderful turntable, that the hi-fi shop assured you was state of the art in balance and majestic motion with the automatic pick up which would rise and fall with the delicacy and lightness of a snow flake, obsolete.

Barry Humphries, when he gets into one of his reminiscent moods, tells the tale when he worked for one of the record companies. He had just left Melbourne Grammar and it must have been back around the dawn of the fifties. The new LPs had come in. These LPs were the greatest miracle since the invention of the electric lamp. They would run for 40 to 45 minutes, you could put a whole symphony on one disc. But that wasn't all, there was a whole new dimension of sound so brilliant it was better than listening to the real thing.

All the old 78 rpm acetate discs were obsolete. Barry said they put him in a room and he had just one job. All day long he had to smash 78 rpms with a hammer. You will remember Beethoven's 9th took six or seven records. He worked his way through all Beethoven. Smash! Smash! Bach. Smash! Smash! Mozart. Smash! Smash! Brahms. Smash! Smash!...

After two days he was knee deep in acetate chips, the ruins of all the great artists and orchestras or Europe. He felt like a man in a mad surrealist dream, and although the pay was good, he quit.

Is there already some university student with the job of smashing LPs? Although I guess it's not so easy. They seem to be made out of some curious plastic. Perhaps you have to boil all Beethoven, Bach, Brahms and the entire orchestras of Europe in one great pot.

Just last year I went to our local hi fi shop and reported that it was time I acquired some new gear. The salesman, who was so elegant he could have been at Sothebys, said too many people made the mistake of not doing things properly. I am not very technical but I think he explained that I would need German speakers , equipment with upper woofer and lower woofer, transient and ambient speakers. I would need a tape deck, a CD player, a quality amplifier. Yes, I could probably get out of it for as little as $2500.

That was when I started to weep. It all made me dream of the beautiful days when the playing of gramophone records was so uncomplicated. There were no such things as discs and you never dreamed of laying down tracks.

I started with an HMV portable gramophone. Classical records were always 12 inches and pop records, 10 inch.

WHO SMASHES THE BEETHOVEN, BACH AND BRAHMS LPs

The HMV was all right for the 10-inchers, but for the 12-inchers you had to give it another wind halfway through and this had to be done with great delicacy so as not to upset Fritz Kreisler.

The next step forward was the electric turntable with the pick up arm. This was fantastic. We had a Mickey Mouse mantle radio. Astor made them and they cost 12 pounds 19 shillings and sixpence. If I remember rightly, you connected one lead to the top of the valve and the other to earth. I tell you, this was the ultimate in sound, as good as being in the Town Hall.

Yet it wasn't long before people considered Mickey Mouse radios not good enough. It was vital to go for a big radiogram complete with pick-up arm fitted with fibre needles.

We went one better. There was no question that the perfect sound was provided by cactus spikes. These had to be sharpened on mother's cardboard nail file. The spike had to be changed for every side. We cultivated so much prickly pear at our place it looked like an outback Queensland cattle station.

Then someone invented the automatic record changer with the sapphire tipped needle. It rendered all old 78s obsolete because they had to be in a special sequence. You put them in a stack of five or six and they would drop down one by one with an appalling clunk.

No sooner had we invested in this remarkable device than out came the microgroove LP which once again rendered our entire record collection obsolete. Oh yes, it's been just one plot after another.

So we proceeded, the fi got hi-er and hi-er. We proceeded on to stereo sound and even quadraphonic sound, where you needed four tracks and four speakers. My mate Alf had the best equipment, 60 watt output and no distortion whatever at full power. It was important, he said, to actually make the windows rattle to receive the full majesty of the highs and lows.

His sound, he insisted, was better than in any concert hall because he could place my ears in exactly the right position. My ears did not work for three days afterwards.

So now we start all over again. For a time we were in danger of switching to a new miraculous digital tape. Apparently that danger is over. CDs are in full command. You can see the ads: "From a mouse squeak to the triumphant sounds of Beethoven you can hear it all on a Nakamichi 550..."

But don't think you are through. I asked at Thomas' record centre in the city what was the next cab on the rank.

CDV, they told me. CDV? Yes, Compact Disc Video. You put on your disc and the orchestra comes up on your video screen at the same time. It should be here in a month or so, gold disc which will cost around $39.95. Except, of course, you will need a new player. They tell me the visual is superb, such definition far better than your normal TV, and such clarity of sound, you will have to get one.

But please don't boil up your old CDs. Keep them. I'm thinking of digging out my old HMV gramophone.

God Save Fish'n'Chips

Yes, I have waited patiently for nearly a week, expecting the thundering editorials but there has been none.

There have been few letters to the editor, no public outcry. You will remember last Wednesday in Canberra the Agricultural Outlook Conference was told that the fish and chip shops were dying. They were being killed off by the fast fooderies.

Come the year 2000 fish and chip shops would be just a memory.

Do we really want this to happen? The greatest things we should be grateful to the English are: Our legal system, the curious hysterical manner in which we conduct democracy, the game of cricket, and, not the least, fish and chips.

For more than a century fish and chips wrapped in newspaper has been a great example of British culture. Back in the 1950s when fast foods first began to sweep the United States some enterprising Poms opened English fish and chip shops in New York.

They advertised that these were genuine English fish and chips wrapped in English newspapers. It was a very serious enterprise and they imported copies of London's *Daily Mirror* to make it possible. For a time it was a huge success.

That has been the problem here. Nightly we are subjected to advertisements from McDonalds, Pizza Hut, Red Rooster and Colonel Sanders, but what promotion do you see for our beloved fish and chips? None.

For my money Melbourne fish and chips always were the best in world because - with a bit of luck - the fish was flake, surely one of the great under-rated eating fish. We used to think flake, purchased fresh on the pier at places like Lorne, then cooked in batter, was one of the glories of the summer.

I don't know which public relations genius back around the turn of the century first thought that it would be nicer, more tactful to housewifely sensibilities, if we called shark "flake" but at the time it seemed to work.

Melbourne became the shark eating capital of the world. Sydney never took to it like we did. In Sydney sharks tended to eat people, while in Melbourne people tended to eat shark.

But flake, to my mind, had a splendid firm texture, it came in good sized pieces, it had almost no bones, and it wasn't one of your anaemic tasteless fishes.

The time has come to give both flake and fish and chips some real promotion. I would suggest they forget the flake nonsense. Crocodiles are all the go in the Northern Territory. We are living in an age of horror and violence. Admittedly most of the flake we eat comes from a shark that is small and harmless, but shark for all that.

Let's advertise "Shark and Chips," "The Shark You Eat Today was Wiggling Yesterday in Port Phillip Bay". I think I would prefer they ate it out of copies of the *Age*, but if they wanted some panache they could import from London copies of *The Times* or even Mr Murdoch's *Sun* which always has an over-developed nude on page three.

At least our fish and chips wrapped in newspaper is educational, not like Mr McDonald's fishburger, which is merely an unnamed, anonymous fish wrapped in a roll so soft it can be eaten without teeth.

American fast foods are swamping everything. I would suggest that by the year 2000 other deeply indigenous Melburnian items will be in deep peril. It is well known that Melbourne is the meat pie capital of the world. We eat more pies than anyone else, even though Four'n'Twenty is trying to spread the message to California, Japan and even England.

This is the centre, we are greater pie lovers than Sydney, Brisbane or Adelaide. But don't under-estimate the danger of the pizza and the chicken invasion. The pie scene is not what it was and a whole generation is now with us that has lost that great art of how to eat a hot pie in a paper bag without spilling the sauce down your shirt.

Other fast foods deeply indigenous to Melbourne are also among the endangered species and should be given a grading by the National Trust. We were the crumpet capital. The crumpet had the superb high cholesterol skill of being able to absorb at least three times its weight in melted butter. Places like the long-departed Glaciarium used to serve hot crumpets, supercharged with melted butter then laden with honey.

Such items "ready to go" are now rare indeed.

The dim sim, too, we should recognise and put on the endangered list. Always there has been the suspicion that the dim sim never came from Canton or Shanghai, it was invented right here by the Melburnian Chinese.

For me it remains one of the most glorious dishes ever given to mankind. If the situation at our house is too desperate to do any cooking it is pure bliss to slip out for a dozen dim sims. This must be protected from the Sanders and the McDonalds.

You must appreciate there are varieties of dim sims. In Sydney they tend to prefer them fried. Here in Melbourne very sensibly we go for the classic, more succulent boiled dim sim, all pale and crinkly. Begging your pardon, it looks as if it has been cooked in a condom.

Other indigenous items born of Yarra-town are Vegemite, the Violet Crumble and the Cherry Ripe. Vegemite has survived and blossomed as a cult spread. It has become a mystic Oz thing essential to our survival, like betel juice is important to the highland tribes of Papua.

The Violet Crumble and the Cherry Ripe are under threat from the American Mars invasion and should be watched. I noticed all through the matriculation and university exam agony period there were advertisements on television announcing that the Mars bar was an essential item for sustenance and survival.

I would have thought that the indigenous Ocker Violet Crumble or Cherry Ripe was preferable. But in the mean time let us first save our shark and chips. Remember how the ice cream shops always sported an illuminated ice cream outside. I would suggest that every fish and chip shop have an illuminated shark. Put a little bite in your day.

Goodbye to the Daily at Dawn

The new creature, the *Herald Sun News Pictorial*, arrived on our doorstep yesterday morning.

GOODBYE TO THE DAILY AT DAWN...

There were mixed feelings. First sadness, an odor of death in the nostrils. Two newspapers not one had died in Flinders Street. Then there was irritation.

Where was the old chook on the masthead? Where was that famous rooster standing before the rising sun and the slogan "Daily at Dawn"?

Gone, that's what. And that title HERALD SUN. Why not SUN HERALD? As long as I can remember the employes at the Sun Pic had a feeling of deprivation. The Herald considered itself the elder brother, the intellectual superior and *Herald* men received all the perks.

The *Sun* didn't even rate in the company title. It was always the Herald & Weekly Times Ltd, but almost from the time of its birth it was the lusty child, the *Sun News Pictorial*, who made all the money and supported the parent.

Now even in death the *Herald* is still lording it over the *Sun*.

Please forgive me for talking this way because I was practically born in that Flinders Street building. My father, William Dunstan, was General Manager of the *Herald & Weekly Times Ltd*. He adored the place. He didn't think much of journalists, but he loved the machine and production staff.

His idea of heaven was to go down to the machine room just before noon when the first edition of the Herald was going to press. He would listen to the huge DRUM....DRUM...DRUM. DRUM....DRUM.... DRUM....DRUM as the presses began to roll. He didn't like Beethoven at all, but he thought the sound of a Goss printing press in full cry was the most perfect sound on earth.

From the age of 12, in school holidays I used to hang around Flinders Street pleading to be taken out with photographers or best of all, out on deliveries with Herald trucks. The Argus had brought out its new evening tabloid, the *Star*.

Sir Keith Murdoch, Rupert's father, had given orders that the *Star* must not be allowed to survive and it did not. One of the tactics was to make sure the *Herald* was always delivered ahead of its rival. Herald drivers were on bonuses if they won the race.

So the race down the Nepean Highway to Sorrento or the Geelong Road to Geelong was more exciting than anything that goes on at Calder. A kindly driver, Mr Milling, used to take me with him. At newsagents along the way there was no time to stop, we just hurled the bundles of *Heralds* out the back.

There were some very regrettable incidents and repercussions when ladies on the footpaths were hit by big bundles of City Extras.

I started as a cadet in 1946 and immediately I had to meet the extraordinary Sir Keith Murdoch. He insisted on interviewing all new cadets himself and furthermore he kept track of them and remembered their names.

One my assignments in the first month was to go through the *Sun*, the *Age* and the *Argus*, count the number of news stories in each, then list any that were not in the *Sun News Pictorial*. If the *Sun* was short on any good stories Sir Keith wanted to know why.

Bylines were almost unknown. Only the very great, Mr Clive Turnbull, Mr John Hetherington, Mr Allan Dawes or Mr Rohan Rivett received bylines. We called our seniors Mister, no bandying round of Christian names in those days. Furthermore Sir Keith insisted every reporter had to wear a good suit, tie and a hat. How could a reporter be taken seriously as a gentleman without a hat.

The *Sun's* leader writer was Mr Harrison Owen. Harrison Owen had a Max Beerbohm *fin de siecle* air about him. Legend had that he wrote plays and some of them had even been staged in London's West End. Mr Owen did not like the radio and I was told he didn't own one. Radio with all those dreadful serials only softened the brain.

Not long after I started Mr Owen retired and the *Sun* dropped its leading article. The theory was that its readers should be able to make up their own minds on political matters. From then on the *Sun* only ran leaders at times of dire emergency or on the eve of elections.

There was nothing politically complicated about those leaders, in their entire history the *Herald* and the *Sun* had backed only one side of the political spectrum.

When I started the *Sun* editor was Mr Jack Waters, or Promising Jack as they called him. Jack was always putting his hand on your shoulder and promising you a glorious future.

But it was Jack who helped push the formula that made the *Sun* such a success in the forties and fifties. Pictures, above all, were important. Jack loved to get a good picture and run it over the entire front page. Good photographers, like Bert Rodda, George Bugden, Frank Tolra and Lloyd Brown were more important than reporters.

As for reporters, we were told over and over, the *Sun* was a family paper, nothing vulgar, nothing horrid that might upset the family must ever appear. We were to use simple words and a *Sun* story should not go beyond 12 paragraphs. The Second Coming of our Lord might be worth 25 paragraphs but only for one or two days.

Above all, the *Sun* had to be warm and human. Mr Waters introduced a bonus system for the best human interest or funniest story of the week. The winning story he cut out of the paper and put it on the office notice board. That was worth an extra five pounds in one's pay envelope, as good as a week's salary. Winning that was better than riding a Cup winner.

Yet what surprises me particularly about those old days was the speed of production. When we were out on Court stories it was still possible to get results of cases into the *Herald* at 4.30 p.m. Those were the days of old fashioned hot metal. But come the days of computerised production everything seemed to slow down. If anything happened after 11 in the morning you were lucky to get it into the paper. I am sure this is one of the reasons for the *Herald's* demise. No news.

If I could just mention this in very small print. In the 1940s I used to double as a football writer and I reported top league matches. There was a twin miracle every Saturday afternoon. All the racing and football news used to come into the *Herald* around 5 p.m The final *Herald* would be on the streets at 5.30. The *Sporting Globe* was the same, and that was a true marvel, an entire newspaper was produced in half an hour with all the results produced accurately.

You might get away with errors in some parts of the paper but not in sport. Those papers disappeared and you wonder if they could be repeated now with all our modern technology.

I wish the brand *Herald Sun Pictorial* every kind of success, but I don't believe this 24 hour stuff. I used to buy the *Herald* every day, I wouldn't miss it. But I certainly wouldn't go to the newsagent to purchase another edition of what I already had in the morning.

I give the afternoon edition six months, the mid-morning three months and then it will be back to being a morning paper like all the others. But Mr Murdoch, would you kindly put the rooster back on top.

The Glory of Grass

The truth is I am deeply fond of grass and this is a last ditch appeal in its favor.

Not the ghastly hash kind, but honest, lovely old fashioned green grass.

Now if you were watching Wimbledon or television you would have noticed the glory of the grass tennis courts. Whenever things got dull they gave us a high shot and there was this panorama of grass activity going on for ever and ever.

You will have noticed further that Australians with their deep grass heritage always do better at Wimbledon. Frequently many of them get past the second round.

But with the advent of the National Tennis Stadium at Melbourne's Jolimont the tennis championships are played on a horrid surface called Plexipave which is heat absorbing and guaranteed on a hot day to barbecue players like a leg of lamb.

This means that grass tennis is virtually finished in this country, our grand slam tournament is plexipaved yet we still have an organisation which laughably calls itself the Lawn Tennis Association of Australia.

This, of course, is tragic. When I was a small boy, back in the days of Bromwich, Vivian McGrath and Adrian Quist - Good Grief - I can even remember Jack Crawford when he wore long whites - yes, back in those days there were grass courts scattered everywhere through the suburbs.

We had several well-off friends with grass courts, and we would assist with the mowing and rolling on Friday evenings. The smell of fresh cut grass was one of those divinely created odours perhaps second only to fresh ground coffee.

On hot days there was nothing to beat grass. You could play in your bare feet and feel the cool grass between your toes.

And there was a marvellous charm about grass. We had a wonky machine which laid down the chalk lines, so that with the passing of the years the lines got wider and wider. Also you were never precisely sure of the size of the court. As for a bad line call, a ball could pick up a flash of white anywhere. Over 20 years of line laying, a chalky line could be anything up to a yard wide.

Just after World War 2 the developers discovered that a tennis court was just space enough for erecting four units of Own Your Owns. So the lovely grass courts we knew became sinister blocks with names like Beverly Mews or

Buckingham Close. Close always meant too damned close to your neighbors.

This murder of the domestic court was the beginning of the end for Australia as a world tennis power. *En tout cas* became trendy and those courts which didn't go under brick and concrete went under gravel.

But the Americans wreaked even greater havoc. I think it was on the second or the third day that Jehovah created grass. But in the early 1970s the Americans decided he had done a bad design job.

Grass had to be watered, fertilised, weeded, nurtured. It was hideously slippery in the wet and tended to tear under running feet. So they invented hard wearing plastic grass which did not have to be watered and when damaged could be replaced precisely like carpet.

It took over in baseball stadiums, football stadiums and (shudder) in some areas they even used it for bowls. Synthetic grass, plastic, rubber, took over everywhere. Grass is still available in some parks but I have the feeling it is discredited and it may disappear altogether in the United States.

There are no major tennis tournaments on grass in the U.S., none in Europe and soon Wimbledon will be the last repository of grass left on earth, a curiosity, a sight to see like the Elgin Marbles or Stonehenge.

I think the LTAA is showing an incredible lack of foresight. We should be putting in more grass courts, not taking them away. At least when Davis Cup matches are played on grass we have a better than average chance of winning. I mean, the last time we won the Davis Cup was at Kooyong on grass and that curious Jeohovah made substance did much to confound the Swedes.

I think the National Trust, the Historic Buildings Council, the Ministry for the Environment, even Bob Hawke, should step in now and declare grass a sacred surface, before it is too late.

We do have one or two small pockets where grass tennis is still played. Kooyong, nigh forgotten, battles on bravely with grass. Meantime, unless the LTAA is prepared to act sensibly with an eye to the future of Oz tennis, it should change its name to the Plexi Tennis Association of Australia. Or even the Perplexed.

COLUMNS ALLIED TO THE GRAPE AND ASSOCIATED BEVERAGES ...

2

Columns Allied to the Grape and Associated Beverages

Let Us Spray

It was John C. Brown, the master vigneron from Milawa, who put his hand on my shoulder and said: "Keith, I will give you some very good advice, it is much easier to get it out of the bottle."

That was three years ago. Foolishly I didn't take note. How could one resist the romance of it all, the wonder of being able to sample one's very own wine, to gaze at one's very own label.

We went ahead and planted 1200 *pinot noir* vines.

Then I remembered a line I once read in the Readers Digest: "Farming always looks better through a car window."

We hadn't realised that every vine virtually was a child. It had to be fed, watered, clipped and trained. Well, more than trained, it had be trellised. I mean Toorak matrons get their hair dyed, teased, twisted, permed and perfumed by Lillian Frank. It's even worse with a grape vine. Every cane has to be trained, nurtured, fertilised, pinned, put into its proper position on the wire.

The tender little things also have to battle against weeds. There are about 240 varieties of weeds all of which are available in our vineyard. Their speed and vigor of growth is beyond belief and every one of them tries to smother your vine.

I remembered one year going to the Department of Agriculture display at the Royal Show. An Ag. scientist was there with a display of all the common weeds, he had them all growing there in boxes and he was watering them one by one, ragwort, oxalis, chickweed, patterson's curse, copeweed, bindy-eye, potato weed, nettles..."

I said to him: "Were they difficult to grow?"

He looked at me with sad eyes: "Were they ever. When you want to grow weeds they are the very devil. The cranky things kept withering up and dying."

I thought as much. Everything to do with agriculture is designed to be difficult. The next problem after weeds was diseases. All right, grape vines are subject to even more pests and diseases than two-year-old humans, all of which require sprays and come with awesome names like chlorpyrifos, dithianon, and chlorothalonil. And the cost? No wonder chemical companies are the richest in the world. The stuff invariably costs about six times as much as Johnny Walker Black Label.

All this is leading up to tell you about Black Monday. The agricultural experts said after the damp soggy Spring, conditions were perfect for almost everything horrid; it was vital at once to spray against black spot, downy mildew, mites and caterpillars. After that look out for powdering mildew and bunch rot.

I waited a week for the right conditions; when it wasn't raining there were 70 knot gale winds. All right, the forecast was good, so I got up at 5 a.m. before the gales got under way, did my mixing, filled the backpack spray and then sprayed with Delan to get rid of the diseases and Lorspan to get rid of the bugs. It was barely light when I started but brilliant sunshine when I finished.

I returned to the garage, started to return canisters to the chemical cupboard and noted something very strange - the square plastic bottle of Delan was still there and in my hand was an exactly similar square plastic bottle of Surflan. How could that be? The terrible truth began to seep into my brain.

Surflan is a pre-emergent spray for killing weeds. Theoretically it stops weeds before they get out of the ground. Ohhh! Nooooooo! I rushed to the bedroom where my wife Marie was just getting up, and blurted:

"I have just done something absolutely terrible."

"What, dear? Tell me about it."

"I have just sprayed the entire vineyard with weed killer."

That sank in, she said nothing, so I added what should have been the right cross.

"What's more, I thought I was doing the right thing. I sprayed all your lovely roses with the same stuff."

She should have committed homicide at that point, but she was marvellous. She took over like General Eisenhower organising the Second Front. "Don't worry about it," she said, "there has to be an answer."

Soon she was organising. We pulled out every hose we could find. She called up friends, good neighbours, fellow vine growers, who came round with knapsack sprays. How could you exist without good friends. For three hours we hosed and sprayed down every leaf.

But even then work wasn't done. I hadn't disposed of the enemy. I had to spray with the chemicals I should have sprayed with in the first place.

That took the rest of the day.

All this happened three weeks ago, roughly the period it should take for a decent weed killer to destroy the lot. Well, all 1200 vines have survived. Indeed they have taken on the most extraordinary luxuriant growth and look very beautiful indeed. They look particularly lovely in the late evening as we gaze through the living room window and the western sun is shining through the leaves.

As for the roses, White Wings, Chianti, Marguerite, Tuscany Superb and Alba Maxima, have never been more prolific. They just keep on flowering.

Grapes are forming. All we have to do is cope with the next problem. I mentioned General Eisenhower. O.K. it has been a remarkable season for birds. Word has got around, rosellas, sulphur crested cockatoos, silver eyes, starlings, every conceivable type of bird, brown, black and brindle is gathering forces now like Rommel's Panzer divisions waiting for the feast. Many of them have even built nests under our eaves, bivouacs waiting for action.

Will any grapes remain? I have tried to work out eventual production costs. I think it will be around $100 a bottle.

But I am very worried about next season. I will have to get rid of those chemicals. Do you think it would be all right to plant garlic and place a religious symbol between each vine?

Getting the Bird

We need psychological help. We are in the midst of a deep emotional crisis over birds.

At our house we have always been bird lovers. We try to identify every bird that comes on the property. We have the beautiful Gould League bird charts pinned up all round the walls of the spare room. So when a New Holland Honey Eater does his incredible acrobatic stuff hanging upside down to get his feed we have his type exactly identified.

We provide splendid washing facilities for all birds, ornate Grecian bird baths, constantly supplied with fresh water so that everything from rosellas through to magpies can go through their daily ablutions.

We hang ceramic bowls of seed from the branches of the wattle in the hope of inviting every type of thrush, tit, fantail or wren that might come our way.

GETTING THE BIRD...

But the worst has happened. Suddenly birds have become, if not the enemy, creatures which are very faintly popular. There was the time when our district was all herefords, apples and chooks. Now everybody is switching to vineyards.

There is nothing that a parrot, a starling, or silver eye, adores more than a succulent fat bunch of grapes. They like shiraz, they love rhine riesling, they are very partial to pinot noir as a dessert and will fly through an artillery barrage to get to a choice acre of chardonnay. It's unbelievable. A squadron of starlings can go through 200 grapes in half a minute.

I tell you, when you have slaved all the year, pruned, weeded, irrigated, fertilised, trained your vines patiently into exquisite canopies, sprayed against invading weeds, sprayed against caterpillars, sprayed against downy mildew, prayed for sunshine, prayed for rain, your bird devotion dies in a hurry, when the attack squadrons move in and take the lot.

Take John up the road. He was very kindly at first. He and his wife built a gorgeous scarecrow. It was most realistic, known to everybody as Bob Hawke. Bob might have deterred one of two birds back last January, but now they treat him with indifference, even contempt. I have suggested to John they might do better if they replace him with Paul Keating, or even better, Wilson Tuckey.

Finally he became fed up with the ineffective Mr Hawke. He started warfare, every day at dawn and every night at dusk. He has a shotgun and you can buy special cartridges call "Frite." First they go off "Phut", then there is a three second fuse delay, and they go off with an almighty "Bang" and a cloud of smoke.

Well, last week "Frite" was failing utterly. At first the birds scooted for their lives. It was a bit like the Toorak folk carting their possums across the Yarra into Hawthorn. John blasted his crows and parrots. They took off to Fred's place up the road. Fred blasted again so they settled on Leon's vineyard. Leon gave them a go and off they went to Reg's place.

Then they returned back to John's vineyard. By last Friday the birds were a complete wake-up. The scare delay before they returned became shorter and shorter, until finally they were like triumphant Spitfire pilots doing victory rolls. Those Frite shells cost a dollar a time.

Of course, if you have a 1000 acres under vine it doesn't matter so much. You have so many grapes you can spare a few for the birds, it's the small growers who suffer. Reg has tried putting up fake hawks on strings attached to tall poles. They sail, swoop and swing across the vineyard. That wheeze works for some of the dumber birds.

A variation of the attack is rocket warfare. He puts rockets into champagne bottles, lights the fuse and lets them go right across the top of the vineyard, so sometimes it is like the last night at Moomba. That too is expensive.

He confesses absolutely the best thing is to get his wife to stand out in the middle of the vineyard and bang saucepan lids. Wives, regrettably, will only do that for a certain length of time.

You can buy a spray which makes the grapes taste disagreeable to the birds. Sadly it also makes the grapes disagreeable to humans, so we have abandoned that. Almost everybody has gone for scare guns. They are gas operated. You set them up in the vineyard and they go off automatically, say, every 10 minutes or so. Our district sometimes sounds like the dawn artillery barrage at Ypres or on the Somme.

The trouble with that system is the neighbors get upset. You have to go round and compensate every one of them with a case of wine.

Oh they're crafty (the birds not the neighbors). The black birds and those pretty parrots actually hide in the trees until you have walked past. Joe has covered his entire vineyard in a sort of permanent cage. It has cost him a fortune. The trouble is if any birds do get inside they are there for ever.

Most growers are now going for nets. You spread plastic nets over every row of vines. It doesn't defeat the little silver eyes. They nick in underneath and you don't even know they are there until the grapes are all gone.

Our neighbor has gone for desperate measures. Not only has he spread nets over all the grapes, his devoted wife, family and friends, have sewn all the nets together underneath, a labor of grape devotion which has taken three weeks.

This week-end, as one bird lover to another, I played a dirty trick. I muffled the telephone and called up:

"It is Fred Avion here, honorary secretary of the Gould League of Bird Lovers. We are making a survey in the district of the birds you have seen and admired this past month. Could I have your comments?"

There was a long pause at the end of the phone, a dreadful silence. Then he said:

"I'd kill all the bastards."

Getting the Bird (Part 2)

The vintage, the grape picking and the battle of the birds is now at its height on the Peninsular.

You will remember a month back in the midst of our agonies we formed the Ghould League of Birds. The Ghould League was the protection society for grape growers who were feeding the seeming millions of starlings, blackbirds, parrots and silver eyes.

There were a number of remarkable calls and letters. From Gingin Western Australia we heard from "Invent Australia" which has sold many thousands of its Bird Deterrent Unit at $74 each. This is a revolving weather vane of reflecting mirrors designed to dazzle the birds with flashes of sun. What happens when you don't have any sun?

We have sent for three of those, but they will not arrive until after the big feed is all over.

A gentleman from Tascott NSW told us that the answer is to grow sun flowers between the rows. When the birds see the huge yellow flowers always they will eat the flower seed before the grapes.

From Balranald a farmer told us: "Give them bowls of fermenting gruel and keep them all drunk. After a few hangovers they will never come back." My experience is that hangovers have never been a deterrent to humans.

Southport Queensland was a real darling. He gave us a design for a sheet of chicken wire connected to positive and negative electricity leads. In the centre was a tin plate, an enamel bowl of sweet bran, and when the birds landed, they made perfect contact...ZAP!

If I were a nervous type and wanted to sooth the greenies, he suggested that I could reduce the charge to 110 volts.

In the end we went for no fancy solutions. We netted the really productive rows with a brand of yellow plastic netting. As reported earlier, we covered individual bunches of pinot noir with panty hose. Indeed we went round the district pleading for used panty hose and came up with some very attractive specimens, green, yellow, blue and even sexy black. You get three bunches to a leg.

The panty hose was a fantastic success, but with the yellow netting we lost 80 to 90 per cent of our grapes. Alas the quality was not good enough and it stretched too easily. We put the nets all over the vines and clipped them underneath. The tiny silvereyes were unbelievable. You could watch them wriggling inside, first one leg through the web, then the other and - bewdee - inside. They just make a needle peck into every grape.

The starlings and blackbirds can't get through the net but they push it against the grapes, then do the job. They are enthusiastic early eaters. I would get up at dawn and run up and down and shriek: GEEDAWAY YOU LITTLE BUGGERS.

The man who delivered the papers would blush as he heard this daily fuss.

Sometimes the larger birds would get tangled in the vines. Last Wednesday we found a blackbird, limp. Was it dead? I freed it from the net and it gave a faint shudder.

My wife said: "We can't leave the poor thing like this, the dogs will get it." I won't say we gave it mouth to mouth resuscitation but we did everything else. We put it in an intensive care unit at the back of the house. We gave it a light spray with water, put it in cool shade and would you believe the ghastly grape filled object made a complete recovery.

When foolishly I reported the tale to our neighboring vigneron he was shocked. "This is an outrage," said he. "I will report you to the committee and have you expelled from the Ghould Birds. I bet that bird went straight over to eat at my place."

O.K. we had our vintage at Easter, such grapes that were left. We had to go over every bunch and pick off all those that had silver eye puncture marks. Yes, once a silver eye has popped in his hypodermic, terrible bacteria can result.

We put the grapes in a large plastic rubbish tin and you appreciate, of course, that the classic method from ancient times is to have the fruit foot-tramped by virgins. Maidens doing the job ensures that the wine has absolute purity.

We do not have a great many virgins available on the Peninsular, but we managed to arrange some granddaughters, Hannah, 7, and Isabel, 4.

They took off their dresses, shoes, socks, wearing only their under things they hopped into the plastic bin and started squelching. Actually it took rather a long time. My recommendation would be to look for heavier virgins, 80 or 90 kilo maidens would be wonderful.

However, these girls did a splendid job and Hannah found it such fun, she didn't want to get out. There was no worry about the red juice around her knees, the strawberry squash between the toes. She thought it was lovely.

A little sulphur, some warm yeast all these things went in. The laundry is the temporary winery and some fine bubbling and very noble aromas are coming from that part of the house. There are suggestions that we should make some pinot blanc, some white wine, and in that case we will need to take over the refrigerator and put a bin there for controlled fermentation. Clothes washing and eating might have to be delayed for four or five days.

And again if the pinot noir fermentation doesn't reach the right temperatures I will have to take electric blankets off the bed to give the brew an extra boost. Wives need to be very understanding at vintage time.

The next step will be to determine a name for the wine. Do you think Pinot Panty Hose would be rather fetching?

This story is rather like Neighbors, Home and Away, or even East End. You might even hear some more gaudy episodes...

What Hope for the Humble Drinking Man

From the Angelic ranks goes forth a groan,
How long, O Lord, how long?

Macaulay.

Yes, O Lord, they are at it again. Is there any hope at all for the humble drinking man?

The persecution began with 6 o'clock closing. The wowsers agreed that the drink was the cause of all evil and it would be no trouble at all to defeat the Kaiser if only they closed the hotels at 6 p.m. We defeated the Kaiser but we kept hotels closed for 50 years.

How long, O Lord, how long?

It was a sin for a cafe or a restaurant to have a wine licence. Such establishments which could serve drinks with meals had a curfew. Remember how you would be half way through your Steak Diane then come 8 o'clock they whipped the glasses off the table?

How long, O Lord, how long?

The new refinement was .05. Driving down the Pt Nepean Highway. "Pull over Driver," and one had to blow into a little bag.

A further refinement was the dry area the MCG. A few rowdies were hollering at the game, but we all had to share the blame. Through the Outer there was a two can limit.

How long, O Lord, how long?

We became the most thoroughly taxed drinking nation on earth. We contribute 2.3 billion dollars to the Commonwealth Government every year. But that's not all, there is a further gift of $100 million to the Victorian Government in licence fees. We do so much more than the non drinking classes. More than half of every glass is a kindly contribution to Government.

In 40 years of drinking I think I have contributed at least half a frigate or maybe the wing of an F18.

How long, O Lord, how long?

This week we are being assaulted again. Dr Carmen Lawrence, the new premier of West Australia, has called for a national ban on advertising. Senator Janet Powell of the Democrats is bringing a bill before the Senate to do just that.

What's more our Victorian Minister for Police and Emergency Services, Mr Sandon, is threatening a levy, a new tax on alcohol, to pay for police and correctional services. He says 40 per cent of assaults and 50 per cent of rapes are alcohol related.

Back in the 19th century our grandparents had the naive belief that if only man would banish alcohol, crime would cease, the gaols would be emptied, lunacy would disappear, husbands would remain faithful to their wives, the enormous wealth spent on drink would be spent on culture, and in the new, splendid dry community, Eldorado would be at hand.

Nothing like that ever happened anywhere, but there are those who still cherish this 19th century dream. It is a strange over-simplification to blame all sin, all road carnage on alcohol. Do the 99 per cent who handle alcohol wisely always have to live in guilt for the one per cent who do not know how to use it?

I say 99 per cent because when it comes to those breathalyser tests we have a pretty good record. The police find that 99.7 per cent of us are below the .05 limit.

Just as a humble user I would like to say a word in its defence. From the time I was born I was told alcohol was a sin. My father, against the wishes of his father, did not think so. From the age of 14 on he started giving me the occasional glass of wine. It has been one of the great joys of my life and I don't want to be penalised at every turn by some misguided politician.

At our place every evening come six o'clock we have our glorious ritual, I have a bottle of beer, my wife has a Scotch. It is the happy hour, the summing up, we discuss the good things, the bad things that happened during the day. Maybe it would go just as well on lemonade or barley water, but I doubt it. The alcohol is a relaxing balm and, besides, it tastes better.

Then whenever friends are around we open a bottle of wine. I don't think I have ever extracted a cork without a sense of anticipation and excitement. This is because no vintage is ever the same, no grape is quite like any other, and if you are looking for the extraordinary glory of creation you get it in the magic subtle variations of a glass of riesling, chardonnay or, ah yes, cabernet sauvignon.

There is not the slightest doubt in my mind of the health benefits of a glass of wine every day, and most of my mates in the wine industry seem quite capable of living for ever.

But now the Demon Drink is under assault again, curiously at a time when consumption is going down. Now look here, the demon, if that's what you like to call it, hit its peak in 1975-76. Australians were drinking 9.8 litres a head of pure alcohol. It is down now to 8.7 litres and that is a mighty drop, better than 10 per cent.

Take beer. In 1975-76 we drank 140 litres a head. It is now 110 litres. There used to be a theory beer consumption would never fall, it would only go up, but that is a drop of 21.4 per cent and the big reason why the beer producers shifted their activities overseas. But those figures don't tell anything like the real story. Back in 1975 we had no interest in low alcohol beers and the consumption then was all full strength beer. Now, don't you see, 18 per cent of all our beer is low alcohol.

Wine consumption is down eight per cent, particularly with the large volume cask wines. Yes, there is a change in the way people handle their drink and I see it in the people around me. I am fascinated by the young, particularly the young journalists. They are a abstemious lot, compared with the rambunctious men of my day. We used to have a group called the Morning Tea Club, and always they would gather in the Back Bar of the Oriental Hotel at 11 a.m.

There was a famous finance writer who always had his first beer at Young & Jackson's on his way to the office. Carefully he would time his arrival by train at Flinders Street for 9 a.m. That was when they opened the doors.

Mr Sandon, don't slug us with yet another tax. Could we ask precisely what you are doing with all the money you are peeling of us already? We don't want to pay more for what we consider our humble joy. Nor do the producers want to charge more. You are close now to destroying the wine industry. Half the producers in Victoria are teetering on bankruptcy.

One might ask whether you are concerned about our health or the billion odd dollars that the Victorian Government has let go astray in recent years.

How long, O Lord, how long?

The Romance of the Home Bottler

You are looking at a crazy character who one time possessed over 5000 home bottlings.

Not peaches, plums, or skinned tomatoes, but top quality riesling, cabernet, shiraz and merlot, all splendidly bottled corked and labelled.

It was the wonderful dream time era of home bottling and I can date for you, almost precisely, the time that it all came to an end, 1969-70.

The reasons? Australians suddenly discovered wine as an alternate to beer. The wine producers, who had suffered so long, did not need to sell in bulk any more, they put all the good stuff in bottles themselves. And, besides, along came the cask, the odious plastic bag.

One is telling you all this, because an extraordinary thing has happened, home bottling is booming again. Oh, the reasons are obvious. One, Mr Keating has discovered that wine, like whisky, gin, beer, and rum, is a glorious device for taxing human beings. Two, consumers in places as far apart as London, Hong Kong, Tokyo and New York, have found that Australian wine is good to drink. So the prices have gone berserk.

But there are other and more subtle reasons. Back in the dream time we were referring to earlier, you could name the available vineyards on a couple of hands. Now they run into hundreds, no thousands. For example, we live on

Victoria's Mornington Peninsular, where 20 years ago we had nothing but chooks and apples. Now I can count at least 90 vineyards.

Wine is now being produced in quantities and varieties we never saw before and there is excellent stuff available for the home bottler. But for a moment, just like the best movies, do you mind if we indulge in some flashbacks?

I began home bottling back in 1960. We used to get our wine from Brown Bros at Milawa, from Eric Purbrick at Chateau Tahbilk and A.P. Birks in South Australia. We used to have an old 18-gallon beer keg. We would send up the barrel to John Brown or Mr Purbrick and he would send it back full, to our local railway station. Heaven knows how many trips that barrel made.

I ask you to believe that we bottled superb wines for a shilling or around 10 cents a bottle, plus two cents for the cork. They were very good indeed and I can prove it because I still have some of those treasures from the early sixties. The most blissful occasions were the bottling parties. Our leading bottler, was Nick, who dealt in the big time, hogsheads. A hogshead would hold around 315 bottles.

All right, Nick had a superb system. He would put his hogshead on the concrete roof of his garage. A large plastic tube ran from the barrel into a refined, begging your pardon, lavatory cistern, controlled by a ball valve.

From the lavatory cistern ran two more tubes complete with taps, so we bottled two bottles at a time, and as we bottled there would be a back up team with brass corkers, corking like crazy. Round about 11 p.m. if you were in Nick's street, you could witness team members pushing home loads of wine in wheelbarrows, a very romantic sight.

Some of us were snobs. We would go to the city's leading restaurateurs like Herman Schneider and Leon Massoni and collect all their empties. Always there would be a vast pile on Sunday mornings. How nice it was to put our home bottled wine into a Lafite, Margaux, Haut Brion or maybe a late departed Mouton-Rothschild.

Nick was a reverse snob, despised that sort of thing. He had an 'in' where he could get brand new turpentine bottles. If you are old enough, you will remember, they used to come in a triangular shape. One time, with incredible courage, Nick took one of his home bottlings into Melbourne's august Florentino. The shocked head waiter took away the turpentine bottle for uncorking, holding it with two fingers, as if it were a dead rat.

I won't say we didn't have disasters. I used to own one of those bottles like old time pharmacists display in their windows. It held about 20 gallons. One sunny February I took it to Milawa and John Brown filled it with his best cabernet-shiraz-mondeuse, an utterly gorgeous blend.

We were almost home, driving through Carlton, and I heard terrible crack in the back seat; expanding gases with the heat had blown my beautiful bottle. Can you imagine 20 gallons of red wine let loose in an FJ Holden? All I could do was pull up at the kerb, open the back door and it flowed like a waterfall into the gutter.

An Australian would have laughed. But an Italian was standing there and he was almost in tears: "Mama Mia, What a tragedy." Oh, it was he who understood our grief at that moment. Losing the wine was bad enough, but it soaked right down into that bowels of that Holden, and the whole car for the next five years had the odour of an old keg.

Storage was the problem in those days. My theory was this; a gentleman should purchase twice as much wine as he could drink, so that always there would be bottles nicely maturing for his old age. So, Heaven forgive us, we had bottles stored under the children's beds. We bought old wardrobes, put them in the garage and filled them with wine. We went without wood so that we could fill the wood shed. The wood shed was not such a good idea. That little weevil, the cork borer, got into the corks. One day I discovered seeping wine coming out of the cartons. The beetles were drinking more than I was.

I went to that great wine expert, Dan Murphy: "Dan, what do I do now?" "Simple, said Dan." "You recork the lot." So one incredible week-end we had to recork 5000 bottles with even the children in the production line. That's another of my sins, the children were expert at bottling and labelling.

One member of our group made the supreme sacrifice. He covered his floor only with mats and rugs, and kept the floor boards loose. His entire house was literally floating on wine. Going to his place for dinner was an amazing experience. He could never remember where he put his prize bottles, so he would be pulling up boards in the living room, in the study....

So fellow wine lovers, all this is returning, except the price is not the same. Golly, these days you pay 20 cents even for a cork, and 10 cents would buy about enough wine to put in your ear hole. In the 1960s wine was the one wonderful liquid that was not taxed. Now home bottling a quality wine costs around $3 a bottle.

But the difference is they do it better now and with better equipment. There are firms which cater entirely for the home bottler. You will find them in all the capital cities. The biggest customers are schools, churches and youth groups, who bottle for charity. It is all done, quite legally, taxes paid etc., and they bottle under supervision.

The groups vary, maybe from a very nice Catholic church school to rowing clubs, to parish churches, to cricket clubs, to young Communists and even policemen. But why has it all come back? There are still serious wine drinkers, who want wine at a reasonable price and they don't want cask wine.

Now, with so many vineyards producing wine, you are constantly getting situations where vignerons have small lots which are not begin enough for a commercial bottle run, ideal to be sold in bulk for the home bottler. You get very distinguished wine makers who sell their wine, at say, $25, but as always happens they have some wine, which is not quite the style that suits their label, good wine nevertheless, so they sell it anonymously, wonderful for the home bottler. Then there are vignerons who have production costs, need money quickly, so they sell in bulk. Great for the home bottler.

I was delighted to note that the domestic home bottler is thriving as never before. The home bottling parties are cropping up again in Balwyn, Chadstone, Vaucluse, Paddo and all over.

The wine goes out in 27.5 litre plastic casks, designed specifically for the home bottler. They hold precisely three dozen bottles.

Which is a pity. When I was home bottling, I always liked three quarters of a bottle left over. I mean, even if it is eleven in the morning a home bottler has to check it out.

Your De-palatisation Guide

You know how we all have our Walter Mitty dreams?

Mine was to acquire the ultimate wine palate. Perhaps you have attended one of these lunches or dinners run for would-be wine connoisseurs. All the bottles are masked, carefully wrapped in brown paper.

So the wine is poured into your glass and from your peerless knowledge, you are asked to identify it, naming the country of origin, the district, the grape variety, the year of its vintage, etc.

Always it is my dream to be invited to speak on the wine of the night, before this distinguished gathering of connoisseurs.

I hold up my glass by the stem, roll it between finger and thumb, sniff, lift it towards the light and say: "Yes, Mr Chairman, I found the wine tonight particularly interesting and I am deeply grateful for this opportunity to taste it." (I taste it again).

"Mmmm. My first thought was that this was a first growth, a great wine from Burgundy. But, of course, it isn't, and you have honored us with something that is perhaps even better. I detect that distinctive honey smell on the noise, the brilliant amber in the color, that smooth almost oily texture, which tells me it has to come from the Hunter.

"My almost computerised memory bank of tastes tells me even further it is a Lindeman's, undoubtedly the semillon grapes came from that superb and famous producer Alfred Bloggenheimer. I can read his careful use of oak and what with that just faint hint of raspberry in the after palate I detect that he picked the grapes from the home paddock on the left side. I have assessed the year. Ahhh, a dry year it was, lot of sunshine, 1969. I believe the grapes were picked on March the second. Thank-you, I am drinking it with great pleasure."

The bottle is unmasked. "Astounding! He is exactly right," gasps the chairman. "How did he do it?"

The truth is I have always been hopeless at this sort of thing. I have picked Minchinbury fizz as Veuve Cliquot champagne, Grange Hermitage as Jacob's Creek, named chardonnay for riesling, riesling for Gewurtztraminer, called Rutherglen sherry for dinkum Madeira; and retired red in the face not from the wine.

What's to be done? You can only begin to acquire a great palate by training like Robert de Castella. Instead of pounding a million hours out on the road, you have to put in a million hours at glass, never giving up, showing dedication and valor, going through bottle after bottle.

There is only one trouble with this program, you get to the stage where you only enjoy the high quality wines, and just lately the prices have all gone through the roof.

Did you notice all the full page Christmas ads from the wine houses? Australians allegedly are running about third amongst the world's greatest lovers of French champagne. You can't get a humble non vintage under $40 and a vintage will set you back nigh on $60. The latest Grange, 1983, is $58.99 a bottle or $690 a case. The best whites and reds from the Yarra Valley are all running at $25 or $30 a bottle.

Then if you like a Sauterne, Ye Gods, just a simple Chateau Guiraud 1983 is being offered down the road from our place at $75 a bottle.

I mean, you can't afford to train any more. We have to return to simple basics. I am offering a training course to all my friends. It is called De-palatisation. For example on Champagne, you start on Veuve Cliquot, Perignon, and Bollinger. Second week you go to Salinger, to Yellowglen, to Seaview until finally you are enjoying Minchinbury and Great Western Imperial Reserve at $3.99 a bottle.

You do the same with the reds, work your way down through Browns, Chateau Tahbilk, Wolf Blass cabernet, Jacob's Creek, until you reach what appears to be your Nirvana; a Coolibah cask at $7.99 for four litres. There are other varieties at $4.99 a cask but my training there might take another three weeks. My de-palatisation program could save any true wine lover anything up to $5000 a year.

I am going to set up a consultancy and my rooms will be in one of these fancy new towers in Collins Street. The de-palatisation program will spread into many fields. I will run a course for golfers, particularly those who disappear four days a week or are never seen all week-end. I could start my de-golfing course with a short lecture from Greg Norman. He could show us how to put the golf ball down in the wrong spot and get disqualified.

We will have a de-Bridging course for those who are far-gone in Bridge. This will not be easy, for Bridge, like asthma, is a disease, marvellous for the doctors and the cure takes a very long time. The answer, I think, is to irritate your Bridge patients. Give them misdeals, always make sure they get poor hands. Then talk a lot during the game. If your patient, by some mischance, does get a good hand and has big six no trumps, think of some good conversation pointers. Just as the six-no-trumper is desperately pondering his/her strategy, say: "Dear, don't you think all this wood chipping in Tasmania is marvellous for the economy?" Or, "We wouldn't be having all these troubles now if only they had made Sir Joh prime minister. Do you think it's too late?" A little of this treatment and I think we can de-Bridge a patient very well.

The sweet-tooth creatures, lovers of Violet Crumbles, chocolates and jelly beans, we can put them through a course of de-palitisation. I would give them a special summer time feast. It is so easy to get the right stock; we could go to a milk bar and buy all the jaded, slightly grey material that they have had in their show case out of refrigeration. Two of three feeds of this and our sweet-tooth fans would be crying for a cleansing bran and yoghurt.

The round-the-bend cricket addict? I think I will force him or her to sit in front of a television set through an entire match, listening to the drone of talk on Channel Nine, taking in all the re-plays, plus all the commercials which come on at the end of every over and at every wicket fall. The student will be crying for mercy, asking even for old videos within three hours.

How do you de-palatise a football lover terminal case? Don't ask for too much too soon. I have been trying to do this for 23 years, and I think I'm on the point of giving up. There is no known cure.

There's Sex in Lolly Water

Maybe like me you are becoming disturbed by the soft drink ads.

I was always brought up to believe liquor was dangerous and utterly evil.

My marvellous old headmaster used to say: "There are three temptations you will encounter in this life - wine, women and motor cars. Any one of these is dangerous, but any two combined is lethal."

There were all sorts of splendid alternatives, lemonade, raspberry vinegar, creamy soda, ginger beer. When I was young barley water was all the go. Stick with these things - and I often wish I had - the perfect life would unfold.

Well, I think something has gone wrong. The soft drink ads that I see on television do not fill me with - how shall I put it? - with wholesome pure thoughts. They are so redolent with sex they bring me to the edge of the sofa. On occasions I have had to push the dimmer switch on the remote control.

The Coco-Cola ads always show young people in a state of frenzy. Boys and gorgeous young females leaping up and down, dancing, throwing themselves into each others arms. All having such a frenetic good time, you feel it would be dangerous to give young people Coco-Cola in mixed company.

Diet Coke has gone for Australian celebrities, Grant Kenny the Iron man, John Alexander and Paul McNamee tennis players and of course, Elle Macpherson, the most curvy and enticing of all Australian models. I mean you would leave home and even drink Diet Coke for her.

Pepsi seduces you with the beautiful Kate Cebrano, Robert Palmer sings "Simply Irresistible" and then they have Tina Turner doing her super sexy writhing, groaning, singing act. Give Tina Turner a Diet Coke and not only does she stay slim but she goes berserk and smoulders.

I can remember, too, one of those Schweppes ads. A very suave young man invites a *soignee* comely young lady to his apartment. You think he is going to show her his etchings but he lights up an entire wall, a library of seductive soft drink and she can choose anything. You tremble excitedly at what is certain to happen next.

I can remember ads for spa water. Yes, just plain old spa water. The voice over keeps whispering "sexy" and then says: "Have you ever wanted your spa water to be sexy?" There's a shot of a girl slowly running her tongue about her mouth. Oh boy. The message is the girl who drinks this brand of spa water will do anything.

Some commercials are designed to depict all kinds of macho masculine violence. Have you see some of those Solo ads. There is one which asks whether you are a Solo man. You see a fellow going through some sort of military daring-do as if he were being trained for under cover work with the Contras in Nicaragua.

He swings on an overhead wire drops his can of Solo, then with a magnificent leap down into a lake he grabs his can of Solo with all the frenzy of a man needing a fix. It worries me so much I would be almost frightened to touch it.

On the other hand, beer and cigarette ads are associated with decent, honest endeavor. The cigarette ads show chaps out on horses - rugged looking chaps in $100 shirts and wide hats. They have just spent all day rounding up 2000 cattle. And as they look across to the blue-tinged mountains they light a cigarette.

The advertising industry on the other hand has to endure a voluntary code of good behavior.

The beer people have a problem. They must not have people in their ads that are too young, look under 25 and never, never, never, must there be a suggestion that sex could be the reward for good drink. They can't suggest either financial or social success acquired by drink, nor can alcohol appear at sport functions or with automobiles and boats.

Although at times I am convinced a glass of this or that has done me a wonderful lot of good. No indeed, the ads must not suggest that alcohol has any wholesome therapeutic qualities.

They can't bring in celebrities. Paul Hogan could promote Foster's in Britain but not here. So what is left? The beer ads tie in with the nobility of work or the spiritual quality of hard-fought endeavor. The theme is that the foaming glass of beer is your reward, you have "earned it". Everything is pure decent and manly.

Soft drink ads can get away with almost anything. However I would humbly suggest they have an air of unreality. They ought to identify much more with the life you and I lead.

- You are sitting there in the evening. The air is warm, the smell of jasmine comes from the garden. "Moonlight becomes you" is lilting from the radio.

  "Darling..."

  "Not tonight dear. I think I've picked up a terrible wog from the office air conditioning."

  Camera zooms in on miserable, frustrated partner. "My God, I might as well have a lemon sparkling spa."

- Or how about this. Scene: Husband in one of those, gigantic super markets. His wife has given him a shopping list of 25 items including obscure things like lemon flavoring essence. The super market has few directions, it is a mind destroying maze with everything superbly hidden.

  Husband in terrible frustration collides his shopping basket with another, but the understanding female opposing driver says: Don't worry dear. All you need is a glass of Mother O'Reilly's Sweet Barley Water.

- Or maybe this. You wake up in the morning. It's Monday. Another day. The boss hasn't said anything nice to you in years. You have to go to the dentist in your lunch hour. Your pay packet is loaded with so much wage restraint and suffering from so many deductions you are working almost for nothing. The female clerk at the next desk is anything but a sex symbol.

  "Aw to hell with it." You have a Black Label Diet Creamy Soda, get back into bed, close your eyes - and a faint look of happiness flits around your lips.

Cut.

Dear Viewer,

During 1990 there were three episodes of the unnerving mini-series "The Dreams of Agonies of a Trainee Winemaker".

Would you please stand by for episode four. When we left you we had endured a very hard vintage. Even though we had placed pantie hose over individual bunches, predatory birds devoured at least 95 per cent of our grapes and we were left with just enough to fill a plastic rubbish tin.

These we had foot-tramped by virgins in the utterly classic European tradition. We strained the juice through a tea towel attached to the upturned legs of a chair and actually produced nine bottles of pinot noir.

In 1991 the word went around the entire bird population of the Mornington Peninsular that it was on again at Dunstan's. We netted the vineyard from end to end, not only netted, but nailed the nets to the ground with a nail to every third of a metre.

But please don't under-estimate the ingenuity of a starling. If a starling had to get in or out of Pentridge, winged or unwinged, it would have no difficulty. These starlings devote endless time to probing defences. They look for the slightest change in gradient or the smallest aperture by a fence post then they burrow their way in. Yes, they actually wriggle and dig.

Once in it is bliss, they have an aviary full of grapes, a feast beyond imagining. When you chase them they are clever at going into hiding amongst the vine leaves. Now we have had poodles for 20 years. During the entire length of that time I have wondered whether there is any possible practical use for a toy poodle.

At last I have found it. Lotte turned into a brilliant starling router. She patrolled the vineyard from sunrise to sunset and the starlings were defeated even more significantly than Saddam Hussein's army. This year we picked more than three tonnes of pinot noir grapes.

We had hoped to maintain purity with foot tramping by virgins. Last year our two virgins were aged four and six, but this season we felt there was a certain difficulty. We needed at least 20 virgins, preferably ladies with big feet and tipping the scale at around 80 kilos.

Even considering today's inflated labor market we believed this a target difficult to achieve, so we settled for a veteran power crusher. It has a large augur which pushes the grapes towards the crushing jaws, spews stems out the back and pulverised skins and juice out the front.

Now with all this mechanical aid we looked at the splendid must, wine and skins, bubbling in the fermenting vat and thought the hard labor was all over. Kevin McCarthy and Kathleen Quealy our wine consultants, said "Certainly not. Every six hours that must had to be turned and pummelled to get the maximum color and flavor."

"But-but, that means getting up every night at 3 a.m."

"Precisely," said Kevin. "In Burgundy really dedicated makers of pinot actually get into the vats and swim around in it to improve the process. If you want a good pinot you have to do that."

Dear viewers, we did actually get up nightly at 3 a.m. shoving the must with a paddle, but as yet there have been no midnight swims."

It was Kathleen who told us we had to do a malolactic fermentation. This she said called for the wine to be held at a temperature between 20 and 25 degrees for at least a week and perhaps two weeks.

"But the barrels hold 220 litres each you can't keep them at over 20 degrees in this weather."

"Yes you can," said Kathleen sweetly.

"How?"

"You use an electric blanket and a blanket off a double bed is ideal."

This indeed was the biggest crisis since the 1960s, when we used to make beer. It was one of those 40 degree days and it was absolutely essential that I get my brew down below 30 degrees. I took everything out of the refrigerator, all the butter, meat, soft drinks etc, and replaced it with the 30 litre beer fermenter. It was a success chemically but a failure socially.

This was even more serious. I have always considered the electric blanket the greatest contribution by science to the 20th century, an item that is vital even in early April.

"Dear, could I please have our electric blanket for the winery?"

I have to concede this wonderful woman conceded the electric blanket almost without a murmur. Thus began a long battle. Before we were getting up at all hours to stir the must. Now we had to get up to take the patient's temperature. I tell you it was easier when we merely had to look after babies.

But there have been other things to cause domestic strain. Careful wine production needs a wide range of equipment. One was forced to borrow the kitchen strainer, the kitchen scales, the kitchen wooden spoons, all the spare clean marmalade bottles for wine samples, the kitchen scissors, the kitchen basin, jugs, the precious stainless steel cooking pot...

It was over the hair dryer that she almost cracked.

"Why do you need the hair dryer?"

"Well, you see, you have this malolactic thing and you have to check whether it has gone through by putting spots of wine on litmus paper. You have to get it perfectly dry and your hair dryer would be really splendid. Honestly."

Marie Rose thought it might have been easier had the winery been shifted into the kitchen or vice versa. Ah but finally you take a sample out of the oak keg. It is in the tasting glass and you sip.

You know how mothers provide glorious instant love to the quite ghastly creatures at birth. You know how vegetable growers pick cauliflowers out of the garden, look at them with pride and triumph, even though cauliflowers twice the size and produced at a quarter the price, are down at the local store.

Well, it's a bit like that. Holding the first glass does give one quite a glow.

And do you know the biggest relief? Getting the nets off those vines. It's like taking off one's corsets. At least I imagine that's what it it's like.

COLUMNS WHICH REFER TO FILTHY LUCRE ...

3

Columns Which Refer to Filthy Lucre

Loving Messages from the Chairman

BHP sent us a charming letter in the mail several weeks back. If we did not wish to be bothered by their regular statements just fill in the form etc. Indeed we have had several of these from other companies.

You know why? They can't afford to send them out any more. Not only do they keep sending you obscure letters about their half year progress, their new issues, and the deep mysteries about new taxation arrangements, but their annual reports are so large they are getting like the telephone books. Very soon they will have to start splitting them into two sections.

Our balance of payments situation gets worse and worse, and some economists have given dire predictions for 1991. But please don't worry. I think everything looks marvellous. My personal survey is this. Annual reports are 31.2 per cent bigger than in 1987 and they show a definite upswing in the number of pictures used, 21.7 per cent; and the quality of the color has never been better. As a company annual report observer, one could say that conditions rarely have been more promising.

Many of them clearly have been inspired by illustrious magazines like *Fortune*, *Vogue* or even *Architectural Digest*, and they drop into the letter box with a heavy clunk.

Now take the National Australia Bank annual report, that was the latest to arrive, an absolutely gorgeous production. Back in the sixties and early seventies annual reports were dull affairs, about as bright as taxation returns. Now the object is to make everybody associated with the company look warm and lovable, like dear friends, particularly the directors. Some of the group pictures have all that warmth and nonchalance they used to show in pictures of Edwardian cricket teams.

The National Australia Bank directors get a full page in superb color. They are wandering easily down a very elegant marble staircase and I believe it is the head office in Melbourne. First down the stairs is the chairman, Sir Rupert Clarke, he is washing his hands in a Shylock motion and beaming at the wonder of the year's profit. Right behind him is the vice-chairman, Sir Peter Finley, and he looks desperately worried. On the landing is the managing director, N.R. "Nobby" Clark and he is giving a benevolent parson's smile in the direction of the staff.

I'm concerned though about Mr W.R.M. Irvine. He is pointing down across the Italian marble baluster. What is he pointing at? Could it be a suspect bank robber?

Then all through the report there are color shots of staff members on location around the globe. They are so artistic National Geographic could not have done better. There's Doug Robertson, National Bank man, deep in frightful traffic in Bangkok. There's Yi Chun Chang amongst bicycles in the great square at Beijing. He is looking solemn. I think he has just left Mao's tomb. But absolutely the best is National man Michael Xu in Shanghai amongst all his customers writhing round doing tai chi.

Absolutely the most beautiful annual report we received came from the Lend Lease Corporation. On the cover there is an almost surrealist picture of Mr G.J. Dusseldorp. It is all a luscious shade of sapphire blue and there way down in the right hand bottom corner is Mr D, his hands in his pockets, half smiling looking towards the horizon and, obviously, a wonderful future. The paper is parchment quality and the picture I liked was site carpenter, Lee Johnson, holding, way up over his head, a stunning ballerina, taken at the National Ballet Centre in Melbourne. You don't get sex like that in every annual report.

The Elders report we enjoyed. That had everything, a picture of the old sailing ship *Alma Doepel*, Australian Rules footballers playing at "The Fosters Oval" in Surrey; the Foster's Grand Prix in Adelaide and mouth-watering shots of beer products around the globe. In the make-your-directors-look-friendly stakes I thought they did well. They are in a sort of bush setting, all looking wonderful relaxed with trees behind them and you suspect they are about to have a very good lunch.

I thought Western Mining disappointing, nothing much to look at beyond pictures of mining, and Mt Isa Mines was no better.

BHP was tasteful. They managed to spread the pictures of their directors across two pages, although Mr Brian Loton was lost in the centrefold. I hope there was nothing symbolic in that. News International was hugely entertaining. We received a report on all the activities at Wapping, including some of the best headlines from the *Sun* and *News of the World*. The one I liked best was Maggie Thatcher's message on the Falklands STICK IT UP YOUR JUNTA and there was a splendid juicy picture of a *Sun* and *News of the World* Bingo girl.

Our National Bank annual report also carried a slip telling us we didn't have to receive it if we didn't want to. But we've voted to keep on the list. Annual reports are improving at such a rate why would you want to spend money on things like Ita's new magazine?

Would a Tax on the Waistline Help?

The tubes are alive with the sound of consumption tax.

John Elliott wants a consumption tax. John Howard almost wants a consumption tax. Andrew Peacock would like a consumption tax when anybody allows him to say it loud enough. John Stone used to want a consumption tax, but now it is great fun not to want it.

A consumption tax really is a percentage tax on every damn thing you buy. Now in my naive innocence I thought that was something we had already. Everything I can think of is taxed and all those things I love passionately, and are not good for me, are taxed abominably.

Taxation in years gone by has been used as a moral weapon to put us on the road to purity. The Government, for example, has always put an outrageous tax on cigarettes, then at the same time heavily subsidised the growing of tobacco.

It has put murderous taxes on beer, then encouraged the production of barley, hops and sugar. It has told us what a wicked thing is gambling, then done everything possible to facilitate the vice as a revenue raiser, by building lovely TABs, running its own lotteries and creating casinos as temples of joy.

Seeing that we have always worked on this principle, let's get on with it. Let us improve our society with just, wise, and truly crafty consumption taxes.

Are we are agreed that the vilest thing in our society today, worse than heroin, alcohol, and uranium, is the automobile? Let us put a violent tax on the internal combustion engine. Any engines which can produce speeds, say, higher than 80 kmh, receive taxes which go up on an ever mounting curve. All cars and engines will receive a pollution, earth-destroying tax. Each vehicle will be assessed on the vile emissions it puts into the atmosphere and be taxed accordingly.

Indeed a lot of my taxes will be interested in the earth and the future of mankind. We will tax spray cans out of sight. We will tax without mercy those paint spray cans and marking pens, so useful for making graffiti messages on walls. We will put a tax on plastic, on plastic bottles, and particularly the madness of all those plastic bags in super markets. There will be a consumption tax too on all those horrid hard plastic containers, which seal everything from wood screws and torch bulbs through to mini portions of butter and marmalade. You know the type, you need a tungsten tipped drill to get them open.

Under the present system take-overs are actually encouraged by providing kindly tax advantages. Under NICK, which is short for New Inspired Consumption Kill, we handle take-overs in two ways. First there will be the 25 per cent tax on borrowings, then we will have the 20 per cent tax on the bid. So that when, for example, a Maxwell, a Packer, a Murdoch, or whoever, bids 800 million for the *Age*, $160 million goes to the Government in NICK tax.

NICK will be brutal on noise and brutal on outdoor advertising. We will create a new era of peace and beauty. NICK will attack all devices that amplify musical instruments. The guitar, for example, is particularly attractive when it is not boosted to 200 decibels. We will tax non silent motor bikes, noisy chain saws, mowers and over boosted hi-fis.

As for outdoor advertising, the bigger the sign, naturally the greater the charge. I mean some of the signs which urge us to smoke super milds or gaze upon our most loved newscasters and commentators, could be worth $20,000 each a year for the mutilation they do to the landscape. Minor signs such as you see on the backs of taxis might be a very good deal to the Treasury for only $1000.

Taxation already is severe on the beer and the wine drinker. Yet the biggest rip off in our society today is the diet industry. We have 16 million people in this country. It would be safe to say that at any one time 12 million of them are attempting a diet with a success rate of maybe 0.15 per cent. Diet books now even outsell books on sex, and diet shops under the guise of health food shops are proliferating across the nation. NICK could get into them.

There might even be money in joggers. They too are growing in numbers, particularly the lunch time joggers who have given up business lunches. We could tax their running shoes, their shorts and, by heavens, their track suits. The women at our super market, 40 per cent of them do their shopping in track suits and joggers. Consumption tax there could be very interesting.

There are so many ways NICK could improve our society. Have you noticed under the new let-em-rip system with advertising on television, the better the program the more the commercials? Ye Gods, sometimes you get six commercials in a row. I reckon that when you get more than three in a row, when you get more than a dozen to the hour, then the NICK tax ought to hit hard.

There could be a NICK tax for repeats. The tax for a repeat should rise according to the numbers of times it has been repeated. For example, the ABC is giving us "Upstairs Downstairs" yet again. Is this the fourth or the fifth time we have seen it? We could have $200 per station per episode for the first repeat, $1000 for the fifth repeat. Putting on "Casablanca" again would cost them almost a million. Would you like, too, a body tax? How about $1000 for every creature who perishes on TV, $800 for every king hit? Sex, copulation? Maybe we will let them get away with that. After all, it is supposed to be an act of love.

This is of course just the first approach. The NICK office will be open to all sorts of suggestions. Give us a month or two and I am sure we could get this economy back on its feet.

The Intelligent Man's Budget Guide

What with this plethora of budgets, Federal Budget last Tuesday, State Budget next Tuesday, it is very difficult to understand money any more or where we are going. We

THE INTELLIGENT MAN'S BUDGET GUIDE...

thought it might be helpful to provide our exclusive Economic Dictionary.

Accord: Blissful state of Employer-Union harmony, just like Israel with the PLO.

Back Burner: Place for putting anything to do with lowering interest rates. (See Front Burner)

Creep: Not a term for any Treasurer past or present. It's just how we all creep into a higher tax bracket every time we think of filing a tax return.

Deficit: Sometimes we despair as the trade figures come in and we observe our balance of payments but there is always comfort in knowing that running a deficit is our one growth industry.

Economists: Ingenious people who know how to solve our problems. They all know how; except history will be made when one economist agrees with another economist.

Front Burner: Immediacy with which Government can raise new taxes. (See Back Burner.)

Gearing: Charming term for borrowing. You can be highly geared, under geared, even negatively geared, or run entirely out of gears like some of our famous entrepreneurs, Alan, George, Christopher and John.

Horror: A technical term usually used to describe budgets.

Interest: Never was anything better named. Once you are on to interest rates they get more interesting all the time and in defiance of all laws of motion, what goes up never comes down.

J-curve: The tendency to call on the Almighty when one sees the balance of trade figures.

K is for Keating, The Treasurer, world's greatest.

K is for Kirner, And K is for Kind, The budget, we craveth.

Liquidity: State you tend to get into when trying to face up to your own micro economic reform. (See micro)

Micro: Economics is just your minor financial disaster. Macro is doing on a majestic global scale.

Nuclear Family: Eventually it all comes back to this. It has virtually no say, it is expected to front in times of war, to be there for every crisis, to shoulder every workload. It is that wonderful group which eventually pays for everything.

Overseas Aid: Going into a decline. As a percentage of our national product we are giving less and less. Perhaps it something required by Australia.

Pipeline: Useful word to describe what is going to happen, when your lot is likely to improve. If it is not down the track then at least it is in the pipeline. And here is a bonus P. That is Privatisation. Selling off everything a Government possesses to pay for what it never had.

Quid: Could it be that everything started to go wrong when we freed the economy and liberated the dollar? Do you ever yearn back to the days when Ming was there, Artie was Treasurer and a quid was a quid?

Recession or Economic Downturn: Useful terms designed to avoid that horrid, vulgar word Depression. And a bonus R is Rubbery, an adjective which marries well with all economic statistics.

States: Artificial economies which have to have journey annually to Canberra to beg for sustenance.

Tunnel: A place where you look for a light at the end of, but it could be an engine coming the other way.

Unemployment: Curious modern economics, the greater the unemployment, the greater the penury, the better the chance of reducing inflation and lowering interests.

Victoria: Former colony which is seeking a gold medal for the world's greatest borrowings.

Wages: Something which is held down to the correct guidelines as long as you are not a managing director.

X: The one area where Canberra is superbly profitable. If it is low on the production of material wealth, nothing beats it as the national capital for X-rated videos.

Yen: We are full of yens, the yen for better interest rates, the yen for a non-red balance of payments, the yen for deflation of inflation. But in the end with the rising sun in the north the yen will overtake us all.

Zero: State of your bank account when you have paid your interest rates.

A Prostate Could Make You AA

You can feel for the poor, unfortunate State Bank and the once illustrious State Electricity Commission.

It seems that they are about to be down-graded by Moody's. Moody's is that snooty, superior, international credit agency which decides what common creatures are worth.

The State Bank and the SEC, at least until last Friday, were Aaa. Where will they head now? Australia already has slipped down the scale to Aa2 and is poised to drop to who knows what depths.

Mr Keating was livid and refused to have any more truck with Moody officials. I can understand his chagrin. This credit monster has become a complete part of modern living. The Big Brother is eyeing us up and down at every turn.

Four weeks ago I applied for an international credit card. They sent such a loving letter in the mail. If only I joined it would be subscription free for the first year and they would send six bottles of wine with their compliments.

Nothing like that happened. Instead they sent an inquisition and a big bill. They wanted to know my employers name, exactly how much I earned. They needed a reference from my accountant, my bank account number and the whole process has taken a month. I suspect now they are checking my church attendance record with the Vicar.

I bet they have also checked with Moody's. Down to AA4.

Then last week I went to get the car filled. I thought it would be nice to use the electronic card. They play weird tricks these cards. I swear I got my number right and I knew there was plenty of money in the bank. A little message came up on the screen: TRANSACTION DECLINED.

The girl at the service station gave me a long slow look meaning: "Ahhh, we know your kind." I paid cash, but I bet Moody's knew about it at once. Bb3.

Then I went to a suburban bank, Saturday morning, long queue at the automatic teller. There are so many crazy numbers you have to remember now, telephone number at home and office, Bass number for buying theatre tickets, passport number, security number in case the alarm goes off and you have to get a clearance with the security agency. Then there's the darned number you have to remember at the credit union.

O.K., there was a memory lapse this awful Saturday morning. There were three attempts with the result. Alas, this nasty machine swallowed my card and refused to give it back. I can't tell you the humiliation. The rest of the queue give you long looks even more meaningful than the girl at the service station. "Uh-uh, another one trying to get a free bob."

Moody's would never forgive that one. Cf7.

There are all sorts of ways of putting you in your place. You go into your favourite store to buy a new pullover for the winter. You have been a regular client there for only 45 years, but it takes a while to break through.

"You would like to put that on the account, Sir."

"Yes please."

"Your, address? Full name.?

Then there is the pause of about five minutes while she rings through to the accountant, Moody's, Bank of Tokyo, or wherever. Five minutes elapse before she gets the O.K. But you feel you have sunk again. Dd8.

We are living in difficult times. Nobody is trusted any more. Every creature is looked upon as a serious financial risk. If late with your payments there was a time when public organisations sent a polite note: Sir/Madam, we are sure you have overlooked your account with us..." Now it is blunt: "If we do not receive your payment within 14 days we will be forced to take legal action..."

We made an error with our rates this year. We misread the awful complication of numbers and fine print on the notice. We underpaid by a small amount. There was no kindly pat on the shoulder from the Shire treasurer, just a blunt demand and a surcharge of 20 per cent interest. I'm sure Moody's understand perfectly. Qr14.

And cheques? There was a time when there was never a bother paying by cheque. Now all cheques are suspicious objects, less loved even than the credit card. I went into a South Yarra liquor store to get a little lubricant which I hoped would smooth the evening.

When I offered the cheque, the refusal was unequivocal. I offered the usual driving licence. "No, Sir."

"You can check with my bank. It is immediately over the road. "No, Sir."

So away I went, no purchase. What would Moody's say now? Zz2.

Everything we do is assessed, graded, catalogued. I am particularly interested by the approval ratings put out weekly through the Bulletin and almost all other journals. Why do these public judgements fluctuate so wildly? Hawke, Hewson, Cain, Peacock, Greiner, they go up and down week by week.

Take Bob Hawke and his prostate. For a very long time I have been an observer of what we can slip in to the paper and what we cannot. I can remember back to the forties when expletives like God and hell were not allowed and such items as brothel and rape were absolutely too horrid for the public print.

But look what we have done to Bob. R.G. Menzies had some appalling things done to his plumbing while he was in office, but no mention of it got into print. The Prime Minister was merely poorly or taking a rest.

Now all is exposed. Last week we had full sketches of a penis and what goes on with a prime ministerial prostate operation. I feel that now we have arrived and as far public frankness is concerned there is nothing more to be achieved.

But what I want to know is this. What will it do for Bob's approval rating? I suspect from here on he will be Aaa.

Do Any of us Get Paid Enough?

Frankly I have a certain sympathy with the airline pilots.

Mr Hawke claimed that flying an aeroplane was easy. He flew one when he was at Oxford. Anyone could do it.

Dear Reader, I always found flying an aeroplane difficult to the point of being unnerving. The biggest problem was returning to earth. Earth was never precisely where I wanted it. Either it came up to quickly - then my machine bounced across the aerodrome like a kangaroo.

Or it came up far too late. Then there was that awesome sinking feeling, descending like a lift in a 60-storey building, climaxing with a resounding crunch on the undercarriage.

The next problem was avoiding getting lost. In an automobile one can stop and ask the way at any service station. When I was flying the only people I could ask were the angels and they never seemed to be available. The best solution was to dive down to a height of 50 feet and read the names of railway stations. This tended to be disturbing for people standing on railway platforms. Nor did one always found out what one wanted to know. There was the time when I climbed away from the railway station with the knowledge that when you took Irish Moss Gum Jubes you could feel them doing you good.

Then came the time during the war when they removed place names on railway stations to confuse the Japanese. You have no idea how it confused mug pilots.

Now I understand pilots don't need railway stations. They have both beacons and computers which are close to black magic. If, say, they are going to Los Angeles, they key in LAX, the computer announces the distance in nautical miles, gives them the course and the aeroplane automatically takes them straight there. But what if the computer breaks down? Of if the luggage door falls off? I never had that trouble.

My ultimate problem was returning home in horrid weather and not being able to see the airport. We always described clouds in the manner of Newman's chocolate. There were soft centre clouds and hard centre clouds. Hard centres were the ones with mountains inside them.

Then sometimes one had passengers aboard. They would have this pathetic look of blue-eyed absolute trust. You did not tell them you did not know where the aerodrome was and you were asking God what to do next.

Yes, flying an aeroplane is a complex and difficult art, but how do you assess the worth of a human to the community? How rare it is for any person, male or female to receive precisely their correct cash rewards?

For example, we have a baker at Flinders, who makes a dark rye bread in old fashioned wood-fired ovens. Because of him every week-end becomes an over-eating joy. His crusty wholemeal is so rich and splendid you don't need anything else, not even butter. I reckon he is an artist. His bread is the best for several hundred kilometres around and his skill is easily akin to that of an airline pilot. But I doubt if he earns much money.

At Montsalvat in Victoria I met a man who makes grand pianos and another who makes violins and cellos. There would not be a dozen, no, not half a dozen in the world as skilled at their craft. The music that comes from their instruments is sublime. They make enough money to live, no more.

Leg spin bowlers are a rare and wonderful breed. I would double their salaries immediately. They never get the publicity, rarely get much co-operation from their captains. Wretched fast bowlers always win the publicity, the love and the devotion. There are thousands of airline pilots, very few leg spin bowlers.

Take teachers. Teaching, I believe, is the most important task of all. Not only do they have to maintain peace in class, they have to fill in and do all those things inept parents, often indifferent parents, have failed to do. Teachers have to be mentally skilled and inspiring in the classroom, then physically brilliant when instructing on the playground. What percentage of an airline pilot are they worth? By my reckoning on an average you can equate their salaries under one third airline pilot.

How about your local priest? He is your spiritual pilot, there in times of life and death, and with a bit of luck your guide to the hereafter. So far as I know there is no Spiritual Pilots Association of Australia which can organise, threaten strike action or even announce that from now on their services will be provided only from nine to five. One sky pilot by my reckoning has the salary of five spiritual pilots.

What is a policeman worth when you call him in the midst of a bank robbery or an armed assault? Or how about your firemen when he is risking his life by a falling wall or coping with a raging chemical fire?

My wife is utterly irreplaceable, a wonderful gardener, a perfect secretary, a superb nurse, she makes the best pasta and the best pie I ever tasted. She has no award, operates only by direct negotiation, and thank heavens, has never threatened to go on strike. I hope she doesn't read this but if she exerted industrial muscle she could increase her salary ten fold.

On the other hand there are those who make salaries so large they are madly over-paid. Are golfers and tennis players worth a million dollars a year? What would you pay a top jockey? Do share brokers, news readers, disc jockeys, anchor men, and bearded TV commentators deserve all that money?

And how about newspaper columnists? Hey, wait a minute.

You Too Can Talk Like a Financial Wizard

You will have noticed that we are perilously near the end of the nineteen eighties. Journals everywhere are preparing their brilliant summings-up of the decade.

One deeply trusts no-one will overlook the surge in interest in money. Back in my day the news stands sported two types of magazines. Those for male interest which always had girls on the cover and those for female interest which always had girls on the cover.

In the eighties there was the astonishing flowering of weeklies and monthlies which devoted themselves entirely to money and to those who were making a lot of it.

Indeed, the biggest difference between the eighties and the seventies this was. Leading money makers became almost as important as footballers and in some cases even surpassed them as beloved personalities on front pages and TV screens.

Nor were the finance writers the dull fellows they used to be. All of us who observed the share market this past week must have been impressed by the eloquence, the excitement and sheer beauty of the language used.

It is something we must not lose. In order to keep up the pace your correspondent has been conducting a seminar for aspiring young money writers. It just so happens that we have a tape of one of the first lessons, which we have transcribed for the public benefit.

Good morning everyone. Today our lesson will be on words. We want to get away from cliches and I want to tell you about all the wonderful words we can use to describe what the market is doing.

Now A'court, you're a smart young man. Tell me, how would you describe a dull week on the exchange.

Sir, normally the important thing is not to make it too obvious that people are losing money. The market fades, it drifts, it slides. It can go off the boil. I think it is a good idea to say there was poor competition.

You are quite right. Easing, too, is a very word. You can say that the market eased yesterday. This implies that everything is more relaxed and the truth is it's actually a darned sight worse than it was yesterday. Then if you haven't the slightest idea what the market is really doing, you can say it is nervous, it is brittle.

O.K. We will proceed. Last night for homework I announced that there had been a spectacular fall in prices on Wall Street and I asked you to come up with phrases and words that you would use to describe it. Now Bondy, you have been to Perth, you ought to be good at this. Tell me what you have.

Yes Sir, the market dives, it sinks, it crashes, it plunges, it plummets, it goes into a tailspin, investors are mugged by reality and there is slaughter of shareholders.

That's a start but I was looking for something a little more eloquent. Spalvins, how about you?

Oh Sir, I have here: Today was Black Tuesday the most fearful day on the exchange since 1892; frenzied scenes gripped the national markets, in three hours of mad excitement when two and half billion dollars disappeared down the financial black hole, chalkies had their most desperate day.

I like that very much. Yes, Elliott.

Free fall. I've noticed that since all these balloon disasters, free fall is all the go. And the market has been free falling all the week.

Sir, Sir, Sir.

Yes, Brierley, what is it?

You've got to get blood into it. I have written, there was a huge bloodbath on the national market yesterday as investors rushed to shed their stocks.

Yes, that's good. But you can't keep it up day after day. If you have a crash on Tuesday it is vital to have a different mood on Thursday and Friday. Any ideas on that one?

A'Court: You have to explain that it wasn't such a bloodbath at all. Actually it was just a rationalisation of an overpumped market and it had to come. The market had been unrealistically overheated and it was a necessary shake-out that was good for all of us. Merely a temporary cash flow crisis.

Bondy: Yair, and we're clawing our way back.

Spalvins: And investors are returning, indulging in bargain hunting.

Brierley: Really Sir, there is a special term for it. You know how it is wrong now to say that people go to gaol. They are merely put into a correction facility. That's what we call a market disaster, a financial correction.

My goodness, you are learning fast. What's that Bond. Were you whispering something to young Elliott?

I was just trying to tell him Sir, that you are never broke or ruined or short of money. The fact is that you are highly geared.

Quite so. Quite so. And you must remember that the market is a living thing, it bounces back, it trampolines, it roller coasters and it shows excessive volatility. And I want you to remember that the financial markets are peculiar, they always operate in cycles. You will need a new range of words for the boom of 1990.

Murdoch, you're a great boom man, what would you suggest?

Sir, that's easy. The market soars, it sky rockets, it splurges, it jets to unprecedented heights, the Dow Jones goes berserk, there is a floodtide of stocks as brokers go mad with enthusiasm and in some cases, prices go into orbit.

Yes, that's nice. That's nice. Tomorrow I think we will have a lecture on the dollar. Back in the sixties and the seventies neither the pound nor the dollar were ever mentioned. Now it gets a position on the front page and everyone loves it even more than the weather.

How do you find the dollar Bondy?

Sir, it is practically human. I have noticed lately that it is weak, ailing, suffering, it's nervous, close to death, and needs a transfusion of liquidity.

A good draught of Fourex eh? (Hah! Hah! Hah!)

Hey, what's that? Murdoch what are doing? What's that you are writing down. Give it to me here. Thank-you. I see, you are making an offer, a take-over bid for the entire class room. Well, it's not on. The class is dismissed. I'll see you at this time tomorrow morning and don't forget to do your homework.

COLUMNS ON DOMESTIC HORTICULTURE...

4

Columns on Domestic Horticulture

Nearer to God in the Garden? The Garden is God

At our place we are addicted to the ABC gardening program on Saturday mornings.

Last week I was listening to "Tom" from Balwyn. He was blaming Kevin Heinz for his matrimonial problem. It went something like this:

"Years ago I married this charming, lovely girl. She was everything I could hope a wife to be. Now, as a result of your program I am married to a garden. We have 4000 pots outside. We have 2000 pots inside.

"When I go into the bathroom, there are pots in the bath. When I walk out the door I get cracked on the head by hanging baskets. When I get out the car I am in danger of scraping it against the wall of the house. Pots! If I go down the other side there isn't even room for a wheelbarrow. Pots!

We can't go away, can't leave the place for more than a day, because we have 6000 pots to feed and I blame it all on you."

Mr Heinz was most tactful in dealing with Tom's matrimonial problem. He said Tom's wife could keep up her enthusiasm but she could give some of her pots away to charity.

"She does. She does," replied Tom. "But every time she gives away a pot she replaces it with another three. You've got to help me. I really need a helicopter now to get away from the house."

Oh, I know exactly how Tom feels, but he didn't tell the half. Hanging baskets? We have a whole line of them on the veranda. Each hanging basket is worth another child, fed, watered, tended night and day. You virtually have to change their nappies. As for banging your head, I ask you to believe we even have one in the bathroom. Each time you get into the bath you bang your head.

We are devoted to orchids. They get moved all around the garden in a quest for the right degree of sunshine or shade. They have to be re-potted, divided and as soon as they bloom they get carted inside. There are the fish tail ferns. They are on a rotation plan. As soon as they look a bit tired inside, they go outside. Plants are like T.S. Eliot's cats. When they are inside they want to be outside and when they are outside they want to be inside.

There are the African violets. They want hardly any water, but then there are the Madonna lilies which like a lot. You do the watering and get into trouble for flooding on to the carpet.

Maiden hair ferns like to be hand sprayed to keep them fresh and, Ye Gods! there are other plants that get their leaves polished. We polish more plants than the furniture. But we are not as bad as some people we know. We have some friends who are mad for *monstera deliciosa* and they have it creeping across the ceiling. Go into their living room and you expect Tarzan to start yodelling from the corner.

It is the fashion this Christmas to have a fair dinkum pine tree in a pot. So that goes outside and inside and has to be watered and loved. You need a personal indoor railway just to keep moving the garden.

This is the year of the herb. Herbs are absolutely all the go, so we have a special herb garden and my wife know all the herbs by their christian names. These have to be tended.

The drying of lavender is "in". Pot pourri is "in". You dry off all the roses petals and make little scented bowls.

We are not allowed to throw away any kitchen scraps, not allowed to throw away a single leaf or twig. Everything has to be re-cycled. In the old days you would have a nice bonfire of leaves in the gutter. We have three compost bins, which all get their turn and if that's not enough we have to make expeditions to the beach for seaweed.

I reckon it's all a plot. The council told these gardening experts seaweed is good for the carrots just to get their beaches cleared.

And I sympathise with Tom over the watering. It never stops. Some require fine sprays, some, like stag horns, the orchids and ferns, require individual special treatment. There are the natives which don't want too much water at all, but they have to be in nice positions where we can see them because they attract the birds.

The up-to-date folk out our way have sprinkler systems run by computers. You get computers now which offer six sprays a day and you can program it for a different watering routine for every day of the week.

Yet there is always that touch of anxiety. We were at a dinner party where the host set his wrist alarm for 9 p.m., then as soon as it went off, sprinted out into the garden. "I just wanted to make certain it was all working," said he.

Oh, I tell you, it is better to live in a flat or have one of these firms that come around, bring the garden in on Tuesdays and take it away on Fridays. Now with the weather getting progressively more peculiar, operations which were labor intensive are now labor manic. Usually by January life is becoming a little easier, but with record rain falls the grass has been growing as if we were living in Lae or Rabaul. This season our mower has been back to the repairman three times from over work and our weeds have been as big as stringy barks.

However, there is a sequel to the tale about the man on talk back to the ABC. His voice was Scottish and definitely familiar. Yes, it was Tom Paterson, former chief of the Road Safety Council.

So we checked to find out the result. "Well," he said, "when it was on Nancy had a transistor and she was at the bottom of the garden. 'Did you listen to the gardening program?' I said. 'I only got on to the tail end of it,' she replied. 'But there was some b... belly aching. He sounded just like you.'"

Rows and Rows of Roses

It is the height of the season and I fear we have caught another appalling gardening disease.

We have been through them all. There was the dahlia disease. I had over 200 dahlias every one of them personally named. They had blooms as big as rubbish tin lids and the idea was to have them nodding over the front fence in order to stun the neighbors.

Then we went into azaleas, rhododendrons and there was a brief bout with fuchsias. During that flood of nationalism when Bondy won the America's Cup it was essential to be Australian native. We pulled out everything that was non Oz, turned the place into bushland and went mad for melaleucas, grevillea, callistemons, eriostemons and all sorts of darned things I can't spell.

Mid eighties was English cottage garden. Sensible garden trendies had to put in a fountain, a gazebo and you were just not there if you didn't have a picket fence. The garden had to be a perfect display of phlox, deliphiniums, hollyhocks, candytuft, cosmos with wafting summer smells of lavender.

And hanging baskets! You couldn't walk around the house without crashing your head on a great suspended wire cage of petunias.

Now roses are all the go and those who have been hooked will understand it is a frightening addiction, possibly worse than heroin. The west side of the house is now like a barbed wire entanglement. It is most difficult trying to pick one's way through Sparrieshoop, Cymbeline, Wise Portia and The Prioress.

Every morning we clean up Rosemary Harkness, Wini Edmunds, and Sweet Mimi petals off the dining room table and living room carpet.

Yes, it is addictive. Once you start buying roses you can't really stop. When my wife is feeling a little blue she says: "I think I will go out and buy a rose."

"You can't buy any more roses. We have 119 now. There isn't room for another."

"Yes there is. There's always room for another rose. We can move something."

In our garden there are more moves and reshuffles than in the British Cabinet. "I have just the spot," she continued.

"Where?"

"The corner of the house by the gas bottles. I'll put in a climbing Iceberg."

"Ye Gods, there's a big drainpipe right under there."

There is no point in reasoning with genuine rose passion. In the end we had to get some railway sleepers, build up the bed half a metre and we have yet another Iceberg. We now have more Icebergs than in the entire Antarctic.

Please excuse me for tossing names around like this. Once you are rose manic you move into a different world and you have to know all the names. I think we have the entire Royal Family: Queen Elizabeth, Prince Charles, La Reine Victoria, Princess Margaret, Royal Highness and Grace of Monaco. We have wine: Chianti and Chablis. We have lots of singers: Helen Traubel, Nana Mouskouri, and Maria Callas. Although frankly I would like to have Ginger

Rogers, Judy Garland and particularly Dolly Parton. Dolly is a beaut hybrid tea, a voluptuous pinky red.

Sex comes into it. There's Love, Lovers' Meeting, First Love, Loving Memory - I get a lot of satisfaction putting President Hoover in the same bed as Princess Margaret, or popping Penelope Keith in some nice soft compost with Charles de Gaulle.

Addicts are beyond belief at rose recognition. If you were introduced to them they would not remember your name five minutes later, but they can remember a rose they met 15 years ago. We had a group in last week. They didn't greet each other at all, they just talked to the roses.

"Isn't Ophelia divine?"

"Did you ever see anything like Just Joey?"

"I think Souvenir de la Malmaison is absolutely my favorite. I'd like to grow nothing else."

You have to understand what they are talking about. They tend to get on first name terms with their favorites. "I am a bit worried about Papa. He is looking a bit poorly.

They are referring, of course, to Papa Meilland who is suffering from Black Spot. There is a whole damn family of Meillands. There's Michele Meilland, Sonia Meilland, Manou Meilland....

On the other hand they might say: "I have to go out and put some water on Derek and Maggie needs tying up."

You must appreciate Derek Nimmo and Mrs Thatcher both have had roses named after them. Mrs Thatcher is a particularly vibrant, vigorous rose.

There are those who are crazy about the smell of roses. I was driving with that TV cook Peter Russell-Clarke. He slammed on his brakes sprinted across to a front garden. "You can't pass a beautiful rose without smelling it," he cried.

You can recognise a rose grower by the scratches and scars up and down the arms. Their houses too have a slight air of chaos, because there is so much to be done outside there is no time left for what goes on inside.

My wife says: "I will just slip outside for two minutes. I have to pick a Pascali."

That's absolutely fatal. She returns four hours later. You can't walk past a rose bed without seeing 40 things to do.

The craze for old fashioned English roses is particularly dangerous. Those Old Fashioneds like to stretch out and spread like blackberries. You have to put in rose arbors, and we have great tripods constructed from Stringybark boughs. It gets so that you can't mow the lawn any more.

However, for the rose addict there is one lovely compensation. The roses bloom for at least nine months of the year. It doesn't matter what happens to BHP shares, interest rates, or whether the price of petrol goes up to a dollar a litre.

It doesn't matter even if England bowls us out for 65, you can still go out in the garden and look at Chianti, or Tuscany, or the latest edition of Peace. You know, I still think a perfect Peace is the best of them all.

Oh for a Cottage Garden!

At our house we are finding life very difficult, no longer are we keeping up with the trends.

Five years ago, when we returned from California, the new nationalism was sweeping the land. In cricket matches against England more flags were being displayed than when John Wayne was winning World War 2.

Nationalism knew no bounds after Bondy won the America's Cup. It even became essential to have an all-Australian garden. The environmentalists told us to plant Australian because dinkum Australian birds would never visit your garden unless they could feast on Australian flowers.

We had to get into melaleucas, grevillea, callistemons, boronia, crowea, eriostemon and all those other things you can't spell. None of your English trees which dropped leaves for three months of the year, we went for beaut gum trees which dropped stuff all the year round.

The pressure was really on. We had three local nurseries which were pure Australia. Ask them for a petunia and they would wince like Paul Hogan before a pink gin or a cucumber sandwich.

We first noticed the change when the folk in our street started to go for picket fences. Not your plain old pickets but the gorgeous old English fences with the sort of fleur-de-lis tops. Would you believe one lady up the road even installed delightful picket fence gates with remote control. Presumably Old English.

We were told, quietly, things had changed. Now the English garden was all the go. Vita Sackville-West, the late Bloomsbury lady, created her dream, Sissinghurst, the perfect piece of aromatic old England. Get into this.

We noticed the all-Oz nurseries were under heavy competition. There was a nursery called "The Britannica", English only. Business too was picking up. They were getting bigger and bigger. One near us is particularly grand, a cross between the Crystal Palace, the Brighton Pavilion and Kew Gardens. The proprietor confirmed there was indeed an astonishing boom in annuals and English type.

Just to prove his words he indicated the English cottage they had built out the back, complete with exquisite English garden. I half expected Vita herself, or Thomas Hardy at the very least, to step out the door.

"Oh yes," said our man, "you must have perennials. Your garden should be filled with phlox, delphiniums, hollyhocks, snapdragons, Queen Anne's lace, verbena, forget-me-nots, poppies, candytuft, aquilegia, and, ah yes, cosmos. Absolutely everybody is going for cosmos. Very pretty.

"And lavender. I have never known such a season for lavender. Incredible how it has come back. I suppose we would be handling eight to 10 varieties, French, English, but the biggest goer is Hidcote, dwarf, deep purple, lovely on the nose."

I have always been a Peace man myself or President Hoover, but he pointed out it was no good meddling any more with modern roses. People were buying the old English ones. "Not the same splendid tight buds," I said, "loose, petals that fall all over the place."

"Oh no," he replied, "they have a delicate beauty all of their own. You must get Buff Beauty, Sparrieshoop or Cornelia. They only bloom once, not twice in the season like modern roses, but you do get wonderful rose hips in the autumn."

Then he waved his hand at the neatly trimmed hedges in the cottage garden. You must have your hedges, English box, dwarf box, Dutch box. One shuddered at the sight of the hedges. They are a license to ruin your week-end, like owning hanging baskets. They should pay child endowment for those wretched things, every hanging basket is like having another child. Leave them for two days and you need a hanging basket sitter.

Worst off all, everywhere in the nursery there was the English garden paraphernalia. You must have a sun dial. Never mind that with daylight saving it is unlikely to get the time right within two hours. You must have a weather vane, complete with brass cock up aloft, never mind if the darned things are always pointing north when they should be pointing south. It's the look that counts.

You must have a lovely curved pergola or arbor for your climbing old English roses. What's more you can spend your entire superannuation check just on old English edging for your flower beds. They come in the form of steel hoops, fancy cast iron or terra cotta slates with beaut twiddledey bits on top.

We inquired about a gazebo, a place where we could sit in the evening by the herb garden and take in the scent of the rosemary. It looked very charming like a grandstand. Ye Gods, the price was $4000. Then there was a garden arbour, a delightful little affair with an iron roof and little steeples. The price, $1280.

Our nursery man explained, too, that there was a boom in garden statuary, nothing over-large; discreet, you understand. Your garden could have Hermes, or Modesty just displaying one breast. Or how about Michelangelo's David. You would put him in a spot where the delphiniums would hide anything that was untoward.

Little fountains with several cupids on top were good and there was an exquisite cast iron wall fountain, the sort you might find in a charming lane by York Cathedral, for $652.

I used to dream it would be good to get out of journalism and become the curator of a splendid garden. In journalism when you make a mistake it is obvious the next morning. If you plotted a garden it would take 20 years to discover your ghastly errors.

Not any more, it is moving too quickly. I bet by the time we converted to an English garden it would all be over, and there would be an entirely new trend. They would be into cactus and desert succulents.

Spring is the Thunder of the Two Stroke

John Keats back around 1820 exclaimed: "Where are the songs of Spring? Ay, where are they?"

I'll tell you where they are. They're with all the latest power machinery. Spring is the thunder of two stroke and four stroke motors.

We don't get bird songs around us so much any more, we get the chain saws. Indeed a really gifted member of the

SPRING IS THE THUNDER OF THE TWO STROKE...

Noise Observers Club can pick the sounds: There is the Homelite Red-crested 30 cc warbler, the McCulloch 50 cc yellow-breasted screecher, and over yonder amongst the crushing boughs one can detect the unmistakable Spring noises of a Stihl 120 c.c. orange-chested, super-throated shrieker.

Oh no, axes are not needed any more, all our domestic devices are power operated.

Remember the old days when the neighborhood was silent. The only noise was the panting and the straining and everybody had a hefty Qualcast push mower.

Not any more. This has been very nearly the wettest Spring on record. At our place the grass is growing so rapidly you have to be careful where you walk or it will actually push you over.

You will notice on the television the fancy mowers are getting almost as many romantic, lovable commercials as the BMWs and Toyotas. What's more, the mowers have the same dreams-of-glory names as the motor cars, names that will give you a feeling of prestige and importance when you get out to do the mowing.

There is the Mustang, the Ambassador, the Whirlwind, the Monarch, for heaven's sake, the Shiremaster, and the Tornado. So far there is not a V.I.P. mower but there is one called the Executive. You get solid state electronic ignition, finger-tip height adjustment and rust free mowing comfort.

But I get envious when I see the 1990 ride-ons being test driven on the screen. Clearly my old ride-on is not up to the standard of what the other chaps and ladies are driving.

I mean, they don't call them ride-ons any more. They are home tractors. Just like the cars they come with two year warranty. They are beautiful with dazzling two-tone paintwork. They have wrap around headlights, presumably so that you can go mowing after dinner in the dark. They have push button starting, single touch pedal which controls forward and reverse, disc brakes, hydrostatic transaxle, no less, and five speed cruise control.

They have little trailers you can attach and bulldozer blades to put out front. Now you can get little mini cabins so that you won't be connected with the horrid outside atmosphere and you can listen to the cricket.

Then you will notice that in almost every mower advertisement for the ride-ons, just to demonstrate the true bliss of grass mowing, they have a female at the wheel. Ah yes, if you really want to give someone the hint there is a model called the Jillaroo.

But it doesn't stop there. The true gardener now requires a machinery shed the equivalent of McArthur Downs or whatever. You can't get by without a five horsepower mulcher. The 1990s models are larger than ever before.

The pure beauty about these is that you can become your own home wood-chipper and turn the entire garden into mulch.

The pick and shovel also is utterly out of date. Have you noticed the range of "home cultivators" on the market. There are devices called Rotahoes and Rotatillers. "Save yourself money time and effort all the year round," the ads coo. "Your cultivator with its lusty appetite for work will penetrate the hardest ground, digging deep and breaking the soil to a fine tilth...flower beds and weeds are culled effortlessly and plant growth stimulated. Your cultivator is an all year round workmate."

What else do you need? You must appreciate the broom is finished, done. You have two choices here. There is the 21 c.c. power-operated blower, which sucks 2000 cubic feet of air a minute and blows at 160 mph. They do tend to be a little noisy and in some areas of California they are now banned altogether. But surely they are no worse than the rest of the garden orchestra and they do flatten the leaves against the back fence.

The alternative is the domestic vacuum cleaner. This too has a two stroke engine, a great bag and looks like an overgrown indoor Hoover. You find half the kids toys in the bag when you clean it out.

Garden shears and scissors also are finished. You must have a power operated brush cutter or whipper snipper. There is a gorgeous advertisement for these things. The scene is a colonial mansion just like the one Vivien Leigh occupied in Gone With the Wind. Out front is a lawn, roughly the same size President Bush has at the White House, perfect edges, obviously done effortlessly in two and a half minutes with the nylon cord brush cutter. There is no mention of the vibration that eventually sends you for treatment to the physio.

You will also need a power-operated hedge cutter, another two stroke motor and one could recommend a power-operated spray for working over the roses, and the vegetables.

By the time you have all this equipment your Mc Arthur Downs machinery shed will be full, you will need to employ a full time mechanic to keep them in working order, and you will be storing so much fuel you will have to put a HAZCHEM sign outside the gate.

And don't think you won't go without exercise. The two stroke motor is the most contrary, quixotic creature ever invented by - ah - personkind, and what with the string pull starting devices you will develop a right arm so powerful you will be able to star in Rocky 14.

Battling the Berry

For my sins I have a little farmlet. It doesn't produce much but it is fantastic at making blackberries.

Of the two acres almost half has been covered with blackberry.

If John Cain has been having trouble in eradicating Norm Gallagher it's just nothing to the problem of the blackberry. According to my handbook one bush can spread up to six metres in a year.

It can spread through seeds, through cuttings or it can arch right over, hit the ground and start all over again, creating a sort of barbed wire entanglement that would do justice to the Battle of the Somme.

Brute force accompanied by bleeding flesh is the best way to get rid of blackberry. You just dig it out root by root. You can poison it by spray. There is a spray which has a charming name with connotations of John Wayne and Ronald Reagan. It is called "Round Up". The stuff comes in a tiny container which sells, Ye Gods, for $45.

Apparently it does no harm to the soil but blackberry plus foliage heads for the last round up. Say you do that and the blackberry dies, but still you are left with a wonderful skeleton still life, a barbed wire entanglement that is more flesh carving than ever.

I am reminded of all this by one of the grand gestures of Victoria's 150th celebrations, Baron Ferdinand Von Mueller had to be remembered. So we erected a bronze bust to him in Melbourne's Botanic Gardens.

Now Von Mueller was a great scientist, explorer, world renowned botanist, founder of the Melbourne Botanic Gardens and a superb eccentric. He had an uncommon lust for meringues, no knowledge of the passing of time, never carried a watch and gave remarkably long speeches.

But also he believed deeply in the blackberry. He thought there should be blackberries along every rivulet and stream in the colony. This was to provide vegetation and prevent erosion. But he also liked blackberry fruit. He thought the Australian countryside provided little survival fruit for the wanderer.

What better then than the blackberry. Legend has it that when he set out on trips he would take with him bags of seed and distribute his bounty.

One wonders how many mega millions the blackberry has cost Victoria in devastated land. According to Eric Rolls in his excellent book *See How they Run* the blackberry was first imported from England to Tasmania in 1843.

He quotes the sheer delight of 1843 Tasmanian blackberry planter, James Fenton: "I put my valued cuttings in my garden on a rich plot of chocolate soil. I watered them! I watched them! I weeded them with all the tender care of a nursery man and had the unspeakable pleasure of seeing them push forth buds in due time...They made wonderful headway, throwing out long arms in every direction."

I appreciate exactly what he meant, but I bet his long arms didn't out-throw my long arms.

Of course, we've had some sinister blackberry hanky panky here in Victoria. Last year some spore smuggler impatient for devastation introduced a virulent strain of blackberry rust near the small Gippsland town of Hiawatha and this has swept through south-eastern Australia.

It has been available for some time in France and South America, but it takes five years or more to put such a disease through all the tests to make sure it doesn't wipe out everything in sight.

The tell tale purple spot has started to appear on some of my blackberries, and despite its piratical behavior I have a feeling we could learn to be friends.

Elegio Bruzzese at the Keith Turnbull Research Station in Werribee, the expert in this field, says there are eight different varieties of blackberry. The rust is effective on six of them and very virulent on three.

So far he has tested 108 different anti-blackberry species which has taken four and half years. He says that they have applied for Government approval, but it all takes time. For example, in Tasmania there is opposition because there are farmers down there who grow blackberries commercially. Could they be relatives of Mr Fenton?

But as I burn my funeral pyre of blackberry roots this week-end I will think lovingly of the Baron. The Botanic Gardens shouldn't stop with him.

We could have a bust to Thomas Austin of Barwon Park who nurtured 24 English rabbits in 1859 and did so, one gathers, with quite some success.

The Acclimatisation Society introduced the house sparrow, the Indian myna and the English starling to eat caterpillars which were worrying the market gardeners. In Melbourne you hardly see anything else but mynas, sparrows and starlings. Eric Rolls thinks they might have been imported by Mr Brown the bird dealer in 1857. O.K. let's have a bust to Mr Brown.

There's seems to be a little doubt as to who first imported foxes and deer, but Thomas Chirnside who built Werribee Park did marvellous things for the Melbourne Hunt providing foxes, deer, hares and rabbits. He almost deserves several busts.

Then how about busts for the characters who introduced the cane toad, the prickly pear, Patterson's Curse, St John's Wort, Oxalis, Bathurst Burr, Boneseed and I am sure there are lots of others.

We could have a gallery of busts which could become one of Melbourne's intriguing tourist attractions.

COLUMNS ON THE GREATEST SPORT—CRICKET!

5

Columns on the Greatest Sport - Cricket

Are Pitches Human?

Our cricket writers haven't accused the Poms of cheating in this Test series, but by heavens, they have gone close.

For example, Rod Nicholson of the Melbourne Herald, has written that England's fear of the Australian speed attack could cost it the chances. He says the pitch at Trent Bridge was prepared "deliberately to blunt the Australian attack of Geoff Lawson and Craig McDermott."

"The Trent Bridge pitch was brazenly out of character," says he.

Now we are told that both captains are knocking the pitch for the coming Test at Old Trafford. The forecast is that the pitch at Manchester will be slower than a one-wheeled bicycle.

I really find it most exciting when our chaps knock up scores around 600, but I get most irritated when Messrs Gower, Botham and Gooch all help themselves to centuries each. There is more pleasure to be had in tumbling wickets.

But it is wretchedly unfair when we always have this trouble with dumb, tedious, ill-behaving wickets. Should some groundsman, curator in Leeds, Manchester or wherever be able to say: "Eeee oi'll fix these lads. Oi'll mix oop a noice concoction of Clag, molasses and rolled oats."

The truth is that pitches are fairly unpredictable. If a pitch is in a bad temper on a certain day almost everything depends on who is going to win the toss.

In recent times I have seen these descriptions of cricket pitches: volatile, responsive fiery, spirited, unnerving, rewarding, quixotic, meaningful and good grief, even a Christian pitch. Some commentators have the suspicion they are human.

Now look here, we are approaching the 21st century. Isn't it time they started designing pitches which are fair to both sides? I mean grass has almost gone from tennis.

Miserably, unreliable stuff, grass. Wears faster than paper napkins. Useless after rain. Hideously uneven after three matches. The Australian Open is giving it away and soon Wimbledon will be the last little cell on earth still using it.

Marvellous new rubberised and plastic surfaces are all the go.

Grass is an anachronism for U.S. sport, either for running, football or baseball. They have artificial grasses which are infinitely more hard wearing, efficient and easy to maintain.

So why do we persist with turf? The mysterious totally unfathomable wicket at the Melbourne Cricket Ground has almost destroyed the Victorian Sheffield team. I mean they have hardly won a game there since the days of Billy Ponsford. They have dug up and buried the old cadaver about 15 times and still they don't know what's wrong.

There is a suspicion that the turf at the MCG is sulking. It has never got over the shock of pyjama cricket.

Now my idea is this, we should have a cricket summit. You can't get anywhere now without a summit. Cricketer Bob Hawke could be the chairman. We would call in all our top scientists, characters from the CSIRO, ICI, ACI, all the universities, plus some old hands like Bill O'Reilly, Ray Lindwall, Richie Benaud and Keith Miller.

Now, we would want them to come up with a pitch that was superb. This pitch would be good for the fast bowlers and it would have just the right texture so that it would be good for cutters, always good for the off spinners and, ah yes, particularly good for the leg spinners.

I would like to see the spinners even opening the bowling.

On the other hand I don't want a pitch that is going to leave the bowlers completely in command, just a nice balance, you understand, a pitch that will be a test of skill for everyone.

It won't crumble and tear up under the feet of the fast bowlers. You won't even have to cover it when it rains. It is absurd the manner in which these sickly cricketers go off the ground the minute a few drops of moisture begin to fall.

My pitches will be capable of use again and again. Their design will be such that a drawn match will be a rarity and you will be able to buy them at Myer, Coles or Woolworths or whoever happens to own everything.

Ah, oh yes, the design will be an international standard accepted by England, West Indies, Pakistan, India, Australia, the lot.

We don't want these Poms cooking up their own pitch that's no good for Lawson and McDermott.

Oh Freddie and Sir Leonard, Now it's the Foster's Oval

From now on it is official. The dear old Oval at Kennington Surrey is the "Foster's Oval".

After the passage of time I have learned to live with the Foster's Caulfield Cup, the Foster's Melbourne Cup and I think I am comfortable with the Fosterised Grand Final.

But just give me a week or two to absorb the Foster's Oval. It is akin, really, to Foster's Westminster Abbey and maybe the Foster's House of Commons is not far behind.

You must appreciate the Oval is in the heart of Pom-land. Walk across the Vauxhall Bridge and you are there. It is practically within a cover drive of Big Ben. But the Surrey Cricket Club, until C.U.B. and Courage offered them $4.14 million, was in dire poverty.

Practically any suburban Australian football ground has better facilities. The seating accommodation is lamentable. In Australia it would have no hope of getting a Test Match. It holds only 15,000 spectators. The roofs leak, the toilets are like those that make you shudder in provincial France. However, every cricketer remembers the glory of playing there. The grass, the turf, is superb.

One time a parishioner asked the late Cardinal John Heenan what he would like to see in heaven. The fine old prelate mused for a moment and said; "I just hope there is a small English lawn to mow."

All right, if the Surrey Oval is up there His Eminence will be very happy indeed.

Unlike Australians the English do not profane their cricket grounds with football. Alex Bedser, when he was here back last February, said the truth was they used the Oval only about 11 times a year. There were the home Surrey games, a Test match or two, and that was it. It was utterly vacant all winter. They would get more customers at the House of Lords.

There was actually a football match there last year. Foster's sponsored a game between North Melbourne and Carlton. The curator almost swooned with the horror of it all. He could not believe that football boots would prance across his cricket pitch.

One would never decry the deep, social importance of Foster's but one hopes they appreciate what they are doing. Cricket was played on the Kennington Common back in 1730 and between 1792 and 1810 Surrey played All England every year and were so good they even gave their opponents odds.

It was in 1844 that the club found a market garden in Kennington, 10 acres and oval in shape. I don't know when they put up the gasometer which became such a famous part of the Oval scene. However Neville Cardus loved the place. He once wrote that the famous "Ashes test" was "The greatest Test Match".

Dear Reader, you will remember Australia made only 63 and 122 and on that fatal day August 29, 1882, England in the final innings needed only 85 to win. Ah, but Spofforth, bowling shall we say, medium pace, had awesome guile and control. He got W.G. Grace for four runs, Ulyett for 26 and the Hon A. Lyttellton for 2. He and Boyle bowled 12 successive maidens, and several respectable English spectators were actually credited with devouring pieces out of their hats.

Eventually England was all out for 77 and Spofforth took a total of 14 wickets at an average of 6.43 with 33 maidens. He was chaired off the ground and even W.G. himself wrote: "The shouting and cheering that followed Spofforth's performance I shall remember to my dying day."

Then there was that fateful week at the Oval in late August 1938 when Len Hutton made 364 out of an England score of 903. Someone did suggest that had Bradman won the toss and not injured his ankle, and had Hitler not intervened that match would be continuing even now.

When Hutton made his record score Neville Cardus wrote these deeply moving words in the Manchester Guardian: "As the ground became resonant with the cheering the thought occurred to me that it was being heard far and wide, all over the Empire, not only in this country. People walking down Collins Street in Melbourne would hear it, and it would roar and echo in Kandy, Calcutta, Allahabad, Penang; they would hear it in the Cocos Islands and join in, and on liners going patiently their ways over the seven seas they would hear it too, and drink Hutton's health. Possibly in some club in Pall Mall a permanent member would wake up and go to the lunch room and have to be informed who was Hutton."

But how about precisely 15 years later, the autumn of '53. It was Hassett versus Hutton and we had the marvellous cast of Lindwall, Miller, Morris, Archer, Davidson and Harvey, yet would you believe the teams played four successive draws.

Freddie Trueman came in for the first time and many critics didn't think "mooch" of him. The august C.B. Fry had said: "He doesn't even tie his shoelaces properly."

Trueman devoured Australia in the first innings then Messrs Lock and Laker completed the task in the second. England won by eight wickets and it was the breaking of a very severe drought. The joy throughout Britain was so profound it was the equivalent of the Relief of Mafeking during the South African war.

But there were other matters to be considered. It was Lindsay Hassett's last Test match and legend has it that the two teams had a joyous time in the dressing rooms.

Denis Compton credits Keith Miller with starting the fun of throwing champagne bottles and the story goes that Lindsay Hassett completed matters by throwing a bottle at the clock. Didn't go down at all well in Pall Mall.

Presumably the clock still needs repairs and, of course, Foster's will attend to that. However just one thing worries me. Mrs Thatcher is a disturbing lady. Remember her attitude to Argentina over the Falkland Islands.

Do you think she will counter attack. We could finish with the Watney's WACA, the Bass Mild MCG or even the Guinness Gabba.

Couldn't the Cricketers Have Hats With Pretty Ribbons?

Have you read the appalling news? Cricketers in one-day internationals will sport names on their backs next summer.

COULDN'T THE CRICKETERS HAVE HATS WITH PRETTY RIBBONS ...?

The Australian Cricket Board made its decision in Brisbane.

What will they do with the rest of the available shirt space? Presumably it will be handed out to Mojo, George Patterson, or some other imaginative advertising agency, then divided up between Westpac, Four'n'Twenty Pies and Toyota. There are no depths these times to which our cricket administrators will not stoop.

The uniforms already are bad enough, clearly designed by someone who does not like cricket. It is difficult to make up one's mind which is the worst, the lime green and blue of Pakistan, those burgundy stripes coupled with the blue sludge grey of the West Indies, or could it be, the red and yellow of South Australia.

In full cry the South Australians look like some brand of indigenous parrot.

The colored uniforms were really the invention of Packer cricket. Color television had not been with us for very long, so there was the naive idea that to get the value out of your set the screen had to be filled with a kaleidoscope of brilliant hues.

They did the same when the professionals took over amateur tennis. The competition now is to find out how many alarming colored shirts a player can wear in a five set match.

During the 1987 season the Australian cricketers wore shirts with a series of horizontal stripes which would have done credit to a beach umbrella. There was the brilliant yellow collar, a green band across the shoulders, then came four green and yellow stripes, next a wide band of white, then four more green and gold stripes, and finally a gold band which went down to the trousers, which were all yellow.

If a red ball was used during day cricket the yellow trousers set off more brilliantly the red marks when a fast bowler rubbed it on his crotch.

Now it will be fascinating to see how they will set these names amongst all those extraordinary stripes. Remember back in the old days when scoreboards were just simple kindly affairs, when players names were slung on boards. At the MCG if you were a great player like Kippax, Trumper or Hammond for sentimental reasons they kept your board for all time.

At the Melbourne Cricket Ground, for example, they had little lights. Whenever a player fielded the ball, the light went on, and you knew who it was. The fellows in the scoreboard were awfully good. They knew when someone had crossed over to the other side to look after a left-handed batsman.

I liked the blinking light system. On a lazy afternoon, when inevitably you went to sleep, it gave you something to do, identifying each fieldsman. Then if that fieldsman dropped an absolute sitter, they were awfully decent about it. They only blinked the light for a fiftieth of a second.

Now with the electronic scoreboard they give the whole works, with four replays from different angles. If the batsman is out for a duck he gets the ultimate humiliation of a little dancing duck on the big screen.

It used to be the British style to have a sense of understatement, to use a little subtlety. Even the footballers only have numbers on their backs. This, of course, is sheer commercial cunning. They put numbers on backs to force the unfortunate spectators into buying copies of the Football Record.

Let's go back to the first international cricket match. It was between Mr Stephenson's XI from England and the Melbourne and Districts XVIII. George Marshall was captain of the Melbourne and Districts team. His XVIII wore straw-colored shirts with red spots and round dove-colored hats trimmed with magenta ribbon. Their trousers were a dove color.

Mr Stephenson's XI wore white shirts with blue belts and white caps with blue stripes. It was the custom too, not to have an open-necked shirt, but to wear a rather charming cravat.

As you can imagine, George Marshall's fielding side with 18 players out there on the oval, was an amazing sight. How was it possible to identify anyone?

Each player wore a different-colored ribbon tied around his arm. It was just like the Footy Record about a 100 years ahead of its time. You had to buy a score card so that you could identify the players.

Indeed I commend the whole system to the Australian Cricket Board. Instead of the terrible vulgarity of their present uniform I like the idea of straw colored shirts with red spots and dove-coloured hats trimmed with magenta ribbon.

And how could they go wrong with pretty colored ribbons tied around the arm to identify the players. They would produce extra funds through the sale of score cards just as they did in 1862.

But, of course, I'm with Bill O'Reilly and Ian Johnson. I have never believed in the one day game whether they wear pyjamas with names on their backs or not. There is a glorious majesty about a Test Match.

Where else can you find something that takes five days to happen? It is like a Mahler symphony, there are lots of times where you can slip into semi consciousness and come alive again. You can become terribly bored then slowly move into a climax of excitement.

Everything else is being speeded up, jammed into shorter and shorter spaces of time. Cricket should be left where it used to be; all white, peaceful, superbly boring 90 per cent of the time, somewhat unfathomable, with no names on the backs.

Would You Kiss a Merv Hughes Moustache?

Yes, I understand why that Alice Springs magistrate can't stand kissing, hugging Australian cricketers.

He would have been in deep sympathy with my old headmaster. Headmaster believed it was the English tradition of pluck and duty never to show emotion on the sporting field.

There was the appalling example one year when a mile runner breasted the tape then staggered forwards and collapsed on the grass. Tremendously bad form, that was. Even though dying from exhaustion, a gentleman athlete should never show it. That was being un-British. He should walk quietly from the field, head high.

After this disgrace to the school headmaster at assembly laid down the rules.

Always remain cool under fire. Emotion was the ultimate sin, a sign of weakness. When taking wickets or going out for a duck headmaster expected us to show the sort of sang-froid of Gary Cooper in "High Noon".

When making a century maybe a faint Errol Flynn smile could cross your lips. Nothing more. Heaven knows what he would have thought of this frightful habit of fist clenching in moments of triumph.

Oddly enough in tennis, back in the thirties, it was the done thing for the victor to jump the net to shake hands with his opponent. But then tennis was considered an effeminate sport, not a game for true Gary Coopers.

Of course, kissing began with soccer. A goal in soccer is such a rare and extraordinary event it is natural that players should get excited. Furthermore soccer players kiss with more style than our Australian Rules footballers.

Kissing in cricket began during Mr Packer's pyjama game. All the old standards disappeared then. It helped TV ratings to have the cricketers in each other's arms.

Dennis Lillee did more than anyone else to promote this new brotherly love. He wasn't a kisser, but a marvellous embracer. When a player took a catch off his bowling he would run 20 metres to give him a good hug.

However it was Prince Charles who made it decent and put kissing under regal patronage. It was back in 1984. Prince Edward had just returned from the Falkland Islands or some place equally hazardous. Prince Charles embraced his brother then kissed him on the cheek.

The Daily Express commented: "Has Prince Charles unwittingly cut a curious taboo? Has he sparked a new fashion for men?" He has indeed. There is now a avalanche of osculatory extravagance for all sexes and in all places.

Kissing was very different in my day. Fathers did not kiss sons, only daughters. My father-in-law used to complain it was disgusting the way young people these times held hands in public. As for kissing that was something males and females did very discreetly and certainly never out in the streets.

Now kissing goes on everywhere. People even kiss each other in the midst of church services to show their warm fellowship. As for the kissing it is practically X-rated stuff. You even see it outside the Town Hall or at the railway station at 8 a.m., virtually eating each other is now all the go.

Mr Brezhnev was a great kisser. In his heyday he not only kissed Dr Kissinger on the lips but embraced him in such a bear hug he lifted him clear off his feet.

President Carter was an outstanding kisser and used to kiss everyone in sight. The Queen Mother was startled when she received a Jimmy Carter kiss. She is quoted as saying: "He is the only man since my dear husband died to have had the effrontery to kiss me on the lips."

Kissing is terribly 'in' on talk and interview shows. When Parkinson or Michael Aspel kiss it reveals at once the wonderful intimacy and rapport they have with their guests.

Time magazine quoted Murray Davis, an eminent Californian sociologist:

"Increased kissing is part of the general inflation of intimate signals. We kiss people we used to hug, hug people we used to shake hands with and shake hands with people we used to nod to. Not to kiss or hug means one is not relating. Everyone is expected to kiss everyone else."

Indeed party kissing is now overwhelming. It is compulsory to kiss your hostess and if it is a gathering of only six or eight you are expected to kiss the female guests also.

There is a momentary second of tension. Should you or should you not? Your wife is standing by with a critical eye to see what sort of job you make of it.

Some hostesses are remarkably kissable. They offer a warm pair of lips and you know you are in for an excellent night. Then it works by zones. If the kiss comes just to the left or right of the lips with a lingering press on the cheek you know things are pretty good.

But from then on you work further and further into areas of frigidity. I know hostesses who give me that Bass-Strait-in-the-winter look and offer me an area somewhere to the north of the ear hole. Then there are those who dance up for the fake kiss. The whole act is performed so that lips and cheek are 10 millimetres apart.

You can get away with hand kissing. That still is considered gallant. However, if you really want to be a success, to prove that you are about to be the wow of the party, kiss your hostess on both cheeks, that sends them.

But I don't know that I am ready for the male kissing. Our most aggressive and extravagantly male cricketers have proved that this is the way to head into the nineteen nineties.

I prefer the cool approach of my old headmaster. I don't think I could bear to kiss a Merv Hughes moustache and

I'm damned if I going to kiss any chap with an Alan Border beard.

The Addiction of Cricket

Could I make an instant confession. I am a cricket addict. We live 50 metres from a cricket ground.

There are all sorts of bird calls, magpies, wattle birds, kookaburras and cockatoos, but the most evocative beautiful sound is that of a cricket ball hitting the bat. Then maybe every 10 minutes there is that wonderful shriek, more staccato, even more aboriginal than that of the sulphur crested cockatoo, the cry of "OWZAT".

Our cricket ground is lovely. It is surrounded by stringybarks, a few pines and a small pavilion. There are no advertisements, no blinking scoreboard which electrically signals WOW when someone hits a six or hands out a blinding congratulations when a batsman makes 50 or 100.

We hand out our own accolades. Admittedly we have our own hazards, the wicketkeeper tends to bring his pet kelpie, which gambols hither and yon through slips and gully. There is thick grass beyond the long on boundary and a good hook will put the ball into a pond beside the bowling green. Watching cricket at our ground is bliss.

The passion for cricket is something not easily understood. It is like skateboarding, appreciating tripe and onions, or even learning the violin, you have to be introduced to it at a very early age. As the Jesuits used to say, put the religion into them at tender years and you have them for life.

It is no good coming suddenly to cricket in one's twenties or thirties. It is quite beyond the adult mind. There are far too many strange subtleties and mysteries.

The disease is common in men but relatively rare in women. Not enough women get the very early Catholic training but there is more too it than that. I believe that the female mind, so used to child bearing and elementary survival tactics, is far too practical and pragmatic.

For example, the non addict's tolerance of a cricket broadcast I have always found to be twelve and a half minutes. My tolerance is longer than that, about 30 hours, roughly the length of a Test Match. If I cannot actually get to the Test match I like to hear every ball bowled.

Not only must I know what is going on but there is something about a cricket broadcast which is good for the soul. It is like fishing, a sort of poultice for the mind, superbly dull for very long periods, it calms down the rhythms and creates a peace.

But occasionally, say every hour or so you get a nuance, a ripple of wonder and, like a majestic symphony, the Test Match works towards a climax. Again perhaps the climax never comes and that is the beauty of cricket, it doesn't matter if a Test Match does not provide a result. It is like the Pyramids or the Exhibition building, you adore it because it is there.

It is difficult for the rest of the house to live with addicts. I find I have to listen with an ear plug or headphones, take a radio out into the garden or even listen in the car with the windows up. Non addicts find all this terribly frustrating. There is nothing worse than talking to an addict, who is tuned in and hears nothing but the game.

The ear plug is a useful device but somewhat uncomfortable in bed. When you turn over you are inclined to get throttled. Sleep is also a danger. My most regrettable episode took place during the Fourth Test match against England at Manchester in 1956. Lock and Laker were bowling on a turning wicket but Colin McDonald and Jim Burke seemed to be handling these gentlemen with remarkable skill. Inadvertently I dropped off to sleep with the radio still on.

It was 2.30 a.m. when I re-awakened after a lapse of more than three hours. Ah Thank God! McDonald and Burke were still there. All was not lost. The Australian thumb was in the hole in the dyke, holding back the flood.

Slowly the awful truth began to seep through the sleep sodden mind. This was the second time round. While I had been napping the entire Australian side had been bowled out. Our cricket writers, who frequently are on our side, had made the suggestion that an infamous curator had deliberately shaved the wicket practically with Gillette blades to defeat Lindwall and Miller.

There was so much dust on that wicket it could have been out in the Mallee. The incomparable Jim Laker had taken nine wickets for 39 and Australia in the first innings was all out for 84. Oh dear, he took 10 for 53 in the second innings.

These days you would say, why not watch it on TV? Too many advertisements, too many interruptions. I like the continuity of radio. Besides they have gone too far with their replays. It is really too much when they start to put little cameras inside the cricket stumps.

The most exciting time for me is the beginning of a Test Match, the very first over. This is so overpowering I get quite sick in the stomach. I like seeing the fast bowlers preparing for battle. Merv Hughes was not the first to go on stage with the remarkable warm-up routine, rolling the arm over, stretching the shoulder muscles and such.

No, it was Ray Lindwall who invented psychological warfare. He did it to scare the hell out of Len Hutton. Ray before taking the ball would do little runs up and down, roll his arm over, do knee bends and on one occasion, I think, he even did push ups.

Then he would take an unconscionable time measuring out his run-up, putting down a marker, finally eyeballing his victim. It was always a most impressive performance.

Fast bowlers exciting? Well yes, but for true excitement you have to go to leg spinners. Australia was always the breeding ground for the greatest leg spin bowlers. Did you see the recent Bradman series showing Bradman hitting a ball with a cricket stump?

I did similar things. Didn't we all? But it didn't do me any good. Back in the old days of the immortal Clarrie Grimmett we all wanted to be leg spinners. I spent hours, days, weeks, tossing a spinning tennis ball towards my father's battered garage door. But dammit. I couldn't get the ball on the spot, not even on the pitch. It was easier to give in and bowl the more accurate off spin.

Remember what Neville Cardus said of Clarrie Grimmett: "The first sight of Grimmett bowling arouses mild laughter. His action recalls the ancient round-arm worthies, or it recalls cricket on the sands with a walking stick for a wicket and a father of six playing for the first time in years. Grimmett's arm seems to creak. But watch his wrist and his fingers; they are sinuous and beautiful. The wrist twirls and swivels; the fingers seem to adore and caress the ball, with the touch of a parent...To play forward to Grimmett, to miss the spin and find yourself stumped by Oldfield - why it is like an amputation done under an anaesthetic."

I used to love watching Doug Ring. He loved to give the ball plenty of sky and he tossed it right up. So there was this delicious temptation for the batsman, like a cream cake waiting to be gobbled. Ah, but one mis-judge of the turn, one error in timing, and he was gone.

Richie Benaud was never such a tempter as Doug. He was a miser with runs. He came in sideways, five shuffling paces to the wicket and those cold blue eyes never revealed his intentions. The late Ray Robinson told the story that even 10 years after he retired, Benaud gave a lesson in accuracy to a cricket class. With uncanny skill he pitched several balls on to a piece of paper. Then he closed his eyes and did it again.

So the Second Test comes to Melbourne on Boxing Day. It always does. Christmas is such a stressful time, just the agony of getting there, surviving the Christmas parties, buying the presents, suffering a guilty conscience over not sending Christmas cards, then finally eating that enormous Christmas dinner.

One needs to atone for all this, to settle into a comfortable seat at the MCG for a doze. That's the beauty about Test matches. They take their time, if they are any good they have a noble somnolent pace.

There have been ugly suggestions that Pyjama Cricket will eventually replace Test matches. We must fight against this. The National Trust must have Test cricket classified and preserved.

Where else can you find something so beautifully slow that it goes on for five days. I love it, but then I was trained at birth.

The Pleasure of Thrashing Poms

It's nice thrashing the Poms. There is a huge deep satisfaction in it, don't you think?

We slaughter everybody; it is not quite the same with the Indians, the Pakistanis, the Sri Lankans or even the West Indians. It's the Poms. We absolutely love to kick them to death.

All through this Test series Alan Border made it clear he wanted to crush England, you know, by an innings in every match. That included State matches, games up country, plus anything they did in one-day pyjamas. I think even if we played them at ping pong, hop scotch or Monopoly we would want to slaughter them at that too.

You could see Mr Border's intense disappointment when two of the Tests were drawn. We could have beaten them five-nil. Nor was Bobby Simpson satisfied. We could have performed 20 per cent better, said he.

I think I have the same savage atavistic streak as most Australians. I am only half listening when Messrs Hughes, Reid, Alderman and Matthews are being hit all over the ground. I turn to the cricket notes with only one tenth of enthusiasm when Dean Jones has gone for a duck. On those occasions when Australia has performed regrettably I have actually gone to the front page first to read about failures in the economy, instead of automatically turning to the back.

But I am worried. I am becoming soft. Or is it perhaps the faint approach of human feelings? This past week I have had feelings of guilt. Has our euphoria over the thrashing of the Poms been a bit too much? Couldn't we say a thing or two about the visit that was actually kind? "Thank-you very much Mr Gooch and your fellow colleagues. It was wonderful having you and we promise not to be so vicious next time."

But no, we had these pictures of Graham Gooch, head down, his black chin even more covered with stubble than ever. He had this look of immense sadness, a felon who had committed the most appalling crime. Greg Chappell commented: "Poor Graham Gooch. The only difference between Gooch's tour and what happened on the Bounty was that Captain Bligh got that bit more support."

Yes indeed, but I felt for Midshipman Gooch. In front of those cameras he looked as miserable as if Captain Bligh had just ordered that he be tied to the mast and given 500 lashes.

Stories have pointed out that the England team was lax in the field, they didn't show the right competitive spirit, they were gutless, whereas every Australian was true blue and showed a "life or death" will to win.

There were such headlines as: ENGLAND'S FINAL DISGRACE and HEADS WILL ROLL. Then the English press gave some quite distinct notes of displeasure. "Pathetic," said the *Daily Mirror*. "Get this lot out," said the *Sun* in its usual subtle headlines. Even the sober *Times* reported that the England team could hardly leave for the airport quick enough.

Why do you and I, Allan Border, Merv and all, carry on like this? One letter writer to the *Age* last week made the quaint suggestion we shouldn't be excited because it is only a game. He's wrong, of course. Cricket was never a game; a ritual, a sacred rite, or even curious national tragicomedy, certainly, but by no conception a game.

It is more like an Aboriginal corroboree. It helps establish our being, our right to existence in this antipodean continent. We have this ceremony with the Poms so that every couple of years we can re-establish our egos.

I have always believed this takes place for the reason that children ultimately want to conquer their parents. I understand that spiders tend to eat their mothers and fathers. We relish the same thing. It has been going on for a very long time and it was even more important in the old colonial days.

Whenever teams won in England they came home to triumphs akin to those offered by Rome after the armies had spent a season slaughtering Goths, Gauls and such. I think the greatest homecoming was in December 1882 after the famous Ashes Test Match when Spofforth took 14 wickets for 90 runs.

All Melbourne was decorated with Welcome Home banners. Then they had one of the most spectacular processions Melbourne has ever seen. They had a torchlight procession composed of several hundred firemen from Melbourne's brigades, six brass bands and they all gathered at the Burke and Wills monument in Collins Street. Then they marched to the MCG, where they had a special display of electric light plus a huge show of fireworks. Every cricketer received a gold medal the size of an old five shillings piece.

Nor did England take kindly to being thrashed by a colony. The Poms didn't like it then and they don't like it now.

Ted Dexter, who has had a big hand in the selection of MCC teams lately, once wrote in Wisden: "I have on occasions taken a quite unreasonable dislike to Australians. Sorry, but it is the truth. And if I blush at the thought, let alone the telling of it publicly, I derive a certain amount of comfort from the knowledge that I am not alone amongst England's cricketers, highly responsible though they of course are. Given suitable circumstances - and there can be few so absolutely right for a spot of disliking than a Test Match between us Pommies...Under provocation...Australians can, and do, quite readily and often in my experience, throw off all their 180 years of civilised nationhood: they gaily revive every prejudice they ever knew, whether to do with accent, class consciousness, or even the original convict complex, and sally forth into battle with a dedication which would not disgrace the most committed of the world's agitators."

Mr Dexter could even be understating the matter here. I would like to suggest that we move forward a hundred years and just show perhaps a modicum of sophistication and kindliness towards our visitors.

Could we perhaps delete 'thrash', 'pulverise', 'murder', 'chastise', 'decimate', 'destroy' and few other unsavory words from our vocabulary?

Yes, I for one feel very guilty over the unsporting way in which we have treated Mr Gooch and his men. Our euphoria had the air of the cannibal just after he had roasted and pickled the visiting missionary.

This doesn't mean to say I would have let Mr Gooch win any of his matches. Certainly not. Perhaps after yet another 100 years.

COLUMNS ON LESSER MUSCULAR ACTIVITIES...

6

Columns on Lesser Muscular Activities

The Theft of an Old Mate

Some creature stole my bicycle last week.

So topical don't you think? It was Bicycle Week. Champion cyclists were giving speed demonstrations in the City Square not more than 20 metres away.

My bicycle was chained to a lamp post outside Capitol House in Swanston Street. I went up to the 10th floor to buy some bow ties from John Deen, the famous tie man. I couldn't have been more than 10 minutes.

When I returned it was gone, bicycle, chain, lock and all. You know how it is. First puzzlement. I'm pretty forgetful. I did leave it there didn't I? Then stunned disbelief.

I got down on my hands and started studying the empty stretch of pavement. How could anyone take it?

Actually I knew darned well how they could take it. Alan Parker, president of the Bicycle Institute, had been warning as loud as he could. There were teams of professional bicycle thieves on the move. They used bolt cutters which could go through almost any chain or lock faster than you could bite a peanut.

Alan Parker says Victoria has very nearly the highest bike theft rate in the world - an estimated 35,841 went off last year, 940 per 100,000 of the population. New South Wales lost 32,766.

Oh yes, if you leave your bike in a parking lot, or chained in the city your chances of having it stolen in any one year are about even money.

So maybe I'm lucky. This is the first time it has happened since I started commuting to town by bike 25 years ago.

I guess it wasn't the best bicycle in the world. Not a $3000 Italian job made out of metal they invented for going to the moon. No, it was a Malvern Star and our relationship couldn't have been sweeter.

We had done at least 100,000 miles together. Except for a flat tyre here and there, no break downs. If you tried to compare it with the reliability of the railways or any form of public transport, you have to start laughing.

Funny thing that. It all started 25 years ago. There was a public transport strike, no trains or buses. So I borrowed a bicycle and rode to town, 10 kilometres from East Malvern. It took 25 minutes, faster door to door than bus, tram or train. Actually with all the parking problems you have with four wheeled vehicles it was a damned sight quicker and easier than coming by your own car.

I pedalled via parks, along the Yarra. The whole experience was so agreeable I never got over it. Before I had looked upon getting to work and back as absolutely the most horrid part of the day. Now it was the best.

And I would keep varying my route for fun. Particularly I liked going home through the Greek and Italian quarters of Prahran. Still do actually, until someone stole my bike. You would get all the marvellous cooking smells. You don't get cooking smells in a car with all your windows wound up and the air conditioning on.

If you don't ride a bicycle yourself it is hard to explain exactly what all this means. You get very well acquainted with each other, you understand each other's strange quirks and angles. Such a relationship takes years to develop.

I used to have a friend from Alabama, an old Beechcraft pilot but an out-and-out bike nut. Marvin understood the personal nature of a bike and he used to say: "Rahdin' somebuddy else's bahk is like wearin' somebuddy else's teeth."

Then, of course losing your bike is bad enough, but losing your saddle is the ultimate grief. That's irreplaceable. Sir Hubert Opperman once advised: "You may one day sell your bicycle but never never does a serious bicyclist sell his saddle."

Begging your pardon, but only does a well worn infinitely softened and battered leather saddle really understand the mysterious curves, pelvic bones and strange things that go on down there.

There is a story about that saddle. Back in 1976 I was riding my Malvern Star across the United States, a trip of 4300 miles. I had ridden as far as Kansas and was suffering. To be frank I needed a replacement behind. There were blisters on both cheeks. A fellow traveller on the ride was Chip Haines, a commercial artist from Florida. He was suffering the same awful intimate agonies.

I said to him: "Look, we can't do worse. Let's swap saddles."

The result was magic. My saddle suited his bottom, his saddle suited mine. It had a strange name, "Cool Seat". Oddly enough the week after I returned to Australia the alloy frame of the Cool Seat snapped. I wrote to the Cool Seat company, a nice letter, told them of the wonders of the saddle, would they send me another by air mail and I would pay the cost.

Americans are wonderful. Three weeks later there was a Cool Seat in the mail. "A new saddle with our compliments" was the message. "Our saddles never break."

Alas, I don't think the Cool Seat company exists any more, so I can't get another. I have the prospect of infinite exquisite agonies ahead, the months and months of breaking in a new saddle.

Yes indeed, I have ordered a new bicycle. How could I live without one? Nothing could be worse than trying to get around the city on inferior modes of transport, unreliable trains in particular.

But as Marvin pointed out, you have to learn how to use a new set of teeth. The old Malvern Star back in the dream time cost about $220. It was a 10-speed. The new job when it arrives will be an 18-speed, costing about $780 with more advanced technology.

It will take six months to a year, however, before we fully understand and love each other. But how will I save it from marauding bike thief gangs?

Mr Parker recommended a U type lock made out of a miracle metal impervious to bolt cutters or even tungsten saws. So I bought one. It is called the Kryptonite K4. Presumably it came from the same planet on which Superman was born.

Good grief! the darned thing cost $75. Once upon a time you could get an entire bike for that kind of money.

But do you know, the strangest part of the entire episode was going home in the tram. One felt odd indeed sitting in a tram, with helmet on one's knees. To say nothing of having lots and lots to think about, a departed friend who had carried me for 100,000 miles.

The Achilles Knee

Every week one of our contemporaries prints a list of all the footballers that have been injured. It goes down almost a full page.

One runs an eye down it very nervously. So many names, it is reminiscent of those huge casualty lists printed in our newspapers after Gallipoli and the Battle of the Somme.

Normal humans live, suffer, die, get run over by motor cars. They disappear in almost total anonymity, but footballers are fortunate, even a bruised thumbnail is sufficient for them to make the lists of the wounded.

I have the latest list in front of me now. There are 101 names and of these 21 are knees problems. Let's see, among the ailing knees, we have Gary Ablett and Andrew Bews of Geelong, Gary Buckenara of Hawthorn, Sean Wight, Steven Clark and Trevor Spencer of Melbourne, just to mention a few kneelights.

Actually I am grateful for all the medical knowledge I have gathered from sporting heroes. Let's go back over some very famous knees. There was the saga of our tennis great Peter McNamara. He tore the cruciate ligament in his right knee and as his tennis career went to ruin we had daily stories on his knee reconstruction. There were shots of him with his knee in an 11kg plaster cast, then smaller casts and as he tackled his comeback his knee was on the job, lifting weights.

There was Graham Yallop's knee. I was thrilled because he damaged his medial ligament, which gave us a completely different ligament to worry about. How I remember the hourly reports on the swelling and whether he would pass a fitness test to play against the Englishmen.

In 1984 there was some brilliant stuff on Rene Kink of Essendon, known as the Abominable Hulk. He suffered from "patella tendonitis" and they gave him a program of running in water to ease the pressure on his knees.

The most rewarding knee year was 1973. Peter Hudson was having fearful knee trouble and we saw some of the most intimate knee reporting ever carried out in this country. Also that year Francis Bourke of Richmond went down with knee trouble. The *Herald* produced the unforgettable headline: TRAGEDY STRIKES RICHMOND.

Des Tuddenham, captain and coach of Essendon, went the same way. In my files I have a piece of deeply moving verse written by one lady fan:

In these days of nuclear testing
Of bugging and LSD
What do I get in the headlines?
The latest on Tuddy's knee.
When the Prime Minister was leaving
On his visit to Buckingham P.
The last thing he said to his colleague:
Keep me posted on Tuddy's knee.

It is generally agreed that Polly Farmer's knee was the biggest news story of any kind in 1962. It was photographed repeatedly and zoom cameras came within 5mm of it on television. Teams of specialists discussed it. There were marvellous sketches in the paper on how knees worked but, best of all, we followed Mr Farmer's cartilage through all its stresses and strains until finally, at the end of the season, it was removed.

It was surprising that the Museum did not seize the opportunity to grab Farmer's cartilage and put it on display, like Phar Lap's heart.

Apparently God did not do a very good job with the knee. Allow me to parade medical knowledge gained simply from studying sporting news for 40 years. The knee is not an efficient joint. The end of the tibia is like a flat plate, the end of the femur is more like a bunched fist and all that holds them together are ligaments and muscle. The cartilage is a piece of tough gristle shaped liked a full moon. It acts as a washer between the joints.

Unless you are like Polly Farmer every knee has two of them - the medial and the lateral. Upon injury it becomes like a loose cog. The cartilage can be removed but the greatest danger of all is torn ligaments. Unless treated within the first week injury can become permanent.

Perhaps all footballers should have their cartilages removed at 17 and given a kneeworthy certificate before teams sign them up.

Some specialists are saying cartilages are getting smaller and smaller and, on the Darwinian theory, maybe in a 1000 years they will disappear altogether.

Almost inevitably all sportsmen eventually retire because of crook knees. We have an Anti-Cancer Council, a National Heart Foundation, societies to fight asthma, diabetes, multiple sclerosis, why isn't there an Anti Cartilage Council or a Society for the Saving of Kneecaps.

No question, knees are the biggest worry in sport. The cartilage is as dangerous to the human as the sesamoid bone is to the horse.

Except, of course, racehorse owners solve their problems with a far greater simplicity. As soon as a racehorse breaks his sesamoid bone they take him out and shoot him.

Champagne is for Inside Not Outside

Do you think we could start a Society For The Restoration Of Dignity in Sport?

I am grieved by the sight of sportsmen shaking up bottles of champagne, then putting their thumbs on top and spraying each other down, like children with water pistols.

The French have been very trying lately. Their activities with nuclear tests have been nigh unforgivable. After the sinking of the Rainbow Warrior we became so angry with the French at our place we declared a black ban on all French products, no more Camembert, no more brie, no more Chanel, no French fashions, no Chateau Lafite. But, Dear Reader, someone offered us a bottle of 1982 Veuve Cliquot Brut. We cracked. You can only go so far...

CHAMPAGNE IS FOR INSIDE, NOT OUTSIDE!

It has been said that champagne is the one alcoholic drink a gentleman can take at breakfast. It is the one drink that is a genuine comfort any time of the day or night. If you go to Veuve Cliquot at Rheims there are 24 kilometres of underground cellars. These the Romans dug in the 1st Century A.D.

When you go down into these cool cellars there is the nice feeling of being surrounded by about 33 million bottles, all quietly maturing. Now, champagne is made with infinite care and love. The chardonnay and pinot noir is fermented in the bottle. Each bottle is racked on an angle so that the sediment goes down to the neck. What's more each one of these bottles, every month or so, has to be given a turn, so that the sediment goes to the right spot.

Finally the sediment is disgorged, a fine cork put in and wired down, to make what some of us think is the most delicious drink in the world.

So what do they do with it? I believe the disgraceful practice of champagne hosing began with the Grand Prix racing drivers. They, of course, are rich. Usually they have big bottles, magnums or jeroboams. They can spray everyone in sight including their quite hideous racing cars.

Now the idea, I am shocked to say, has spread to cricket. I noticed on TV the triumphant Australian team was having a spray orgy with both beer and champagne. The champagne was the real thing. My eyesight is poor but I can read a bottle label at 200 metres and they were spraying with Moet, which around here costs at least $50 a bottle.

Our Society for the Restoration of Dignity believes champagne should be put inside one, not outside, and the cricketers would get as much satisfaction with more fire power, better aim and soaking capacity by using soda siphons.

Now this dreadful, wasteful game is spreading like a virus. Everyone is doing it. You may have noticed that when Irene Goonan had her triumphant victory this week-end and was elected to the Doncaster and Templestowe Council in place of the Mayor, Bill Larkin, what did she do? She opened a bottle of champagne and sprayed it all over herself and her husband.

Champagne spraying will become the practice at all victories, from the passing of examinations to successful take over bids. Could you see Messrs, Bond, Elliott, Spalvins, Packer and Murdoch spraying each other down with appropriate vintages?

We were told it was the first time Australia had regained the Ashes in England since 1934. This was misleading. It gave the impression we had suffered more than half a century of miserable cricket degradation and suffering, when the truth was frequently we went to Britain with the Ashes already won.

There was greater national euphoria over winning these Ashes than anything since the America's Cup. The Dignity Society would like to make a number of points. From now on, when a bowler takes a wicket, instead of throwing a fist in the air and exchanging indiscriminatory embraces with everyone except the umpire, could we not just have a bowler and his captain exchanging respectful bows?

Could fieldsman who take catches, please remain unkissed?

When the batsman has hit the winning run, need Messrs Marsh and Boon run headlong into each other's arms like a long parted Romeo and Juliet? No. The Dignity Society would prefer that they quietly walk up the wicket and give each other a firm handshake.

I think the practice of cricket kissing has had its effect on the public. Their hysterical behavior has caused national and international hysteria. How do you explain the national hate that the British Press has heaped on Gower. He looks a very nice, blonde, clean cut young man, who, unquestionably, would be very good to his mother.

You would suspect from the headlines he is guilty of terrible crimes, like raping 80-year-old nuns, or writing filthy graffiti on the walls of Westminster Abbey. No, all the poor man has done, is to lose consecutively a number of cricket matches. There was a time in England when that was quite an honorable occupation. There was once, a nice masochistic joy in losing.

There is something to be said for the old 19th century English gentleman we read about in comic books, the one who showed little emotion either winning or losing, but just preferred to play the game.

Come to think of it, the older I get the less I think it matters who wins. The real joy to be had is in watching a truly great player, no matter what side he is on, bowling beautifully or batting with such grace and skill you just hope he stays there for the rest of the afternoon.

For that sort of a performance, English or Australian, I will drink a glass of champagne and certainly not pour it over my head.

Our Muscular Christianity Beats Everything

As we enter a week of agonising sporting euphoria, could one put forward a theory.

In homage to Isaac Newton we could call it the Fourth Law of Motion. If I remember my schoolboy physics there were three laws of motion. The suggested Fourth Law is this:

The Greater the Victory the Greater the Hometown Publicity. The Greater the Loss the Smaller the Hometown publicity.

I have taken out my ruler and I think the ratio for a grand victory is usually 10 times that for a loss. In some sports the feeling back home is so chauvinist it is difficult to discern who actually won the event.

The usual practice is to report only the triumphs and sufferings of your own beloved competitors. Others don't really exist. I have always treasured one sporting headline which appeared in London's *Daily Telegraph*:

Injured Divina is 18th Despite Wrist in Plaster

Divina was an English skier. It was important to stress her grit, skill and courage in coming in 18th. It was not really important to discover who actually won, who was a foreigner anyway.

Yesterday we had some fine headlines reporting that Australia finished a magnificent ninth in the 100 km team time trial cycling. Did the Germans actually win? It doesn't matter really.

We have been playing a Test match in Pakistan. Admittedly there has been some other competition this week but there have been no broadcasts or telecasts. The truth is we have been mercilessly thrashed and the Fourth Law of Motion has been well applied.

And I appreciate the feeling. I hate stories about Australians being beaten. I had heard on the radio news that Pakistan had batted first, Miandad had enough runs to satisfy most humans for an entire season, then having reduced the wicket to something akin the Gibson Desert, the Pakistanis devoured the Australians on a spinning wicket.

Even though I am a passionate cricket lover I tried to drag my eye across to the columns that recorded all this, but in the end I could not. It was far more satisfying to read of an Australian victory against Kenya at hockey, a sport which in my school days was considered on the namby if not the pamby side.

Ah, but had it been an Australian victory with nine wickets from Tony Dodemaide and 300 runs from Dean Jones the Fourth Law would have applied. The Pakistani cricket would get a live telecast on Channel Nine and big columns on page one.

Back in the 19th century there were many fine theories about the nobility of sport. One of the most interesting, which seemed to be inspired by Dr Arnold and Rugby School, was that of the "muscular Christianity". If one was good in muscle then one was also good in mind; sport helped purify soul. Sport spread decency, honor and good fellowship and this was why Britain and its Empire was so great.

Well, muscular Christianity has suffered some fearful schisms lately. Britain is only slightly talking to India because eight members of its team have played in South Africa and the chances of an imminent tour taking place are slim.

Relations between England and Pakistan are similar to those between Britain and Germany after the treaty of Versailles. There have been accusations of cheating and vile umpiring. Indeed one notices even during the current Test we have made formal complaints against Pakistani umpires and the state of the wicket.

In football, I understand, international relations are so congenial that English teams are now banned from Europe. Or take the America's Cup, a sport designed for the rich and the, allegedly, sophisticated.

It brought out such aggression in Australia's dealings with the United States that boxing gloves were placed on the gentle kangaroo. Now, from what one can gather, New Zealand, having departed from the ANZUS alliance, is almost at a state of war with the United States. We witnessed a slanging match on television between the American Dennis Conner and the New Zealander David Barnes which even Messrs Keating and John Howard would have been proud to possess.

One report from San Diego which impressed me stated that the intrigue going on there was worthy of the Manchu dynasty and a pledge of undying support had a shelf life of about six hours.

Simple examples of muscular heresy can be found in most sports. One would not want to go too deeply into Australian Rules football but we have just witnessed the annual execution of coaches who have failed to bring their teams to victory. Victoria is not talking to South Australia and there are further rumblings of a secession movement in West Australia.

However I am particularly interested in applying this Fourth Law. Every affluent nation on earth is spending millions to gain success in sport. We maintain a full time muscle camp in Canberra called the Institute of Sport. The United States, Russia and two Germanys spend even more than our national deficit.

The belief is that through sport you gain international publicity and evidence of national superiority. But what if YOUR victories are only slightly reported in the foreign press, what if the big space goes to the local girl who came 18th in the downhill ski event.

What if other countries get bitterly angry at seeing all your fellows on the victory dais all the time? Maybe Russia, the United States or even Australia should send away teams which get themselves slightly defeated at tennis, football, athletics, hockey and basket ball.

After every defeat they would get x times as much publicity in the foreign press than a victory would earn. And if they went down proudly and magnificently they would be deeply loved instead of causing controversy. I bet you if the Australian teams wins in Pakistan the publicity won't be over attractive.

Keep notes during the next fortnight, apply the Fourth Law of Motion and I assure you, the result will be fascinating.

Why Not Retrospective Wilkies?

The Victorian Football League has had a lovely time this past week handing out Brownlow Medals.

It discovered that back in the days of yore many players tied for the medal. But then they went through a countback system and awarded it to only one man.

Now they have rectified this terrible injury. Anyone who should even faintly have received a Brownlow is to get one. They have been able to drag back old heroes, evoke tears to the eye, have more Brownlow Medal parties and gain a further two or three thousand hectares of newspaper space for football.

This, naturally must be taken as a precedent. The Anti Football League, for example, always awards the Wilkie Medal for the human who did least for football in the fairest manner.

We too had a number of ties with very delicate countbacks so now we will have to award a number of belated Wilkies. For example there is 1971. Kate Baillieu won the Wilkie that year for refusing to play in an all female football team for GTV9.

She tied with Kerry Packer. We thought Mr Packer had nobly contributed to the cause by digging up VFL Park so that his teams could use it for Pyjama Cricket. Mr Packer will have to get his Wilkie in the mail.

Again in 1984 we had a three way tie. Ranald MacDonald and John Elliott were advocating a national competition and they wanted to reduce the number of VFL teams to nine. The AFL thought this a step forward. The more teams that could be removed from Melbourne the better. Ultimately Anne Le Grand won on a countback. Mrs Le Grand had endured incredible suffering by being wife of Peter Le Grand, a 3UZ football commentator for 14 years.

Furthermore we did consider one year that we might give a Wilkie to Harry Beitzel feeling his dulcet tones on radio had done much for our cause. Is it too late to give him a medal now? It could be a very sentimental occasion.

But don't you see the VFL has created an extraordinary precedent. The brilliant idea for flashback awards could spread into every field of activity, all the ghastly Oscars, Logies, Gammies, Yummies or whatever they are called.

Now take the Hawke Government. It is in a serious trouble. According to the latest polls only about one in three electors is interested in voting Labor. You will remember Gough Whitlam, when he came to power, abolished the old imperial system of handing out Knighthoods.

Clearly Australians adore receiving awards. Mr Hawke could pick up lots of love and enthusiasm by handing out all the Sirs and Dames that have missed out these past couple of decades.

I don't know who he would have in mind but here are some suggestions, people who should never have missed out.

- Dame Susan Renouf for services to marriage. Over the past 20 years she has given us some of the most beautiful and colourful of weddings.

- Sir Norm Gallagher for staging the great battle of the MCG and helping to return the Cain Government to power.

- Sir John Cain for services to women. He got women into the inner sanctum of the members betting ring at Flemington and into the most sacred seats of the Long Room at the MCG.

- Dame Florence Isabel Bjelke-Petersen for services to cooking and returning scones to their rightful place in the culinary diet.

- Mr Derryn Hinch for services to the legal profession and litigation.

- Sir Clive Robertson for compassion on television and ability to extract tears from a Prime Minister.

- Sir Jack Herbert for telling so much about fellow Queenslanders and keeping up newspaper circulations week after week.

- Sir Warwick Fairfax for services to banks and banking.

- Sir Robert Hughes for writing "The Fatal Shore" and for making so many Australians so proud that their forbears were convicts.

- Dame Germaine Greer for never forgetting her beloved Melbourne and making its qualities known to all around the Commonwealth.

- Sir Patrick Cash for services to the language and umpires and not letting American players have it all their own way.

- Sir Paul Keating for services to antiques and horology.

- Sir Russell Hinze in gratitude for defying all dieticians and eating fads.

- Sir Mark "Jacko" Hudson for services to advertising and promoting the necessity for remote control TV monitors.

- Sir Andrew Peacock for services to Telecom and promotion of the car telephone.

- Lord Bill Hayden for his wonderful example in showing the value of travel and tourism and because we can't continue with just a plain Mister Hayden as Governor General.

- Sir Donald Dunstan for breadth of human spirit. After resurrecting South Australia from the dark ages, he tried valiantly do something for Victoria as Tourism director.

In the old days if you were boss of the Army, Navy or Air Force, on the High Court bench or even Lord Mayor of Melbourne, automatically you picked up a splendid gong. We will have to have Dame Winsome. Then ex-Prime Ministers were a "must". Arise Sir Malcolm Fraser. That would be handy for him in illustrious posts with the Commonwealth or visits to Texas.

There are some special awards I would recommend. As Freddie Trueman pointed out, Sir Francis Drake was the only bowler ever to get a knighthood, so we could have one for Ray Lindwall. Sir Raymond had the most beautiful action of any bowler I ever saw. I would like also to see Sir Keith Stackpole. His citation would point that he was the first opening batsman who thought there was no harm in immediately making runs without the classic hour or so of digging in.

Here we have just a few recommendations for knighthoods. I am sure you can think of many more. But what a party we could have, what a dazzling investiture. It would be so brilliant it might even return the Hawke Government.

Then we could quietly say "Goodbye" to Bob by shifting him to the House of Lords.

SEXY AND VULGAR COLUMNS...

7

Sexy and Vulgar Columns

Spare Us the Arsehole

You may have noticed there has been a well-publicised war amongst Melbourne's radio personalities.

Interesting that, you don't have people in radio, you have personalities.

There is nothing unusual in a personalities row is there? They do it from time to time when their ratings are ailing. It is a means of generating publicity. Politicians have always done it. Prize fighters have always done it, immediately before a fight when the sale of tickets is required. Characters like Ali even expressed their loathing in verse.

But I am fascinated by a bout between Derryn Hinch and John Blackman of 3AW. When Mr Blackman departed from 3AW Hinch said on air: "Personally, I should say 3AW hasn't lost its soul, it's just lost its arsehole."

Now arsehole is a most uncomely expression and Melbourne's *Herald*, one time an august and sensitive newspaper, broke out the phrase and printed it in large type in their front page lead.

When I picked up my paper it sent a quiver of shock from the eyeball into the brain. "Hey," I shouted to my wife, "There's nowhere they can go any more. Now we have arseholes."

How difficult it is to get over one's old fashioned deeply instilled training. I had an editor who used to thunder: "You work for a family newspaper and don't ever forget it. There are good Methodists, Presbyterians and Baptists out there. Every piece of vulgarity you let slip into the newspaper costs us readers."

All blasphemy, bodily functions and sex were on the black list. Sex actually didn't exist at all in the nineteen forties and fifties. Arsehole? Heavens above, we didn't even have anuses. It was almost impossible to describe any part of the lower anatomy. Bums, no. Posterior was too pompous. I used to contrive the word "sit-upon". As for penis that was a male member, not be confused with member of parliament.

Females were too ladylike to have anything at all. Genitalia, certainly not. Indeed, it was very hard to describe copulation. I think the nearest you could get to it was "relations", you had "relations", certainly not sexual relations. Or sometimes you would commit a certain act.

If you were raped you were indecently assaulted, but if you were good and properly indecently assaulted, you were outraged. Homosexuals? What could you do with them? There would be court cases which referred darkly to "unnatural acts". What on earth did they do to each other, one thought.

An abortion was an illegal operation. Women didn't even get pregnant, they were in a certain condition and as for brothels, they were houses of ill fame. I still can't go down Little Lonsdale without thinking: "My God, that place was a house of ill fame." You couldn't get a name more fraught with sin.

And that's another thing. You couldn't have "My God" in the paper. Yes, you had to be very careful how you treated God. And Jesus. I was severely reprimanded for putting "Geez" into the mouth of an interviewee. Just a cheap way of getting blasphemy, I was told.

Nor could we have damn or struth. It would only offend our readers. Hell wasn't popular either. We must have been frightened of offending him. Then bloody was a dark and terrible word, you got around it with "blunky".

That's the way it was, right until the nineteen sixties. I wrote a daily column and there was a competition to be first with every obscenity and blasphemy. I had a break through with God in 1962, damn made it in 1964.

We had an abortion in the paper in 1968 and good grief, in 1972 a woman was raped. In 1976 we achieved bloody. Until then we had to make use of George Bernard Shaw when things were always "Not Pygmalion Likely" but you must appreciate bloody was an enormous breakthrough, and I believe it had to go all the way to the Board.

The old English term for copulation had a difficult time. In 1975 it was in Parliament. In a discussion on pornography the members condemned a book titled "The Big F..." You see, still, I can't get myself to say it.

In 1979 there was a case and oh, shock, the word actually appeared in the *Age*. This was a watershed decision, like freedom for slaves in the U.S.

Oh dear, in 1980 we acquired shit, bullshit, bugger and since then there has been nothing to which we will not stoop, even arsehole. The inflation of profanity however is worrying.

Say something really disastrous happens, say you are stung by a bull ant, say the TV goes on the blink, or your backhand at the net fails for the umpteenth time. What do you say, how do you release your cooped up emotions? Do you use some dreary word like 'arsehole' which even appears on the front page of the *Herald*?

You need something vile, filthy, outrageous, which really applies to the situation. But you can't. They're no good any more. They have all been on radio in the breakfast programs.

I believe a special resarch unit, composed of language experts, should be established at the National University. It will be their job to find a whole new range of outrageous swear words, unfit for newspaper or radio. I believe there are some words in Hungarian that would shrivel your hair off. Maybe we could use some of those.

This could do much to restore our national stability.

Mr Blackman, no doubt, is deeply grateful to Mr Hinch. There used to be a song: "There's No-one Quite As Famous as Harry James." Now we could say: "There's Nothing As Famous as Blackers Anus." I beg your pardon, arsehole.

The Crafty Creature's Guide to Sex

I have nothing against Boy George, he is the prettiest English pop star we have had here in a generation. He is infinitely more wholesome than the Beatles. Also I am quite moved by Marilyn. His languid pallor is appealing.

It's just that - well - I was brought up in a terribly heterosexual household, and went to a boarding school that was so guiltily male we didn't even allow females to wait on the tables. Now the 'in' trendy word is androgynous and we are told what a beautiful thing it is to sink the difference between the sexes, for all of us to be one.

I can understand all that and I think it puts life on an elegant serene plane. Alas, I cannot get these beastly urges out of my system. I like to know that's MALE and that's FEMALE. Creatures in the animal kingdom have an instinct for these matters. For example male and female crocodiles may look exactly the same to you and me, but I am assured a male crocodile knows instantly when he sees a female crocodile.

I have a male friend who stood in a queue last week outside the Melbourne Cricket Ground. He was hoping to get into a lavatory. It was only after he had been in the queue for five minutes that he realised that he was waiting for the lavatory of the wrong gender.

THE CRAFTY CREATURE'S GUIDE TO SEX...

You used to able to tell by clothes. Not any more. Boy George has fixed all that. The males are wearing dresses. You used to able to tell by smell. Messrs Chanel, Lanvin etc made sure of that. Not any more. The male deodorants are so divine all the girls are going for them. My daughters love the latest after-shaves.

You used to be able to tell by shape. Not any more. Two out of three females are now bigger and stronger than I am. When I bicycle they bicycle past me. When I jog they jog past me with the speed of light. I did manage to overtake a female last Tuesday but I think she had stopped to do up a shoelace.

You used to be able to tell by their narrow shoulders and their wide hips. Not any more. You see hips that are curiously narrow and what with them all going to muscle building gyms they have shoulders like Mr Barry Round.

Maybe some of you folk out there, like me, are losing your grip, so to speak. Well, I have organised my own guide to form, a set of clues which enables me to identify male from female crocodiles.

Jeans:

Females wear them shorter up the calf. Furthermore the female of the species can endure much more pain than the male, so it tends to wear the garment much tighter, particularly about the crotch.

Tops:

Very sloppy at the moment. This makes it impossible to identify breasts. The I-have-just-escaped-from-Afghanistan look is popular with females this week. Both sexes tend to wear shirts hanging out, but trendy South Yarra males like to have the cuffs of their shirts unbuttoned and slightly rolled. The males are also going for holes in the elbows of their sweaters. Females are deep into harness at the moment. They are wearing a lot of leather around their middles.

Sneakers/Joggers:

Female gym/jogging shoes are just slightly more vulgar. Male sneakers are bigger and dirtier. If you can stand the cold it is considered right not to wear socks.

Smoking:

The young creature with a cigarette is more likely to be female. Look particularly for the angle, if it is held up in the classic little finger teacup style, three to one on it's female.

Hair:

Not easy. Both sexes are going for Apaches, both are going for lavatory brush styles, spikes, candy colors. However, male hair tends to be more aggressively bleached and longer.

Ear Rings:

Very good clue. Most males, still, are only wearing one ear ring. There are certain messages to be read from which ear, but I am told this is notoriously unreliable.

Newspapers:

Males almost invariably start reading the newspaper from the back page. Females tend to talk about sex more, but their conversation is often more intelligent.

Posture:

Now this is a delicate subject. I once knew a hostess who said you could always tell where males had been sitting, because crumbs were left in the middle of their seats. What's more my mother used to say a lady never went outside unless she wore hat, gloves, and most important of all, always she kept her knees together.

That knee business doesn't apply. I mean, have you noticed some of the dummy models in the shop windows? However, males do, more often, stand with their legs apart.

Handbags:

Another excellent clue. Male handbags are much neater and smaller than female handbags. But, alas, many females are not carrying them at all.

Make Up:

The females definitely are better at it. Not many chaps are skilled at doing up their eyes. And it is still considered not done for a male to make up his face in public.

Not one of these clues that I have given you will prove anything. Consider yourself like a detective in the CIB, amass and sift all the evidence. Then, when it is all put together, I think I can guarantee you an accurate result.

I find now that I am right, better than 90 per cent of the time.

Please Can We Continue to Have Sex?

You can see it all, there is a move at a high Government level to wipe out sex.

I present, as just a small part of the mounting evidence, two news stories this past week.

1 The Commonwealth produced *A Style Manual for Authors, Editors and Printers*, which de-sexed the entire English language. We no longer have fishermen, we have fisher persons; we no longer have aldermen, we have alderpeople; the ombudsman is an ombudsperson. Ye Gods, even manholes are out. Now they are access holes.

2 There is a formal complaint that females are being exploited, used as sex objects and there is too much sex in advertising. The Minister Assisting the Prime Minister on the Status of Women, Senator Reynolds, has found that one in 10 television ads exploit sex to promote the product. What's more, one in seven ads show scantily clad female characters.

Frankly, I could not be happier that there are two sexes, and I will be delighted to march, carry banners, even live in a tent outside Parliament House for the purpose of continuing the idea. Just as a test case I asked my wife if she liked being a sex object. "You bet I do," she said, "and don't you contemplate the idea of finding another."

What annoys me is this. Virtually from the time of my birth I noticed that there were official attempts to eradicate sex in this country. I went to schools where there were no girls. I learned English, French, Latin, history, geography, geometry, trigonometry, calculus, algebra, chemistry, physics, theology, music, botany, carpentry, metalwork, tennis, football, cricket, and golf, but never did we have one lesson on the most fascinating and important subject of all, sex.

I left school with the ability to measure a female with a slide rule, the ability to exchange with her a few phrases in Latin, and the ability to make a stool for her to sit on, but that was the limit of my knowledge. I knew nothing of her functions.

I smuggled a book on the subject into class by a Miss Marie Stopes and was nearly expelled, yet it received most dedicated interest and attention from all my friends. Then when I started as a journalist, fire, murder, armed assault, assassination, automobile carnage, bank theft, extortion, child beating, parliamentary vilification, embezzlement, criminal libel and treason were matters greeted with much enthusiasm by my editor, but sex was a subject never to be mentioned in his respectable newspaper. The clubs I joined were male only, and females were kept out of hotel bars.

Often I wondered wistfully what females were really like.

Now, glory be, at last when there is a possibility of finding out, when the school I went to is co-ed, when women are being allowed into clubs and pubs, when I am even allowed to use words like copulation in this column, when Elysium seems to be at hand, they want to eradicate sex.

All right, I am prepared to accept the de-sexed language. I concede the possibility that God might be a female. Indeed the chances are around 6 to 4 on that she is, but I will fight to the death to keep females as sex objects.

Just to give you the real truth I have fought for nigh on 60 years to get sex off my mind and I haven't succeeded. In my worst, or shall we say, better moments I have walked down Collins Street mentally undressing lovely females. It improves the day no end. Oh dear yes, even in Church sermons, I have thought of things which are certain to provide hell fire. They helped pass time also.

I have always adored sex mad artists and sculptors. One thinks of artists from Michelangelo through to Norman Lindsay who liked to paint and sculpt humans with no clothes on. I am passionate about Botticelli who liked his females big, round and generous, or how about Rubens who could get such an irresistible lovely pink texture to human flesh.

Rubens would have had no time for joggers, weight watchers, or Pritikin. He didn't go for any these emaciated anorexic models which are so popular today. He liked his sex objects to have a gorgeous plumpness and roundness. There is a Noel Counihan nude on my living room wall. Lovely picture it is. I prefer it to his political paintings of the nineteen thirties, and it beats the hell out of male sex objects.

But look here, there are persons in Government who want to eradicate sex from advertising. Hells bells, if they take the sex out of advertising what is left? The television is so appalling most nights often the advertising is the only thing to lift one's eyelids when dozing on the sofa.

Thank God for the sex objects. I think I find my best sex in the soft drinks. You used to get it in the beer and whisky ads but the liquor people were accused of tempting the young. The soft drink people can get away with anything. I remember one ad which had me on the edge of chair, the young fellow who very suggestively wanted to show this girl something in his apartment. He swung a wall which revealed backlit, all these fascinating bottles of soft drink and you could see, immediately, she was his.

Hair ads are redolent with sex. There is seductive material almost every night. This poor girl has dandruff. She is as bald as Von Stroheim, but she takes this stuff, suddenly she has this marvellous, enticing head of hair and she is throwing it around all over the place.

Ice cream ads also make you perspire. Have you noticed this girl who just moves her tongue in and out on to the ice cream. Good Heavens!

That's the interesting thing about sex objects. No matter how long you spend on this earth you never lose your interest.

How to Love Female Muscle

Just looking furtively this way and that, and just not trying to say it too loudly...

I think I am turned on by Martina Navratilova.

Oh I know what your thinking. When Martina was at Wimbledon this year there was a Mrs Pam Nelson in the grandstand. Time magazine in the old days would have described her as a "great and good friend" or "Constant companion Pam Nelson"

That is not the point. Martina Navratilova symbolises the new breed, the athletic woman. If there is one creature I cannot stand it is the model, the created clothes horse of the nineteen seventies, the anorexia nervosa look.

I saw one on the stage at the Melbourne Regent Hotel last week and she was modelling swim suits - I beg your pardon - apparently we can't call them bathing togs anymore. Anyway her hip bones were sticking out as if they were about to penetrate the skin. Her arms and legs were like pieces of spaghetti, she was a type of creature designed to inspire the fat matrons of Toorak and South Yarra. Not me.

It's the new breed that's got to me. Last week I was at the dentist and there was a pile of magazines, including a copy of that way out German mag, *Stern*. They had a whole feature on American female weight lifters. The centre spread showed a blonde, clenched fists, arms pulled back, doing the classic muscle flex, and she was stripped to the waist.

Oh friends, she looked fantastic, breasts round and hard like chariot wheels, biceps like young pawpaws. Wonderful.

I also see the new breed when I am out jogging. They are all tall. Hells bells, it is amazing how big they grow females these times. They have big shoulders, they wear tiny shorts, often two colors, red on the left, blue on the right, legs so long they seem to go up to the shoulders with beaut calves ... And remember how girls used to run in our day? They used to do a pretty waddle with hands dancing from side to side.

All right. You see these girls on the tan going round Melbourne's Botanic Gardens and it is a curious thing. The new breed is captivated by this athleticism, there are more females than males.

The way they run is beyond belief. No waddle, they stride. One morning early I thought I would match it with one of them, a splendid 185 centimetre Boedicia of a brunette. Alas, she went past me with the speed of a space shuttle. It is safe to say that in three years of jogging I have never managed to pass any of them.

Now Martina Navratilova symbolises all this modern athletic wonder. Admittedly there are some things about her that distress me. If she is going to carry me off under her arm I would like her to grow her hair down her back. Those Victa motor mower blonde hair styles simple won't do. Nor do I approve of her indifference to fashion, those little wrap round skirts and those awful shorts. If she could borrow some of the styles of Chrissie Evert I would be happy.

But sometimes when I need inspiration I go to the photographic library and take down the Navratilova file. Wheeee, here you find really something.

There is one photograph that comes up again and again. It shows Martina stretching for a forehand drive, knee bent and her mighty left arm reaching almost to the camera lens. Obviously photographers are devoted to that arm as I am. One could only describe it as magnificent, an ultimate weapon of power.

Her biceps brachii is a noble mound and when it is truly flexed there is a lovely vein that comes up like a piece of electrical wiring. Ah, but all those muscles on her forearm, the extensor carpi ulnaris, the elegant extensor digitorum, to say nothing of her brachioradialis and her extensor carpi radialis brevis are something to behold.

As for her legs, I stand back in adoration. Look at those upper thigh muscles, the splendid adductor magnus, the noble rectus femoris and when you get down around the calves how could any photographer resist her gastrocnemius or her tibialus anterior.

Hana Mandlikova said some very unkind things about Martina during this year's Wimbledon. One quote comes to mind: "I don't respect Martina for her achievement. When you see how she looks now, I think people should be asking the doctors how she got that way."

The truth is that Hana has not worked hard enough at her weight lifting, her serious iron pumping, and she wishes that she had a biceps brachii or even a triceps brachii to match that of Martina's.

There is one aspect about her that is a little disturbing. She is advised by Dr Robert Haas who keeps her on a peak performance diet, which rules out all dairy products, all red meats, all eggs, sugars and sauces. Not for her any hamburgers, chips or ice cream. After all, one does like to break out into an ice cream or a fried chip occasionally.

Then in the midst of all the controversy it was suggested that Martina should play the 100th male on the world computer rating. Alas, the challenge was not accepted, and with good reason, Martina would swallow him like a Sydney oyster.

Ah yes, to me Martina is the Queen of the new upsurge of womanhood. No need to stand up in the tram for such a power lady. No need to open doors for her or carry her shopping baskets. Such deeds would put her biceps brachii out of training. She would be there to protect you or as a powerful ally when you walked the dog through the darkened park in the evening.

There was a time when my ideal female existed between the 15th and 18th centuries. I adored those lovely large Rubens females, or even better those magnificent Boticelli nudes. This was an era before diet, before bikinis, before sun tanning, everything was large pure white and very round. You had a feeling of immense, female pneumatic comfort.

However all that now is behind me. I am into muscle and power. Martina is superb.

Melbourne's Most Virginal Bosom

The Princes Bridge, alias Young & Jackson's want to put up an illuminated sign featuring Chloe. It is causing trouble with the Melbourne City Council. At 4.30 pm yesterday Keith Dunstan managed to obtain this exclusive interview:

D: Chloe, I wanted...

Chloe: 'Ow dare you call me Chloe. If you call me anything, call me Mademoiselle Chloe or Madame Chloe. I deserve some respect. I am no ingenue. I am Chloe, painted by the great Jules Lefebvre in 1874. I am 125 years old.

D: I beg your pardon, Madame. I have always loved you and been your greatest admirer. You have the most virginal bosom, the most exquisite skin, that enchanting haughty look in your eye.

Chloe: Mmmmm yes. Of course. I am not Melbourne's greatest tourist attraction for nossing. When people think of Melbourne, Chloe ees the first thing.

D: We-ell yes. It has been said that Phar Lap up at the Museum is number one. Or these times even the Arts Centre. I know more people come to see you than Captain Cook's Cottage.

Chloe: Pfui! You compare me with CAPTAIN COOK'S COTTAGE!!! What pictures are there in the Arts Centre! Ze great critic Anatole de Montaiglon wrote of my glorious youth, the delicacy of my wrists and ankles, the immaculate whiteness of my body.

And what ees zis Phar Lap? 'ees not even a 'orse. Ze skeleton ees in New Zealand, ze heart is in Canberra. Ze tourist attraction you talk about, it ees nozzing but a stuffed piece of skin. I am number one by a 100 kilometres.

D: All right. Yes, of course. I understand that the management is planning to put up an electric sign outside, three and a half metres long, brightly illuminating your...ah...wonderful outline.

Chloe: And why not?

D: Well, I think there are objections from the City Council. It is somewhat distracting having a naked female opposite St Paul's Cathedral when people are going in to pray.

Chloe: 'Ow dare you! Me distract. Rubbeesh. What do they 'ave there now, an 'orrible four metre 'igh glass supposedly full of beer. It's enough to make people run off the road. I would be much better. Me on the outside would give taste, *chic, je ne sais quoi.*

Eet is better to sink of female beauty than ze beer, No?

D: Yes, I think you're so right. But it is not the first time you have been involved in controversy, is it?

Chloe: I am such an important personne, always zer is jealousy. Yes, zer was this terrreeb-le row in 1883. I 'ad been brought 'ere from Paris as ze prime attraction at ze international exhibition. I was on show at the National Gallery and when it was opened on Sundays, there was a chorus of stupeed complaints. One woman wrote, "Can it be right zat a mother cannot take 'er daughter to a public gallery, nevair to speak of 'er sons, without 'er cheeks tingling with shame." But then I was defended by Monsieur Longstaff and Monsieur McCubbin and they said my divine figure rather than a corrupting influence, was intensely moral and inspired all ze young men to matrimony.

D: Well, how did you get here?

Chloe: Sir Thomas Fizgerald, ze famous surgeon at the Melbourne Hospital, owned me. When 'e died in 1908 'enry Figsby Young of Young & Jackson's bought me for 800 guineas. Mr Young, veree nice man. 'e great art collecteur, not like 'otel people these times. When 'e put me in the saloon bar Young & Jackson's became Melbourne's number one drinking 'otel.

D. You don't think being on the corner of Swanston and Flinders had something to do with it.

Chloe: You infant no nozzing. I tell you. During ze last big war zer was a famous trial. Hans Runnich, a crewman aboard ze germany luxurie liner Bremer was accused in America of being a spy. 'E had alibi. 'E said he was in Melbourne at ze time. 'e could remember ze place because it had an 'otel opposite a railway station and inside zis 'otel was picture of nude woman. Zats all anyone ever remembairs about Melbourne. Me!

D: That's not all that happened. Didn't someone throw a glass of beer at you.

Chloe: Zat was an American serviceman in 1943. Very poor shot. It 'it me up zair above ze shoulder. Zey put glass over me after zat.

D: What's it been like, I mean, standing here under glass all these years.

Chloe: I tell you. Before we 'ave six o'clock closing. I 'ave to show only between nine and six. Then zey bring back late closing. I'm 'ere from 10 to 10. And remembair when I had to show at ze gallery on Sunday. Now 'ere I am in ze pub on Sunday. Seven days a week I am on show. Very tiring for a 125-year-old.

D.: But you've gone a bit up market haven't you. You're not in the saloon bar any more. Before you were only with the blokes and diggers downstairs.

Chloe: Blokes and diggers?

D: I mean it was a men only bar.

Chloe: Yes, I preferred ze men. Now I 'as all zees women, eating lunch, avocado salads and gins and tonics. Pfui.

D: I agree, ruined the place. Just so that I could talk to you I bought a Swan Extra Light, 0.9 per cent alcohol. Do you know what they charged, $2.30. In the old days you got a beer for threepence.

Chloe: Are you complaining? You say zats too much, a meeeserab-le two dollar thirty. 'eeet is worth a million francs to talk me. Allez vous en! Get out! Get out!

So I fled. I warn the Melbourne City Council. They had better let her have her sign. She is a very touchy lady.

COLUMNS WHICH DEAL WITH DOMESTIC BLISS...

8

Columns Which Deal with Domestic Bliss

Your Intimate Guide to the Dangers of Marriage

You will have noticed that an extraordinary survey has come out of Monash University.

Professor Maurice Balson has shown that more than 80 per cent of families fight over breakfast.

Admittedly breakfast is a sensitive time but at our house never have we found it quite as potent as the professor suggests. There are other occasions that are even more lethal.

So on your behalf this column has spent the past week making its own independent survey. First it was necessary to invent a unit of scale, which we will call MSF, Marital Stress Factor.

If we take 100 per cent MSF as finding your spouse in bed with another then we grade all MSFs back from that.

We found that the two worst ages for children are two and 17. These are times when offspring are totally uncontrollable and cannot be told anything. It is terror getting them to perform even the simplest of tasks. This can cause anything up to 95 MSF.

The automobile is lethal in a number of directions. There is a time when children aged between nine and 18 need to be almost constantly driven and picked up, Parents spend 80 per cent of their time as unpaid taxi drivers, MSF80.

Driving with your spouse is like walking in Belfast without a mine detector. One spouse always knows more about driving than the other, MSF75. However, driving when you are lost, spouse shows inability to map read, appointment time already past...Oh, Heavens above take care of that. MSF99.9.

Indeed partnering spouse in almost anything but sex is tricky. Tennis mixed doubles MSF52, Bridge MSF65, Golf MSF70, watching football MSF80. However it is even more dangerous if you don't do it together. Playing golf, or fishing takes an unconscionable time. Fishing widow, widower, MSF80, Golf widower MSF95.

There are MSFs that have to be watched very carefully. The Garden is far more dangerous than is generally realised. Have you noticed how husbands and wives rarely agree on the placement of an azalea, callistomon, or camellia? Once one has the treasure in position, inevitably it has to be moved two metres to the right. Or if it doesn't have to be moved, really, it should have been turned round the other way. MSF68.

Picture hanging too, I am, told has to be watched. The Arthur Boyd looks ridiculous beside the Looby, it should be in the sun room. You might get away with that Counihan if it were six inches higher, and now that you have it up there, you would get more balance if it were two inches to the left. It is no trouble drilling into cast iron brick. MSF65

Oddly enough television is not a cause of marital stress, except in getting children not to watch it. Our survey found that 90 per cent of husbands and 60 per cent of wives sleep through most programs. MSF22.

The telephone is an MSF cause. Many spouses need a telephone fix sometimes as often as every 15 minutes, which makes Telecom bills astronomic. But the highest MSF comes from failure to use the telephone. Our survey found, that when apart, spouses need to communicate at least four hourly. Otherwise there are suspicions as to what the other is up to. Failure to do so, MSF89.

The Professor did mention the bathroom and quite rightly so. We found the size of the hot water service, the number of females, the quantity of washable hair, the number of males likely to spend time reading in lavatory, all were high risk items. MSF70-90. Happiness in a marriage is many bathrooms and many lavatories.

Then it is clearly understood that the highest MSFs are involved both with going out to parties and having them. There is the MSF "You accepted the invitation I didn't, normally I wouldn't go to their place in a fit" MSF72, "and anyway the baby sitter should have been here half an hour ago." MSF80. "What's the difference if you take so long to get ready?" MSF85. "Me ready, you could have been locking the garage and getting the car out." MSF92.

But even more delicate is having your own party. Nothing quite equals the MSF in arranging the guest list, and we found remarkable consensus in our survey; the most awesome time, when the stress is so fearful the long stemmed glasses on the dinner table almost shatter under the strain, and that is five minutes before the guests are due to arrive.

Lack of communication is a problem. Our survey discovered that 95 per cent of wives complain that their husbands never talk to them. There were serious charges from wives that husbands could actually be sitting two metres away across the breakfast table and not hear instructions that had been given. Husbands countered that when one is involved in serious creative bread-winning thought it is not always possible, even in the presence of a loved one, to be on the proper receptive wavelength. MSF58.

And again, why was the professor so down on breakfast? It is true that with the glories of the public transport system there is a certain drama in getting away, but interviewees reported that the evening meal could even more colorful and Shakespearean, particularly when husband and wife are working.

"You could have stayed at the office all night." "Wasn't it your turn to cook the dinner." "You might have vacuumed and done the dishes before you left this morning." "Before you sit down I want you to thrash Harold. He has been appalling, hasn't done his homework." "I don't think we can go out. Ben backed the car into a tree."

Indeed I think breakfast has been hideously maligned. You get to a stage when breakfast is really the best meal of all. As the *New York Times* used to shout, every day is a fresh beginning, every day the world is born anew. What's more you have made it for another 24 hours, and it is so marvellous, so lovely, to still be together.

Adjusting the Set after Grandchildren

They have all gone home after the Easter holidays. Eleven grandchildren were here.

The quiet is sepulchral. I suspect there was a quiet like this in Hiroshima after the Americans dropped the bomb.

I am disconsolate. I need an adjustment period. I wander around the houses picking up momentos. Always they leave so much behind.

There is a baby's dummy by the telephone. Amazing how they came back into vogue. When we had our third child the doctors, or was it the dentist, warned: "Give a child a dummy and its teeth will be deformed." Just another of the great medical theories that never came to fruition.

Under the television set I find a Ford Thunderbird. In the corner of the spare bedroom there is a U.S. Army jeep and under my armchair there is a compactor garbo truck. This garbo truck comes from France and has the markings of some arrondissement in the City of Paris. Marvellous little toys, I might have a play later.

There is a boomerang up on the roof. I will have to get out the ladder and retrieve that when it stops raining. Walking in the living room is hazardous, there are bits of Lego here and there and under the cushions of the sofa there are assorted lengths of Tinkertoy. This fills me with floods of nostalgia.

Tinkertoy, I think, with the possible exception of Meccano, is the one toy that has survived right through from my childhood. We used to tinker with it by the hour, windmills were the favorite. You can still build windmills, but the trend here is entirely for space ships. They build huge elaborate tinkertoy space ships exactly like those in Star Wars.

I sit down and Lotte, our little black poodle, jumps into my lap. A few hours ago it would have been a four year old granddaughter. I find it absolutely marvellous to be admired by a four-year-old female. The same one, and others, invaded our bed at the very first suggestion of dawn light.

Well, at that hour you try to calm them and suggest that they could have a little doze. So I say: "Shssssh, we are still asleep."

This granddaughter replies: "Don't talk so much, you will wake up my dollies."

This brings back further memories. Was it her mother? No, of course, it wasn't, it was her aunt - back around 1958. It happened several times. There was that dreaded cry at 2 a.m. Mother was already feeding another child, so out I got into the cold, fumbled in the kitchen for a glass of water. Delivered it.

"I don't want a drink. I'm not thirsty. Dolly wants a drink."

There's another indication that the grandchildren have been here. The digital clocks have gone berserk. The microwave is saying: HELP! HELP! Our bedside digital clock is behaving very strangely indeed. We didn't even know it had an alarm. It went off at 3.37 a.m.

Suddenly we awoke to this disembodied BEEP BEEP BEEP. I thought it was having a computerised nightmare. When I discovered it was the clock I didn't know how to turn it off. It ran for 30 seconds, then turned itself off. But the damned thing was a thinking alarm. It assumed we hadn't awakened properly, so off it went again five minutes later.

Oh I tell you, we are in an entirely new world. We have a video with a remote control monitor. This monitor has about 15 buttons on it and you need a genius rating before you go solo.

O.K. we have an Alice in Wonderland video tape, very nearly our best keep-em-quiet line. My wife suggested I put it on. The video machine absolutely refused to work. So I cursed: "It's barely a year since we bought it. The damned thing will have to go back to the shop to be fixed."

It was a seven-year-old male who stepped forward. "Give it to me here," he said. He took the monitor, inspected all the buttons, found one down at the bottom and pressed it. Lo, the video started working and Alice came up on the screen.

"There you are, " he said. "You had it on 'child lock'."

It's like trying to undo child proof bottle tops. It takes a child to understand these things.

Computers are the beginning and end of everything. One young man is working diabolical hours at a newspaper round so that he can save enough money to buy his own computer. We have a computer game called "Dark Castle", which is complicated beyond belief.

You put the soft ware into the Toshiba and on comes this castle, complete with lightning flashes and haunting computer music. The theory is that you are a warrior and you have to enter this terrible castle to defeat the wicked black knight who lives there.

It is infested with vultures, dragons, gargoyles, fiendish torturers with whips, burning eyes, mutants, and plague infested rats. One nip and you are dead.

Well, you get a shield and a bag of 60 rocks with which to protect yourself. But working the keys to keep yourself alive is a nightmare in itself. For example, if you want to throw a rock you select keys one through to eight just to get your arm position right, then you have to push "Insert" to throw. You push D to Duck and move direction keys to walk. But there are other keys for jumping.

Last night only two minutes after I crossed the draw bridge I died from a plague infested rat. On my second attempt I was trying to avoid a deadly vulture. I had to do a Douglas Fairbanks jump from the castle wall to a rope. I misjudged the gap and fell to my death.

But it's no trouble to the young boys, they rack up thousands of points and smash down mace-wielding torturers, no worries.

They are not as good as we were at making go-karts, fashioning bows and arrows, and building cubby houses in trees. Ah, but they are much better at art works. Our refrigerator and the entire walls of bedroom number three are now covered with paintings and drawings, which I swear would be the envy of Sid Nolan or Arthur Boyd.

Also, very interesting, their sex education at five is better than ours was at 16. What's more, they wander the house with complete freedom. Take yesterday morning. A young man aged four wandered into the bathroom while I was having my shower.

He looked at me for quite some time and commented: "You haven't got much fur have you?"

That remark will keep me disturbed for at least a fortnight.

Auctions Are Close to Rape and Murder

Extraordinary things happen in Melbourne as soon as the football is over.

1. Eleven out of 12 coaches are taken away and shot.
2. Back lawns gets mowed for the first time in seven months.
3. The auction season commences and four out of five people move house.

We have just moved again. On the scale of human misery, rape and murder ranks as number 1. Armed robbery, number 2. Losing your spouse, number 3. Having your house auctioned is number 4, and maybe losing your luggage on Qantas is number 5. Locking your keys in the car number 6.

The real estate men told us the house would have to be on show for six weeks. There would be two public viewing times a week and other buyers would come through by appointment.

We had lived in our street for eight years and maybe we had met five per cent of the residents. Come auction time we met them all. Some went through our house three times.

One lot came through while we were having breakfast. "Your kitchen's not up to much is it?" they said.

"It depends on what you cook in it."

The worst part was keeping the place in show condition for six weeks. There's no greater hell. I have always believed bedroom seats are for hanging trousers on and dining room tables are instruments for supporting outspread newspapers. Beds are devices for covering assorted shoes.

"You realise that when they go through the house, they look in all your cupboards," said my wife. "You aren't honestly going to leave your singlets and underpants like that. What will people think?"

So I had to stack my singlets like a display cupboard at David Jones. Even worse the carpet had to be vacuumed every morning..."I don't want you going into the living room, you'll disturb something. You'd better stay in the kitchen."

I tell you for six weeks the place was like the British Museum at opening time.

Then the morning after we decided to sell, come 6 a.m. "BANG! BANG!" That was an enormous board going up outside. In the dim early light we read the beautiful prose. It made our house sound like the type of noble establishment in which Governor Sir Brian Murray must have wished he had lived.

"This most beautiful Victorian residence, superbly renovated throughout to perfectly blend with all the outstanding character of its era."

It mentioned that parking was provided. It was too. You could get a council permit to park in the street.

This board was so inspiring we have become students and in my retirement I hope to set up business as a board writer.

Here is a glossary of terms:

Excellent home for young married or investment.

Translation: Two days camel ride in a suburb even the map makers don't know about.

Renovators dream.

Translation: A nightmare dream actually. Don't lean against the weatherboards you might fall through.

Ideal purchase for imaginative buyer.

Translation: You have to use your imagination to overcome the view of the tip.

Character and charm with high ceilings.

Translation: There's a colony of possums in the high ceiling but the real character and charm comes with the dunny out the back.

This home superb for decorating to your own individual taste

Translation: Owned until last week by a 90-year-old widow. Nothing has been done to it since 1908. Even the National Trust would be frightened of the chip bath heater.

It is interesting to interpret language.

Delightful bush setting means bloody miles from town.

Charming, quaint means it has seen better days.

Outstanding modern environment means it is absolutely surrounded by flats. *Interesting and unusual environment* means that the current owner's taste is nigh beyond belief.

Breathtaking views means that when the southerly blows you get the full smell from the oil refinery.

There is no experience as unnerving as the auction day itself. A vast crowd gathers. Some turn up in Mercedes, BMWs, Volvos and you think you can't go wrong. The entire street arrives with their dogs. Some are in shorts and thongs.

The auctioneer gathers them all together and gives an opening address. I doubt if King Harry at Agincourt, Abe Lincoln at Gettysburg or even Churchill on the eve of the Battle of Britain was more eloquent.

"Why are we selling," said my wife. "This place is so wonderful, we must be out of our minds."

But all those people are only there to look. Ultimately there are only one or two bidders. Finally with a sick feeling in your stomach a deal is done with last minute haggling.

And the hardest part comes later. It is a curious thing you never actually leave a house. A part of you stays there for ever.

I can remember the precise layout, almost every floor board of every house I ever lived in. I wander through those houses in my dreams.

Oh yes, Midge the Corgi was buried over here, Sam the Siamese was interred there. That's the window we mended at least 15 times playing cricket. And my God, those gutters, you could reach them with the paint brush on the 12 foot ladder, teetering at full stretch.

Every morning a little fat willy wagtail would dance by the pool and say "hello" and the silver eyes would bathe in the bird bath.

I hope the newcomers are kind to Willy.

What Hands Did They Have on the Titanic?

You will have noticed that people are "into" things.

They are into mud bricks, into home brewing, into tatting and weaving. Dear Reader, at our place we are into the most deadly disease of all, we are into bridge.

The boom has spread amongst all our friends, although I get the impression the passion is rather stronger with the women than the men.

Indeed I know lots of chaps who are bridge widowers. Their wives play at Beryl's on Mondays, Joan's on Tuesdays, Lorraine's on Wednesday's, Olivia's on Thursdays and Marge's on Fridays. And if Marge's finishes early enough there might be time to go right on and have another session with Doris in the evening.

There is one rule. All else is secondary to bridge. The girls bring their own sandwiches and they have only one gin or sherry.

Oh, I tell you times have changed. I have watched all the various "In" activities. In the early fifties it was French lessons or learning Japanese, then it was the thing to study upholstery; everyone in the sixties was going crazy for spinning wheels and making their own jumpers out of black sheep.

The seventies were just marvellous. The girls were going to Madame de Doop, or Madame Chung Woo to do courses in Continental and Chinese cooking. Husband Pierre would be on hand to tell them how to marry the dishes to the right wines.

They would have to do their homework between lessons, so this was a glorious period, something to be remembered like the Italian Renaissance. Now they don't finish bridge until 5 p.m., so everything has become more desperate and urgent. A bridge widower might be called to the Chinese take-away or the friendly neighborhood pizza.

Actually it hasn't been easy. Bridge is a bit like giving up smoking. It is 15 years before you are relaxed with what you are doing. There are various methods of study.

There is a hideous little game called Auto Bridge. You feed cards into it and you have to play your cards with dummy and two opponents provided by the machine. At the end of each game the machine explains how you made a fool of yourself.

My friend Hilton has a home computer. You can now purchase special software and the computer plays an impeccable game against you, like a world master, never hesitating, all decisions made in a fiftieth of a second.

The big problem is should you play bridge with your wife as partner? This is a matter of some delicacy. Our local bridge teachers, Jim and Norma Borin, both world masters, compete as a team.

However, it needs to be a strong marriage. It is like teaching your wife to drive or playing as her partner in mixed doubles, if you can survive that your marriage has an excellent chance.

The major crisis comes when you doze off while she is going six no trumps or when you renege by failing to follow suit.

On those appalling nights like Fridays and Saturdays when the TV stations provide programs designed only for the people who have not seen the unendurable repeats, my wife and I get down to training.

We have two imaginary characters, Basil and Shirley, and we play two hands each. I get along remarkably well with Shirley and we have very few disagreements. And it assists my bidding no end because she always allows me to have a peep at her hand.

The ultimate act of courage is to go up to the local bridge school for the duplicate sessions. On duplicate nights there are prepared hands, and it is all done at high speed. Each hand must be got through in around four minutes and after each one you change tables and play with another pair.

The stress is terrible. Not a word is spoken. The first time I went there the lady who was playing East at my left was so quiet I thought she was a deaf mute. She was writing down all her bids.

Then it was explained to me that this is utterly the done thing. Back in 1965 a British pair was accused of cheating in international bridge. The suggestion was that they were making signs to each. It became a long battle to prove their innocence and the Dreyfus case was trifling by comparison.

Jim Borin reports that there were equally dramatic events several months ago at the North American Summer National contests in Washington DC.

Edith Rosenkratz, one of the competitors and wife of the famous George Rosenkrantz was kidnapped from the hotel precincts. She was dramatically rescued several days later, yet even though the Rosenkratz team was depleted by one pair, it still went on to win the championship.

At the same time one team was accused of cheating and for the first time the investigators used video evidence to back up the charges.

Jim was distressed that the cheating story made headlines in every newspaper in Britain. Nobody gave a thought for poor Edith Rosenkrantz. That was just a mere kidnapping.

Oh, you don't have to stick around playing bridge at home any more. Jim Borin has a pile of pamphlets offering Bridge week-ends at Sale in Gippsland, at Crow's Nest in NSW, at Albury, Port Macquarie, Glen Innes, Gold Coast, Dalby, Rockhampton at the Taronga Zoo for Heaven's Sake. Then he's running one on Melbourne Cup Day at the English Speaking Union in Melbourne.

There should also be one available to help one avoid Melbourne's Grand Final.

Then, of course, there are bridge tours all over the globe; bridge with Cunard on the QE2; 17 nights of bridge on the Mississippi Queen down the Mississippi to New Orleans; bridge with Sitmar to the Caribbean; bridge to Japan, Asia, South America, Scandinavia...

Then one always remembers the story about the bridge players who kept on playing when the Titanic went down. They didn't know it had sprung a leak.

I wonder what hands they had.

Don't Dare Knock Clocks

Mr Keating has had it now. I have been very tolerant of his escapades in Parliament, his arrogance over economics, but once he attacks clocks, he's through.

He had what the critics call a human, cosy chat on radio, the other day. Leo Schofield asked about his devotion to clocks. Oh no, he just wasn't interested in clocks. His mind spread much further than that. He was a connoisseur of the entire French neo-classic period.

"It is a terrible thing to be written off as a clock collector," said he.

A terrible thing, eh! I don't collect Louis Quinze, Chippendale, Sheraton, old English oak, or even beer cans. It just so happens that I collect clocks, nothing classical like Mr Keating, not French, nothing in ormulu, mainly humble 19th century American with names like Ansonia, Waterbury and Seth Thomas.

Actually I am quite berserk about clocks. There is nothing more beautiful than three or four of them on one wall. I like at least three in every room, all ticking and chiming. There is something about the ticking of a large clock which is like the beating of a heart. It is a comfort; it gives a feeling of life eternal.

Digital clocks are horrid. They do not have the kindly round face, they work silently and have these numbers that click over. There is a terrible inevitability about those numbers which keep coming up 6-7-8-9-10, and sometimes you just sit there waiting for the next one to form out of its horrid liquid crystal dots. Instead of reminding me of life, they signal doom. Each number is one less to go.

The world is divided between those who adore clocks and those who can't stand them. My wife is very tolerant, but she says, "Fair go! No more, than two clocks ticking and chiming in every room." So I do have a rationing program.

They vary in grandeur. We have railway clocks, little steeple clocks and long solemn regulator clocks. There is a ship's clock, no pendulum. It would still keep going even if the house should list at 45 degrees. It has a very busy industrious tick.

We have one regulator which has a noble deep-voiced, resonant tick, which tries to sound like Big Ben. My wife can only live with it provided the television is going at the same time.

But I like listening to them, particularly I love to hear them chiming through the night, two o'clock, three o'clock, four o'clock. You know God is in heaven and all is right with the world if the clocks are chiming. But they must be right, so one tinkers all the time to get them operating dead on.

The chiming period is the crisis and this actually is the test, one listens carefully and counts. I know each clock by the tone. It is bliss when they all go off and chime at the one time, so many bells you would think Mafeking had been relieved or Queen Elizabeth had been crowned.

The senior clock is a dear old thing, a grandmother really. She was made in Cornwall about 1820. Yet she tells the time, the date and the phases of the moon. Tell me a digital clock that gives you the phases of the moon.

You know the old wive's tale that Grandfather clocks don't like to be moved. It is true. Grandma has had a number of moves lately. Last time she was particularly cranky. She didn't settle down for several months, but I think now she has decided to accept the new area and for the past few months she has been surprisingly amenable.

She has one special way of showing her rage. She operates on a weight, one great hunk of lead, attached to pulleys. You haul this up on a hand-made chain which has stretched with the centuries. This has to be done every 24 hours or she stops. Ah, but sometimes, if Grandma is feeling disagreeable, she can throw this weight.

Invariably this happens at 3 a.m. or during a dinner party. I can't tell you the noise it makes, a couple of kilograms of lead crashing over a metre to the floor. You immediately think, "My God, somebody has murdered Aunty."

Many people just have their clocks as decoration. Is Mr Keating like that? Nothing I hate more than a clock that is just sitting there idly, not working, doing nothing for its living. It must tick. There is something superbly admirable about a piece of mechanism which will go on working for hundreds of years.

Yes, much more reliable than those damned digital clocks. You get blessed with those too. We have one by the bedside, that looks at you red-eyed, constantly blinking with dots.

There is one on the stove, one in the TV and even one on the electric heater. You need only a half second blip in the SEC power and they give up. We get plenty of blips in our electric current.

The bedside clock goes berserk and flashes its misery. The electric heater sits there flashing on the one time, telling you precisely when the SEC had its misdemeanor. The stove is quite pathetic. It turns off its numbers and flashes H.E.L.P....H.E.L.P....H.E.L.P. So you have to do a complete digit walkabout, setting them all again, and every one is full of complications. You have to get out the manuals.

It is interesting that the grandchildren are much more interested in the digit than the old fashioned ticking devices. One of them - very crafty - he is the only creature who knows how to set the alarm on the bedside clock.

He sets it so that the alarm goes off in a series of hysterical beeps at 3 a.m. Terrible that is. I'd rather have Grandmother shedding her weight.

Could I Be a Token Male?

Some of my best friends are women.

Indeed, if you cross examine and point a strong light in my eyes, I will say something even more outrageous, I actually prefer women to men.

It is not generally realised the incredible advance to power they have made in Australia. When I was young the female was totally subjugated. We kept males and females apart in schools, clubs, parties, Government, we never gave them executive jobs. We thought it wasteful to educate them properly. In Australia I don't think we even approved of sex. We preferred mateship.

It was recently as 1969 that we would not tolerate them in hotels. If you allowed them into a hotel at all you carefully isolated them in an area called the Ladies Lounge.

You isolated them in a special apartheid area at the races and the same at the cricket.

Now they are full members at the Melbourne Cricket and they are even standing for the committee. It is just a matter of time before we have a Ms President.

All the male clubs around town accept women at dinner, but some have gone further and they allow them for lunch. Once they come in for lunch that is the beginning of the end. However, when they are around the conversation is usually better.

I am reporting all this because now, apparently, it is compulsory to have women members of cabinet. The Prime Minister, well aware of backlash, made sure this was so. Admittedly he gave them positions only where men were still in command, but he has established a precedent. The next Government will have four women, the one after that five, and so on.

A similar situation applies in Victoria. Almost every board appointed by the Cain Government has to have its representative women.

I do hope that when the position is reversed, say, around 1999 the powerful female prime ministers and members of cabinet will be kind enough to appoint token males.

The very week when Mr Hawke was appointing his token females, we had the awesome picture of female power from Los Angeles. Here was a typical down trodden husband, Peter Holm, tossed out of his million dollar house, separated from his $80,000 boat, bereft of his beloved BMW, and not even allowed to spend his $17,000 a month dress allowance. There he was at the divorce trial, pleading to Joan Collins - never once referred to as Mrs Holm - for his male alimony and just $80,000 a month so that he could survive.

This modern position of the male should be carefully observed. Already I have noticed that many of my male friends have taken over domestic duties; minding children, operating the washing machine, working long hours over their Webers, cooking the dinner. Many stay home while their wives work.

It is interesting that rising female power has become a favorite subject with science fiction writers. There is one famous novel which has gone to many editions, *Five to Twelve* by Edmund Cooper.

This book is set early in the 21st century. Towards the end of the 20th century, many distinguished statesmen found the agony of office was simply too tough. The incidence of nervous break down was one in three. Few presidents or prime ministers were keen to accept a second term of office. Fascination for power was waning, so women stepped in and took over. This, you might have noticed, is happening already.

The pill took over completely. Marriage no longer became a social necessity. It was possible to program births. Females were more socially desirable than males. So before long the number of males shrank to a minority in the community. In the year 2043 the ratio of females to males was twelve to five.

Males were necessary only for stud procreation purposes.

And it was quite fascinating, as the females became dominant in the community, progressively they became more powerful physically. (Already I have noticed this. Many of the young girls now are bigger and stronger than I am. And when I go jogging in the park at 7 a.m. they go past me with the speed of light.)

Edmund Cooper reported that in the 21st century it was no longer necessary to separate male athletics from female athletics. In all forms of sport women were superior, and dominated. They revelled in their physiques. Cooper talked of "six foot six inch females, beautifully proportioned, muscles rippling with power" and of course, they preferred to walk around almost naked.

(This worries me also. I get quite a thrill looking at pictures of big girls pumping iron at body building competitions.)

Eventually the males were just reduced to serfdom. Kept at home to do menial chores and used for sexual fun.

The story is about a poet, become male prostitute called Dion Quern, who decides to fight back in a valiant attempt to recreate male power. He has a tough trot.

The women all use longevity pills, which means they have long life spans unshackled to child birth, but the pills do have an awkward side effect. They tend to cause nymphomania. So the poor Dion is overworked. These super powerful females rape him at will and there is one tragic scene where hulking female louts beat him up in a bar.

I am not suggesting that all this is certain to happen. But one humbly submits that things are not quite what they were. If it is not "Five to Twelve" now, it could be a quarter past eleven.

And when twelve o'clock comes I want it remembered that I said I preferred females and I would like to be appointed to a board here and there as the token male.

The Bliss of Owning a Pool

How is your domestic-possessions-social-rating? Are you moving forward, gaining the proper envy of your neighbors? Kindly write down points for these assets.

Mercedes, Jaguar, BMW:	12
Rolls-Royce, Ferrari, Porsche:	15
Tennis court:	10
Mansion in exclusive suburb with ducted heating and air conditioning:	15
Private quarters set in the grounds suitable for domestic staff:	15

Sauna lined with divine smelling timber:	19
Sunken rock pool with articulated fountain:	8
City penthouse pad coupled with glorious farmlet with horses, Aberdeen Angus and white fence rails surrounding lush green paddocks one hour by Merk or Jag from town:	25
Lock up flat on the Gold Coast or Noosa:	16
Jacuzzi set in exquisite Spanish style grotto capable of seating six with bar service:	10
Private gymnasium with ergometer, pulse meter, exercise bike and weightlifting gear:	15
Personal jogging track:	12
Swimming pool:	3

If you have scored above 30 then your life is a private hell, and it is practically impossible to dispose comfortably of the Irish Wolf Hound, the Aberdeen Angus and the Rolls, so that you can conveniently take the usual annual holiday at Cannes or Aspen.

You will notice the pitiful rating received by the swimming pool. I think swimming pools are definitely 1980 or even 1975. We visited a friend at Moorabbin last week. He showed us a fascinating free-form garden down the back. It was all freshly dug and he had planted standard roses and clumps of chrysanthemums all around.

"At last we have done it," he said.

"What have you done?"

"I've got rid of the swimming pool. It was a large fibre glass affair. I didn't even bother to sell it. I gave it away. They came and took it away on a truck. Best thing I ever did in my life. I feel so relieved. Don't you like my new garden?"

I knew exactly what he meant. My heart went out to him and I was chlorinated with envy.

We moved into our present house in 1977. Swimming pools were all the go and I pined for one. I have the piece of blurb on the subject now:

Your swimming pool should be more than just a water holding construction in which to swim on hot days. It can become the focal point of your garden and a very attractive oasis with thoughtful landscaping. Some shade areas are necessary for relief during the hottest part of the day. Whether it is built in or above ground the sheer luxury of being able to swim in your own backyard is pure bliss.

He then went on to say:

Your swimming pool is an investment. Real estate experts say the value added to your house is at least three times the cost.

That was the line that got me. Actually the swimming pool was already installed. The block was so narrow the fibre glass pool had to be lifted right over the house by an enormous crane. It was the talk of the street at the time.

The man who sold us the house said: "And this pool is actually labor saving. It's in your back garden. It's paved all around and unlike other people you will never have a lawn to mow."

"Yes, yes," I said excitedly, "where can I sign?"

Even before a month had passed there were suspicions that swimming pools were not total bliss. First I needed a swimming pool consultant, he was a gentle kindly man. He visited regularly dressed in white like a brain surgeon.

He demonstrated how to keep the water healthy and pure and he ran his stethoscope over the pump. Unlike brain surgeons there was no medicare to meet his bills. Immediately he diagnosed that the pump needed replacing - $220, the pool light didn't work - $85, a new can of chlorine $120 - more diatomaceous earth - $25.

But worse I discovered that owning a swimming pool was like owning an acre of vegetables, it had to be tended and worried over daily. Even worse, when you had guests you had to clean the thing to prove that your attractive oasis was the focal point of your landscaping.

Swimming pool owners are competitive. My brother-in-law's pool always sparkles better than the Olympic Pool. "What's your problem? Having trouble with your Ph?"

Oh yes, we had thoughtful landscaping all right. We have a liquidambar - have you ever met a liquidambar or a silver birch - or a jacaranda, or a lemon scented gum? You wouldn't believe how those trees can contrive to shed stuff all the year round.

Marcus Clarke condemned gum trees because they give no shade. It's all falling into swimming pools, that's why, plus the bark as well. I sit in our living room and I see leaves sailing overhead, 50 metres up, and you can almost see them thinking: "My God, there's a swimming pool. I'll drop down into it."

We went overseas, rented the house, by the time we got back into it again, the swimming pool was a beautiful green and it cost $300 to have it cleaned up to brother-in-law standard.

But what am I to do? I can't afford a crane to lift it out again. It is no good as a garden with a fibre glass base. It would, I think, make quite a nice wine cellar. But would it still be an attractive oasis and focal point of the garden.

Don't Hang Up on Phone Callers

After long experience with a family I have learned this much, there are two areas which are lethal, where you never interfere: hair and telephones.

Oddly enough hair seems to be connected to some strange emotive part of the brain. There is no sex difference. Suggest to another human that an hour in the bathroom plus draining the entire hot water system is quite sufficient to wash the hair and the Richter earthquake scale goes up to three or four.

Tell them further their hair is too long, too short, the wrong color, that beards look better on Moses, Karl Marx and Methuselah, that no-one in a fit would give them a job if they do creative things like coloring their crowning glory in the shades of the union jack, complete with spikes, you go up to Richter scale 10. There are slamming doors, explosions and they leave home.

The telephone is no different. This is why I cannot understand why a Government would dare to suggest such a thing as time-charging for local calls. Our Minister for Communications, Senator Evans, clearly is an innocent, who has had no experience with teleholics.

The telephone is one of our most serious addictive drugs, perhaps not as bad as heroin, but clearly ahead of alcohol and tobacco. We have members of our family who need a telephone fix at least every half hour. I am not quite so bad I can go as long as 40 minutes without feeling guilty that I am not communicating with someone. You get that nervous twitch in the right hand.

Parents have a desperate need to communicate with their children when they leave home. In the 19th and 18th centuries they would write them letters and eventually they would be published into books. Lord Chesterfield was very good at it. Letters are finished, it is all telephone calls. I know one lady who telephones her daughter in Melbourne

DON'T HANG UP ON PHONE CALLERS ...

from Brisbane every day. Her husband shakes a little when I say: "Hello Fred, how you doing, how's the phone bill?"

Even worse, I know a truly pathetic case, mother in Australia, daughter in Minnesota. I think their last phone bill was $1400. A Government with heart and compassion would provide compensation for this sort of thing.

Oh, I have tried to exercise discipline, pasted notices on the wall, doesn't make any difference. Telecom sends out little charts done in pretty colors, telling you rates are cheaper round dawn, or lunch time, or when everybody is in bed, or on Sunday. So one thunders; ring in off peak or I'll have the bloody thing cut off.

Doesn't work. "Look, if you don't mind, I'll ring her right now. Just this once, because she's always home with the baby at 10.30." What do you do? You can't fight someone who is panting for a telephone fix. I know because I am doing the same thing at 11 a.m.

But timing of local calls, how could they do this thing. I have several aunts who have always made calls to their mates as soon as they have finished breakfast and are ready for action. One has this daily call and it goes for a full hour. I know, because just try to call Aunt Freda before noon the phone is always engaged. It wouldn't matter if the roof was on fire you wouldn't get through.

Sometimes I used to wonder what two human beings could say to each other that would keep them involved on a telephone for a full hour. It is simple really. It is just like radio talk back without the commercials. They are a couple of Derryn Hinches, John Laws or Margaret Peacocks. They give each other some pretty swift comments on the shortcomings of Susan Renouf, the Princess of Wales, the striking capabilities of railway workers and sensible economic advice to the likes of Robert Holmes a Court.

And what is Telecom doing to help? Is it asking us to economise on our telephone calls. Does it offer any advice on how to cure our telephone addiction. Not on your life it doesn't. It produces exotic telephones as inviting as lollies. It runs nightly commercials showing children ringing their suffering, weeping mothers in Turin, London, Vladivostock or elsewhere.

It keeps bringing out new fangled telephones, so that you can ring from anywhere: in your car, in a park, in an aeroplane or even on the dunny. It has telephones with memory banks. Instal 30 or 100 of your favorite telephone numbers. So when you want to call Kate, Sarah, Mardi, Jane, Joan, Judy, Marge, Adrian, Sylvia or Bill - Zap! - you have to press only one button. I reckon it's infamous.

I even have a word processor with a modem that can take an infinite number of telephone numbers, press the button and it dials for you. It is just a matter of time before the telephone becomes a permanent part of the human body.

So what do you? Do you train yourself to give up the telephone. Start in short bursts. Try not using the phone for a full hour, then work up to a full day. Join Phoners Anonymous. Seek help. But what do you do when you are really desperate and feel a phone call coming on. Do you telephone a member of Phoners Anonymous for help?

However, if I could offer some simple advice. This is the big chance. If Dr Hewson is serious in his desire to be Prime Minister and sometimes he has almost acted that way, don't time local telephone calls, go the other way. Make local phone calls free. It has been done in some U.S. States.

We would all remember Dr Hewson as the man who gave us the Phoners Eldorado. He would probably remain P.M. for a generation.

COLUMNS OF CANINE AND FARMLAND WONDER...

9

Columns of Canine and Farmland Wonder

Bessie We Thought Was 'Super' Human

Bessie died on Saturday. We took her down to the vet. A very sympathetic young lady gave her a needle and put her to sleep for ever.

Actually I didn't have the guts to go through with it. I sat in the car while my wife took her inside. Simple, really. Price for death and disposal, $25.

Perhaps right-to-lifers would not approve, but we are really kinder to animals than humans. Bessie was 15, half blind, an epileptic and all systems had begun to fail.

As I sat in the car, rain running down the windscreen, I had memories. Bessie was a toy poodle, the color of milk chocolate and tiny. The way we carried on about her was absurd.

She would sleep in a basket in our bedroom and at 4 a.m. - you could almost set your clock by it - there was a ritual. Bessie would jump up on the end of one of the beds. We sleep in single beds and for Bessie it was like conferring an honor, a C.B.E. I scored the honor only one night in seven and I was terribly flattered when I made it. But once on the bed, she would stay there motionless, asleep at the back of your knees.

Oh, we were worse than that. Bessie went everywhere with us, in trains, out to dinner, away on holidays. She was so small she could fit in my wife's handbag, the one object she could always find. So it was no trouble to sneak her into motel rooms. We had to be careful though, she would always bark at the arrival of the breakfast tray.

We went off to California for three years and this was a heartbreak. We left Bessie with out eldest daughter, who loved her as much as we did, but the worry was, dogs are said to have short memories, so would Bessie ever remember us. And she didn't, not for five minutes. It was not visual. It was her sense of smell that set off something in her memory bank.

Suddenly she let off a loud squeal and started doing spectacular Warwick Capper leaps all around the room. From then on she followed my wife at the range of two millimetres just in case she might try that California trick again.

The day Bessie was spayed was dramatic. We had to take her to a vet in Prahran and as we left her she was shivering. She knew something appalling was about to happen. Half an hour later the vet telephoned us, very alarmed. He said Bessie had jumped out of his arms and with the speed of light dashed out the door. The whole staff had set off in pursuit. There had been an incredible chase, down Chapel Street, in, out and around the Housing Commission, up and down corridors, but she had escaped. He was terribly sorry.

As he spoke there was a yelp. Bessie was pushing her nose against the front window. Now Bessie had covered four kilometres, crossed at least three roads of heavy traffic, and come straight home. She had never been across that route before. She didn't need a Melway street directory to find her way round.

Yes, last Saturday morning was very bleak and the memories kept coming faster and faster. There was the extraordinary episode of West Wyalong. We broke a windscreen at West Wyalong and the man at the garage, said 'Leave her in the car with me, you go get a cup of coffee and all will be ready when you return.'

It was a big mistake. Bessie did another Prahran flit. This time straight through the shattered glass hole and when we returned the desperate garage man had given up his chase. For 24 hours we hunted. You don't know how stupid you feel wandering up and down strange streets, pathetically shouting "Bessie". I had an appointment in Forbes, we had to drive on. The next night at the Forbes motel we were both in tears. "I can't stand it," I said, "we're going back."

All day we hunted. We were just about to give up, when suddenly there was a familiar yelp, she hopped into the car. She had been waiting on a street corner close to the point where we first lost her. Captain Cook when he returned from his first voyage wouldn't have received a better welcome.

There were certain things she would not do. Chasing sticks was rather pathetically childish. She loved long walks and adored the beach. She would whimper with joy at the first smell of salt and seaweed. However she would not tolerate jogging. She thought jogging totally unproductive and probably bad for the heart.

You just had to treat her like an adult human being. Even at 15 she was not smart enough to read or write, but she understood perfectly the English language. So sensitive matters, like we were having chicken for dinner, or the existence of a Violet Crumble, we would spell in front of her. However, tell her it was time for her epilepsy pill, and she would front up immediately.

Her absence will be noted by a host of other creatures. Flat dwellers have to indulge in very firm procedures. There is an incredible exodus across to the park at 6.45 a.m. daily. There Bessie would meet an English Sheepdog, a Cocker Spaniel, two German Shepherds, an Airedale and best of all, her own size, an Australian Terrier. The same ritual would take place about 10 p.m., peak hour would come immediately after the best TV program was finished. The dog report amongst the owners was always more interesting than the Carlton-Walsh report. It always seemed ridiculous waiting a for a tiny poodle to do what was expected.

So my wife returned into the car, alone. Nothing was said for a while. She too had her memories. You always feel guilty after a death. There's a feeling, no matter what, you never did enough.

Poodles Are Irrational

Regular readers of this column might just possibly remember an embarrassing account two years ago of the death of Bessie. Please stand by for the regrettable sequel.

Bessie was an apricot colored 15-year-old poodle, who on a black terrible day, had to be put down by the vet. We were very sensible about it. No creature could ever replace Bessie. Never again would we allow ourselves to suffer such dog domination.

Six months went by then a friend, who understands our sometimes not very rational behaviour, telephoned: 'I have just been to see 'X' and she has a little baby poodle, one of two in a litter, the other died. Lovely little thing, an only child."

"Oh well, poodles do get born, " I said, sounding terribly disinterested. "Well, we're actually going right past X's door today," said Marie, "no harm in just looking, we can see how dog breeders go about things."

"Yes, of course," I said, "we will go merely on an education exercise." We called on X. Like all true dog breeders there were few concessions to the human world. She was in jeans, boots, shirt, no make up, intensely practical, and all loving for everything on four legs. She went away and returned with a tiny poodle the size of two tennis balls. It was a coal black poodle with intense black eyes.

As an old hand in these matters I saw immediately that Marie was gone, so did Madame X and she gave us the treatment. "I don't just sell poodles to anybody," she said. "Money is of no concern to me when I handle dogs. First I have to be absolutely sure you are poodle people."

That was a worry. How was I to prove that we were up to proper poodle standards? I did point out we had 15 years training, but I don't think she was listening.

She continued her assault. "And anyway when did your poodle die?" "Six months ago." And I gave her the precise date.

"I don't think you have gone through the proper grief period."

"I beg your pardon."

"After your poodle has died," X continued relentlessly, "you should go through a grief period of at least a year. It is absolutely necessary if you are going to handle the next poodle properly."

X said she would let us know in six weeks time and then, "possibly", we could purchase the black creature which she called "Puppity." In the mean time I suspect inquiries were made similar to those the FBI conducts when an American president chooses a Defence Secretary or a Secretary of State.

The call did come and, suffering strange feelings of disloyalty to the late Bessie, we hurried round to Madame X. She was there all prepared. First we received a lecture on the care and handling of poodles. I ask you to believe that not only was puppity washed, brushed, and ready to go but also she had her worldly possessions supplied by X. These included all sorts of potions; de-worming pills, puppity's favorite cushion and blanket, puppity's toys and an electric warming cushion for puppity to sleep on.

Madame X proudly gave us a run down on puppity's elegant pedigree and announced she would be pleased if we called her Tiffany. "You don't HAVE to call her Tiffany," said X, "but that is her name." I felt this was an order.

Madame X took an unconscionable time to hand over the little black creature but eventually Marie took puppity in her arms and we went off to the car. I had the strong suspicion that Madame X was crying.

As we drove home Marie said: "Of course, she can't be Tiffany. You can see at once that she isn't a Tiffany." So for the first week we checked over maybe 2984 names, all of which failed. We even consulted baby books and went through the Birth columns of the *Sun News Pictorial* which is very strong on baby names. The only one that seemed to fit was Charlotte, Lotte for short.

I think that dogs, like many humans, have been on this earth before. Lotte proved immediately, that she was a strong independent spirit. How shall I put it? Immediately she took command. She was not interested in any of the things that Madame X gave her on departure.

We had for the grandchildren a large, soft, furry mouse about three times the size of Lotte. It had big button eyes and a long tail. Lotte immediately fell in love with mouse. Where she went mouse had to go. She slept with mouse and still does.

But we were strong. Never would we display the weakness that we did with Bessie. Bessie was a creature of immense guile and intelligence. Whenever we packed up we would find Bessie sitting in the car waiting to go too. We even smuggled her on railway trains and into motel rooms in handbags. She slept on the end of our bed. No, there wouldn't be any of that nonsense.

So Lotte, at once, received firm orders. Her place was to sleep in the laundry and we prepared a superbly comfortable basket with soft bedding which would have done credit to a Royal baby.

I can't tell you the complaints. There were piteous cries that went on and on. I called it "doing a June Bronhill." It could have been Mimi in La Boheme dying tragically of tuberculosis.

We both cracked at the same time. "She can't stay there. Just this once." She has been there in the bedroom ever since. Just like Bessie we never allow her to sleep on the bed. Craftily she waits until she is sure we are both asleep then she creeps up. Being all black you can't see her in the dark. You find this lump beside your feet in the morning.

Like all poodles she is quite irrational. Bessie detested children. Lotte adores them. However, adults you want her to like, she snarls at. Then out of the blue, for no reason at all, she takes a fancy to a visitor who is virtually a stranger, say the plumber, and jumps on to his lap.

She prefers human food to dog food, apples, peaches, cheese, and the Pritikin bran muffins we eat when dieting. She will absolutely kill for avocados. So you can see we are stuck with Lotte. I fear for the future.

Dog Dialogue

Aren't you amazed at organisations which keep conducting research into matters we know already.

At the week-end we learned that the Petcare Information and Advisory Service had called in market research to discover that 80 per cent of Australian dog owners admit to talking to their dogs.

There is only one thing wrong with this figure, it is absurdly modest. I would suggest 99.9 per cent of owners talk to their dogs and presume utterly that they are human. What else is a dog for if you can't talk to it. Your dog is your perfect listener.

All our dogs have been human. We have had Skipper, Judge, Claude, Basil, Midge, Bessie and Lotte, all human. During the war years my father named dogs after my brother. He was always getting promoted so we had Bombardier, then Sergeant and Major. Dad would have loved a Brigadier but he never got far. But those military dogs were human too.

We have conversations with our Lotte which can go on for anything up to 20 minutes. We ask her questions about her day, whether she has seen Ernie the Labrador up the road, whether she has noted any good smells.

I won't say we always get answers, but it is not difficult to define Lotte poodle language. She has a noise for when she wants to go outside, a pathetic beautiful plea for when she wants to come inside.

She can be most eloquent about food. She always believes, seeing she is a human dog, she should be allowed to eat human food and she says so.

She has a special throaty noise when we have chicken. The throaty noise takes on the tone of a Joan Sutherland aria when we have avocados. Lotte is round the bend about avocado. She coos also for apples and loves bran muffins.

Her disgust is extreme when we give her that dry carbohydrate dog food. We point out to her that it is recommended by three out of four vets and on television you see dogs bolting it down as if it were caviar, but that does not make any difference. She eats the meat then separates the dry stuff and leaves it on the plate.

We have long conversations too about her sleeping habits. We point out to her firmly that dogs sleep in their own bed and not on our human bed. She has an aria for this too, not the Mad Scene from Lucia like she does for the avocado. It is more Barber of Seville.

We are as stern about this as you can be with a poodle, but then she sneaks up on the bed at 3 a.m. when our resistance is not strong enough to fight the battle.

There is another thing, all 99.9 per cent of humans who talk to their dogs are aware of this. They never let you out of your sight, and seeing that they are perfectly literate in English they eaves drop all the time and they know precisely what you are saying.

For this reason we have to spell things in front of Lotte. Lotte, even though she is now two years old, has been slow with her reading and writing. If we want to discuss that it is time for her worm pill, or time for her bath, we have to spell that out.

But there are some things you cannot hide. If you are going to town, or going away for the weekend, instantly she picks this up and makes her own preparations. She goes out and sits in the car.

If you explain to her that she is not going, she is capable of that withering look, which says: 'Don't you ever stay at home. For God sake, this is the third time you have been out this week."

Bernard Shaw used to say that he talked to himself because this was the one way he could get an intelligent answer. I am sure we talk to our dogs for the same reason.

The answers we get are supremely intelligent.

The Morality of Chookery

There is a dreadful moral crisis that comes to all those who keep chooks.

What do you do when they get too old? At our house we are weak, sentimental creatures. We cannot face up to the role of the executioner.

I have been to the State Library seeking guidance. There they have 222 books on keeping chooks. I sought out *Backyard Poultry Raising*, which Mr John F. Adams wrote in 1930.

He was clear on the subject. Hens are excellent layers for the first year. A splendid fail-me-never white leghorn, says he, will lay 150-250 eggs in her first year, six to eight times her own weight.

Next year the performance is down 25 per cent, and so on, there are diminishing returns. Never keep your hens more than two years, said Mr Adams. Butcher them or they merely become boarders.

Boarders indeed. What about kindness and pensions for faithful long service? Perspiration was forming on my forehead as I read on. First separate out those fowls you want to butcher, said Mr Adams. (I see, chooks have their own special death row.)

Do not feed them for 12 hours before butchering. Give them only water. (Good Heavens, they don't even get their last condemned cell banquet.)

Mr Adams explained there were three ways to kill chooks.

(a) You can wring their necks. Grab the bird by the neck and give the body a couple of rapid and determined swings. A good method is just hold the bird firmly at arm's length and pull about nine inches. Adjust your pull carefully. Pull too hard the head comes off. Don't pull hard enough and the hen will remain alive. "And VERY disturbed," says Mr Adams.

(b) Stretch the head and neck on a chopping block. Sever the head smartly with an axe or a hatchet. The headman's stroke requires a little accuracy. You must have a firm grip because fowls are very muscular. After the chopping there is always a vigorous reflex action for several minutes. "I always thrust the body into a large bucket," explains the calm executioner Adams..

(c) Mr Adams likes this one best, but it sounds even worse. Hang the birds by the their legs and using a sharp slender knife, cut their throats.

I went home feeling ill. We love our chooks. We have four white leghorns which we call "The String Quartet". They are beautiful creatures, haughty, proud, pure white with fiery red combs.

We let them out on parole from 3 p.m. until dusk every day. The first time we let them out, there was terror. Nobody told us Leghorns could fly. They took off and settled way up in the top of the old prunus. I had to climb up and fetch them down.

No trouble any more, they follow us around to see what we are doing and they are much easier than the grandchildren. After an hour or two they just wander back into the chicken house to bed.

We take a childish pleasure in collecting the treasure. I mean, inevitably we go up to the fowl house three or four times a day to see if there are any more eggs. It's marvellous to pick them up while they are still warm. The String Quartet give off contented little clucks, pointing out: "We did that."

Sometimes on cake-making day there is an egg shortage. Marie stands over them, "Come on girls, faster, we need more." Inevitably they oblige.

We don't stand for any of this nonsense about cholesterol. Could anyone seriously believe that anything as natural and as pure as the hen's egg could be bad for humans? Now my friend Mr Adams is eloquent about this. He says: "How can you describe the wonder of the taste of the genuine fresh free range egg."

"You can always tell the difference," he says. "The yolk has that rich deep color, like a hunter's moon just coming over the horizon." As for the shape, "a genuine farm fresh egg will reveal a yolk tall and perky as a young breast, almost a perfect hemisphere."

But the non fresh ordinary egg, ugh. He says the breast has gone flat, the color is pale and the white is mere water around the edge.

You know the best way to eat this gorgeous creation, the farm fresh egg, just boil for three minutes then empty the contents onto a slice of hot buttered toast.

My grandmother used to keep chooks. When she had a choice piece of gossip, and that was often, she would say:

"All right children, go outside and see if the chooks have any water." It's a ploy that remains very useful.

Our Henry, rising four, is fascinated by the String Quartet. Several nights back he complained that he had left his Match Box Ferrari outside. O.K. we get the torch. "Where is it Henry?" He leads me straight to the chook pen, where he inspects the four chooks all cuddled in side by side on their roost, tucked up for the night.

"Oh," said Henry. He didn't even mention the Ferrari, he too went off to his roost and to bed.

They have been through everything with us. Last winter, when we went off on holidays, we thought it best to leave them with a daughter in Maldon. So as we set out we put them in all in the boot, each chook in a bag. As we approached Maldon we had horrid feelings of guilt. "There wasn't any air in those bags. They'll all be dead."

No trouble at all. They were their usual perky selves, and would you believe, at the bottom of each bag there was an egg.

I mean, I ask you. What are we going to do? We have another book on backyard poultry by Andrew Singer. He is even more ruthless than Mr Adams. He would knock them off even after one year and he says: "You must eat your own backyard poultry. They are not the tasteless variety you get now. They bring back all the wonderful memories how chicken used to taste when you were a child."

But I don't think we can go through with it. Eat the String Quartet! That's cannibalism. I think we will we be running the Eventide Chook Retirement Home. But if you will forgive me I think I'll just nick out and see if there are any eggs.

The Murder of the Three Graces

Just before we went off on two weeks holiday this column raised a deep moral question.

What do you do when your chooks are past two years old, not laying with the correct machine-like verve. The experts say no longer are they are an economic production unit. They are ripe for murder.

The text books, we found, gave all the utterly correct methods for execution. How to hold them when you put their heads on the chopping block, how to string them up by their legs to cut their throats, or simply, the smooth even way to stretch them and break their necks. Yes, the books even tell you how to stop them running around headless.

We were so in love with our friendly faithful chooks, weak creatures that we are, we could not go through with it.

Fellow chook people, letters came in from all over. "Gawd love ya", said Anna Marsden of Emana Park, Riddells Creek, "At last we've found someone who's as potty about chooks as we are." She referred to the Emana Park Chook Retirement Home and it is clear that apart from crook financiers, Chook Geriatricism is one of the greatest problems facing this country. You wouldn't believe how many Eventide Chook Retirement Homes we are supporting.

Then there was another letter titled "henpathy". It came from Joan Sampson Tucker of Sandy Bay, Hobart. It was in the form of a nursery rhyme:

Three Blind Mice!

We skipped and sang
biffing threes on the can
on the way to fetch milk
from the farm -
we were running to look
for the farmer's wife -
would she cut-off our tails
with the carving knife?
Huh! we felt no real cause for alarm.

Three, Four...
We knocked at the door

and shouted but nobody came
so we peeped through a crack
in the fence round the back
and witnessed the terrible game:

Ring a Ring o' Roses!
A gruesome Dance of Death;
each brutalised fowl
wore a sugar-bag cowl
to stifle its last gurgled breath.

See How They Run!
We watched them all hurtle
around a red circle
unable to screech-out or cluck
till each feathered clown
with its starched-paper crown
fell down, bloody down on its luck.

He Diddle Diddle!
She stood in the middle
wiping the knife on her frock
- the murderess who laughed
to see such fun - till
everything came to a stop.

Whee! Whee! All the way home
We went; shocked
by the shriek in her laughter
then we hurled down the can.
How it rattled and rang!
And the questions came tumbling after.

Now one has to report the sequel to our chook saga. Off we drove on the Monday morning. The four beautiful white creatures had food stocks in depth and regular chook-sitter visits were arranged.

We telephoned from Mollymook, New South Wales. It is incredible how children always are first to the phone. Grandson Tim, aged four, answered with the strident announcement: "Your chickens are dead...Your chickens are dead."

Tim was the first to discover the bloody scene. Hey Diddle Diddle, indeed. Ah dear, we used to call our chooks the String Quartet. They used to follow us around, more devoted than children.

A fox had torn a neat hole in the wire, and wriggled into the cage. The scene of carnage was terrible. He bit the head off the first chook then delivered the swift coup to grace to the other three. White feathers everywhere, four stiff inert bodies and blood.

Tim and his father quietly buried the String Quartet under the pittosporum tree at the top end of the garden. Young Tim, aged four, had his first lesson in the frailty of life.

But why? If the fox - that's if it was a fox - had killed for food you would understand, but none of the chooks were eaten. Two years earlier a dog entered our bottom paddock and savaged our two sheep; Petal was all lacerated and bleeding but Bottlebrush was so mutilated the vet had to shoot her.

Again chasing those sheep around the paddock and tearing at their throats with sharp teeth was simply huge fun.

How often have we heard it said that humans are the only species that kill for the pure joy of killing. It isn't true. Hey Diddle Diddle.

Sequel 2: But you should never give up. It's like getting all the trainee pilots into the air immediately after the air crash. Confidence has to be restored. Therefore we have rebuilt the chicken cage, covered it in steel mesh, so that it is a virtual Alcatraz and installed String Quartet Two.

They are four gorgeous White Leghorns. Rather nervous, yes, but just this morning, God Bless them, they produced their first egg. It was only the size of a ping pong ball but it was the triumph of the week.

O Ring a Ring o' Roses!

COLUMNS WHICH CONFRONT
TECHNICAL MARVELS ...

10

Columns Which Confront Technical Marvels

The Problems of Being Faxed

Aren't you fascinated with the news that Andrew Peacock has a fax machine in the back of his car?

He also has cellular telephones. These are the latest cordless phones. He can take a call on the run almost anywhere in Australia.

So the minute Bob Hawke makes a statement Andrew can think up a reply, put it on the fax machine which is in the car boot and send out the instant press statement, which presumably chats into faxes in newspaper offices, radio stations and such all over.

I feel terribly underprivileged and out of touch that I don't possess a fax. At least three times a week I get a call from some P.R. man, some Government department or organisation and the conversation goes like this:

"O.K. We'll put it on the fax to you this afternoon."

"I don't have a fax."

(Long shocked silence). "YOU DON'T HAVE A FAX!!!"

"No, I haven't got around to one of those."

"Oh dear. Um. That's difficult. What will we do? Look, could we fax our message to your local post office and you could pick it up there."

So they do that. You drive down to the Post Office and for the privilege of picking up their message, which you didn't want anyway, you have to pay something like $5.

There are firms all over the city now, that are so excited with their fax machines, they don't use the mail anymore. Everything has to be instant. Give us another five years, the mailman will be totally obsolete and everything will be delivered by fax. The damned fax will do nothing else but pump information into your living room.

All right, here is the Dunstan 1990 survey to check whether you are electronically aware.

(1) Do you have your own personal fax machine? 25 points. With special fax line of its own? 10 points.

(2) Do you have a telephone in the car? 15 points. Is it a cellular, carry around, go anywhere phone? Ring up your stockbroker while walking the dog in the park? 20 points.

(3) How about just a plain cordless phone which allows you to take phone calls anything up to 100 metres from your base phone, say, while pruning the roses or dozing by the swimming pool? 10 points.

(4) Do you have an answer phone? 10 points. Is it one of these particularly flash phones which has a special coded signal. You can call up your answer phone from Portsea, Antibes or Bali and retrieve all the recorded messages. 10 points. Or do you have one of those ultra vile phones which will only deliver calls direct to you if your privileged caller dials your secret coded number. All other calls go on to the answer phone and you can decide whether or not you want to call back? 20 points.

(5) Do you have a P.C.? If you don't know what a P.C. is dock yourself 10 points. If you do have a personal

computer add 20. If it is a lap-top with hard and floppy plus full color, compatible with the master computer at the office and you use it for all household accounts, records, tax etc. add another 20.

(6) Of course you have a garage with a door that operates by remote control. You have your little black box sitting on your dashboard, you press the button as you turn into the street, and lo, the door opens. 10 points. If you have a remote which also opens the security front gate add another 20.

(7) Talking of security you do have a horrid little phone system at the gate or door, don't you? And you let people in by pushing a button. 10 points. With video screening another 20 points. Burglar alarm system with heat sensors in every room and automatic alarm connection to security service or police. 20 points.

(8) One can only presume that you have a video. 5 points. With remote control 10 points. Then you have a hi-fi system with C.D. You don't know what a C.D. is? Go back 10 points. All right, you have a compact disc player. Add 10 points. It is one of the latest C.Ds. It has not only remote control, but you can take your pick of any one of half a dozen discs in the machine and you pick off any track you wish from any of those discs and even arrange them in the order you want. 20 points.

If you have scored over 250 points you are in the super executive class and I would advise you have to have a live-in electronics genius to keep all your gear in action. If you have scored over 200 you are an outstanding class yuppie, heading for your first triple by-pass. Well then, 150 to 200, you are a normal 1990s victim.

If you haven't scored any points at all, or even magnificently minus 20, I suspect you a very nice civilised human being.

Making Your Life Remote

We learn something every day. Now we know how to murder by video.

Did you watch "Mother Love" on TV? Diana Rigg in the old Emma Peel days used to beat people up with karate and judo. Now as Helena, the darling mother, she is a sort of Lucretia Borgia, poisoning everyone who gets in her path.

One of the heart-warming scenes, showed her with video monitor in her hand. She had taped a television interview with the hated second wife Lady Vesey. Smiling sweet, villainous smiles, she played back this TV show, then going through it frame by frame, she studied how to impersonate the Lady Vesey voice, she noted how the lady had a dark room in an old air raid shelter.

She could see that it was possible to close the air vents, lock her in. Then, by pretending Lady Vesey's voice on the telephone, she got an innocent friend to drive over to the Vesey house. As he locked the door and closed the air raid shelter air vents he did not realise the woman was inside. For 20 minutes the ABC showed the nice entertainment of Lady Vesey slowly suffocating to death.

All done by push-button TV monitor, an absolute first for TV thrillers. Technology triumphs again.

Actually, at our place, we have three remote control monitors. There's the remote that controls the straight television. There's the remote that works the video and, incredibly, we have a remote for the compact disc player.

They all look alike, long thin black boxes covered in buttons. I suspect that the television remote is the most useful invention in the entire 20th century. I would put it slightly ahead of the electric blanket, even a few notches in front of 10-speed gears for the bicycle.

There are two buttons, which are absolutely beyond price, there is the button that gives you instant quiet and button that turns the whole thing off. There's no quibble, no beg your pardons. Instant obeyance. I just love the omnipotent power. Goodbye Daryl Somers. Be quiet Graham Kennedy. You're talking nonsense Derryn Hinch. ZAP!

Our problem is this. The buttons are so small and inevitably we are operating these things in the dark. Not only that, two times out of three we pick up the wrong monitor. We go to squash Derryn Hinch and we turn on the compact disc player. We try to kill poor Paul Cronin in the midst of a Mitre 10 ad and we put the Video into fast forward.

We are watching our carefully prepared video of the Wimbledon final, Edberg has just won his serve, we try to squash a Toyota ad, press the wrong button and dammit we're back on regular TV with Mr Burke teaching us how to prune hydrangeas.

Our friends Hilton and Olivia are in an even worse situation. They have an extra remote for their radio and hi-fi, which makes four remotes altogether. Fred down the road has a remote for his garage doors and Lindsay even has one for the front gates.

Heavens knows how they get on. I wouldn't be surprised if they too have terrible trouble. Very likely, when Lindsay tries to kill Derryn, he opens the front gates or when hopping from Brian Naylor to Jennifer Kyte he closes the garage doors.

Then there is another problem, you can never find the darned things. I'm inclined to leave a remote or two in the kitchen when I get up to make the tea. Or there are those times of sheer desperation, when a belter is flogging Fords out at Moorabbin, the much required remote has slipped down under the sofa cushions. Sometimes it can take four days to find a lost remote.

There must be a simpler way. Yesterday in the mail we received one of these fancy color catalogues, offering every extraordinary gadget you need. But one caught my eye, "The Universal Remote Control".

"This will replace all the remote controls in your home or office," it said. "It will work an infra-red controlled audio visual device, television, video, CDs, cable TV, digital tapes, sound amplifiers, in fact up to eight separate components."

This little black box costs $145, and complex? I noted that it had 68 buttons. You would be pushing the button to get Joan Sutherland on to a bit of the Mad Scene from Lucretia and lo, the microwave would start cooking breakfast.

No, I'm not going to buy. I think we will wait until they improve the technology. I would like a remote with a sound zapper which I could use in all directions. Screeching motor bikes. ZAP. The character that never stops talking at dinner parties. ZAP. The rock'n'roll party next door. ZAP.

It could be used for even subtler purposes. Instead of long kicks under the dinner table the re-activate button could go into action. It could be used to awaken one at dinner parties. ZAP. A remote would be good for letting the dog in and out the back door and useful for changing baby nappies at 2 a.m.

It would be wonderful to make use of the fast forward or fast reverse buttons. It would be nice, for example, to throw into fast reverse and go back to that beautiful time when you could get a bank loan for around four per cent. I would like to return to the time when you could take it for granted that an Australian was going to win Wimbledon and no doubt there are misguided creatures who would like to fastback to when Collingwood won a Grand Final.

Yes, we could fastback to watch exactly how the young Don Bradman handled Larwood in 1932-33 series, or observe again the grace of Ray Lindwall in full cry when bowling to Len Hutton. Or perhaps one could re-do one of those summer holidays when the surf was warm, when the sun never seemed to stop shining and one heard "In the Mood" for the first time.

On the other hand I'd just love to push the fast forward button and see how those 1990 vintages are going to taste in 1992.

How to Murder Your Computer

Oh yes, I am an absolute, almost violent, member of the anti-gun lobby.

But I am wondering whether I should change my mind. There is a character named Paul La Vista who lives in Marietta, a suburb of Atlanta, Georgia. I have just read about him in an issue of New Scientist.

Paul runs an indoor firing range called Bulletstop. He hires out at all kinds of horrid firearms and supplies the ammunition, even machine guns. The idea is that you can indulge in your own fantasy.

You can take your own target into Bulletstop and fill it with bullets. Get rid of all your violent urges in the harmless atmosphere of a target range. Now here's the point, particular favorites at Bulletstop are personal computers and computer manuals.

When I read this a tear ran down my cheek. I understood perfectly. I have had a love/hate relationship with personal computers that has gone on now for nine years. It all began in the United States with a PC called a Teleram, which weighed 20 kilograms and was laughably described as "portable".

When you turned it on a message came on the screen: "Hi, this is your Teleram P.C." Then when you turned it off it announced chirpily: "So long, that's all folks." It had one appalling characteristic, it was sensitive to static electricity. I would have written a 1000 words or so then suddenly a spark would come from fingers to keys, the screen would go blank and everything I had written irretrievably disappeared.

HOW TO MURDER YOUR COMPUTER ...

If only Paul La Vista had been available then, Rambo would not have known such fury. I would have blasted Teleram with a bazooka. Finally I discovered the only safe way one could operate this PC was to work in bare feet.

The manufacturers of computers know damn well they are, peculiar, fickle, untrustworthy, strange. The absolute law of computers, is BACK-UP, BACK-UP, BACK-UP. In other words never do more than half an hour's work without copying everything on disc.

I had a serene six months and became dangerously over confident. I overloaded a disc and one terrible morning, I punched the keys and all that came back on the screen was "Data fault". The same thing frequently happens with my own memory, whenever I try to remember a dear friend's name, press the mental buttons and back comes "data fault".

But on this disc were 17,000 words of a book and there was no back-up. I didn't become violent and attack the computer, I think I began to cry. I went to the local agents, all the top computer doctors, surgeons, experts on disc cardiac failure. The disc was sent to computer psychiatrists in Sydney, but the data had all gone, gone to some mysterious PC black hole where all computer data disappears.

It was one of the agonies of my life and quietly I had to start all over again. It is not generally realised that computers are sulky and have moods. That is why they talk so much about compatibility. I live in the country and daily send data by modem through telephone wires, and my computer talks to the big brother computer in the newspaper office. But some days either one computer or the other is in a bad mood and they play games of no speak. Not even the greatest experts can explain why.

Paul La Vista reports that one group brought into Bulletstop an enormous computer manual, 2000 pages. They rented three machine guns, an Uzi, an M3 and a Thompson. They proceeded to cut it to pieces with bullets until it was like confetti. This done they went away with happy smiles, rid of a terrible frustration.

If you have had anything to do with computer manuals your sympathy for this act would be overwhelming. I have an entire shelf load of these things. They are written by boffin mathematicians as a puzzle, designed deliberately to confuse. Ten pages will be used to cover a simple act which could be explained in a paragraph.

There is an entire industry now, in trying to explain what computer manuals mean. For example, I use soft wear called Microsoft Word; there are at least four books available which try to explain what the official manual is talking about. You can never get them under $50 each. I have *Microsoft Word Made Easy*.

I bought one item of ingenious software, the manual so indecipherable, I used to ring the manufacturer in Pennsylvania, asking him what the hell I had to do next. He was utterly charming and we became such good friends, but the expense was awful.

Yet I haven't mentioned the most maddening thing of all. You know how Detroit invented built-in obsolescence for the automobile? It is as nothing when compared with computers. You don't get new models, you get new generations, for God's sake.

Already, in nine years, I am on my fourth generation. They keep coming out with brilliant new advances, hard discs, mini discs, extended memory where you can have two or three Bibles on the one disc, lightning speed, facilities where alphanumeric skills, where you can index a book practically in an afternoon, automatic dictionaries, thesauruses, even genius inspired devices that will brush up your grammar.

Unfortunately I found every new gadget or device irresistible. So now I have a room full of aged vintage computers. They don't pick up value like vintage cars or old gramophone records. I would like to shoot them, gun them down while they whimper, but I can't do that either, because they are not compatible and I need them to get data from my library of old discs.

It's very frustrating. Looking back it would have been easier to continue with my dear old Remington, and hire a team of secretaries to produce my copy.

And I strongly doubt whether I would have wanted to murder any of them with Paul La Vista's machine guns. However, four nights out of five I think I could be persuaded to gun down our television set.

COLUMNS ON THE PROBLEMS OF SURVIVAL...

11

Columns on the Mysteries of Survival

When I'm Sixty-four

I was driving home in the car last week and on came that sing-song plaintive tone of the Beatles:

> *Will you still need me, will you still feed me,*
> *When I'm sixty-four.*

Good grief! It was my birthday and I was sixty-four. When the pink-cheeked, almost innocent, long haired Beatles wrote that song a sixty-fourth birthday seemed a date so distant in the future, it would never arrive. Oh, but it has.

The marvellous nostalgic song droned sweetly on:

> *When I get older losing my hair*
> *Many years from now*

Oddly enough I don't feel any different. None of this business of serving and sprinting to the net any more. Indeed sprinting is gone for ever. Do you know what I notice particularly, everybody is bigger, particularly the girls. If you go out jogging all the girls seems six feet tall and they go past as if you're standing still.

> *Will you be sending me a Valentine*
> *Birthday greetings a bottle of wine.*

Yes, she did that all right. As for the bottle of wine, the standard has improved no end, particularly the whites, the chardonnays and the champagnes. But dear friend, what has happened to the price? In our pre-Beatle glory it was untaxed and remember how we used to home bottle our reds for a shilling a bottle?

If I'd been out until quarter to three
Would you lock the door?

Problematical that. She just might, the shock would be so profound. My normal problem is just keeping awake past 9 pm, particularly when television is going through its 240th repeat of "Upstairs Downstairs" or "Executive Stress." Quarter to three! She might even lock it around quarter to eleven.

I could be handy mending a fuse
When your lights are low.

I love that line. About the only brilliant handyman things I could do were mending fuses and changing washers in taps. But time has moved on. We have a brilliant new fuse box now with these fancy pop-up fuses. If we use four heaters, the TV, video and washing machine all at once, you just turn off a few heaters, push it back into place again. She doesn't need me for that job at all.

Doing the garden, digging the weeds,
Could you ask for more?

Not really. Funny thing that, in the first years of marriage gardening is far too slow-moving , no time for that. But then you discover that planting a bottle brush, raising the passion fruit, nurturing the hydrangeas through another season, gives a nice feeling of continuity, even eternity.

As for the weeds, I knew a great journalist, Arthur Richards, who would say: "I always like to come back home, stick a fork in the ground and pull out weed, its long root still intact. It gives a feeling of satisfaction. Pulling out a weed in your garden is the true sense of ownership."

Every summer we rent a cottage
In the Isle of Wight, if it's not too dear.

Don't know about the Isle of Wight, but Lorne, Palm Beach, Sorrento is now off the graph. They are selling little places on the foreshore at Portsea for three or four million and even Susan Renouf had to play two million for her shack at Whale Beach. My father always used to say, never try to live in two houses. You don't know where anything is. Inevitably your trousers end up in one house and your shirt in another.

We shall scrimp and save
Grandchildren on your knee
Vera Chuck and Dave.

Scrimp and save is correct. We had to scrimp and save to pay the babysitters, then drive them home at 12.30 a.m. Now we are the baby sitters, maybe twice a week. Rather nice really. We keep the fridge full of ice blocks and Eskimo Pies. The spare room walls are covered with astonishing drawings of Grandma and Grandpa. We don't have to discipline Vera, Chuck and Dave and we can package them off home. Then when they have gone you find hunks of playdough, bits of Lego under the sofa, and little Chuck has changed all the digital clocks and even set the alarm for quarter to three.

Send me a postcard, drop me a line
Stating a point of view.

Not many people drop a line any more, more likely a fax. But if I did drop a line in my sixty-fourth year I would point out that things were infinitely better. Remember a city riddled with wowserdom? Remember six o'clock closing, wine glasses compulsorily removed from the table, the sepulchral Sunday, when everything closed including the local tennis courts? Remember (shudder) staying at some of those country hotels? When you dropped a line there were two postal deliveries daily plus a delivery on Saturday mornings but the telephone was awful. Sometimes you would wait five minutes before the girl said: "Number please" and when you got the wrong number you started all over again.

As for entertainment there was the Hoyts suburban theatre and the Lux Radio Theatre on the wireless on Sunday nights. As for sport our tennis players seemed to win more often, our cricketers I am sure were better, and as for football, that is infinitely worse. There was a time, particularly in Melbourne when the clamor went for only six months in the year. Now we start it at the height of the bushfire season.

Give me an answer, fill in a form.
Mine for ever more.
Will you still need me, will you still feed me.
When I am sixty-four?

Oh, I hope so. It would be a desperate situation otherwise. It's not only the feeding. Who else would find car keys, and reading spectacles 45 times a day? Who else could remember the names of the people we went out to dinner with last night? Who else would find all the column ideas and who else would help with all those weeds?

When I'm sixty-four.

When I'm Sixty-five

The terrible truth is that this columnist has just become an official geriatric.

Tram conductors and railwaymen get their early retirement plans and whizz off in their fifties, for most the official geriatric figure is 65, judges hang on until they are 70, many politicians refuse to be gagged even when they are 80, Popes can still be there when they are 90, but look out for writers.

Writers keep going until they drop nose first on to their word processors. I think it was Thea Astley who said they should be given some sort of pill which would force them to stop.

Perhaps one should give a report to the shareholders on the state of the company.

Mind:

It has been an average year, the greatest difficulty has been memory. Often it has been like putting a disc into the disc drive of the computer pressing the buttons and nothing comes up on the screen. Names are the very devil. It would be a great help if it were compulsory for all human beings to wear name tags.

But memory is such a precious thing. I was reading an article the other day by a famous author...oh dear, what's his name, it's right on the tip of my brain. He wrote a book...I'll have the title in a minute if I just start thinking of something else...Anyway you must have read it.

This author ...you know who I mean...confessed that he went into his library, looked at the great expanse of books on all his shelves, every word a treasure, a life time of absorbed knowledge, then he said to himself: "Do you know I don't think I can remember more than a line that is in any of them." Oh, I know the feeling.

Sight:

Still operable, except that glasses now have to be tied permanently around the neck or 25 per cent of the day is spent looking for them. Telephone books have become outrageous, but the worst are street directories. Have you ever been out in the car, 7.15 p.m., fading light, trying to find Finschafen Road, Highett, Map 264, K7. It's all a blur and you start to swear it's not there and Melway got it all wrong.

But then there are times when the quality of eye sight is truly amazing, perhaps world class. I know immediately when a tennis linesman has made an error even though I am 15,000 kilometres from the event. At the MCG my eyesight is perfection. Umpires rarely know what they are doing. I can detect an error in an umpire's lbw decision, even though 100 metres off in the grandstand.

Should my host be carrying a wine bottle I can read the fine print on the label at 20 paces. Then at dinner parties post 10 p.m. it is absolutely not done to look at your watch. The trick is to look at other people's watches. I can read the time on a lady's watch, upside down, right across from the other side of the dinner table.

Sleeping:

Very curious. You tend to sleep when you don't want to and can't sleep when you want to. I mean sleep is almost impossible after 4 a.m. , but it is easy in railway carriages, trams, concerts, plays, dinner parties. One notices also on television that mini series are becoming more and more mini. Some of them are all over in five minutes.

Hearing:

Becoming distressingly conservative and unadventurous. I think I have come to the opinion that little noise produced after say 1910 or 1920 is worth hearing, except contemporary stuff orchestrated by our magpies and wattle birds.

Particularly worrying is the music provided in many restaurants. I have an old friend who always calls up first: "Do you have music in your restaurant?"

"OH YES SIR, WE DO. WE DO."

"Thank-you very much. I'll go somewhere else."

We have a mutual understanding in our house, the intensity of our lack of hearing increases in proportion to what we don't want to do. It is remarkable how difficult it is hear important information when one is reading the newspaper.

Physical Activity.

Actually improving. There is more time now to do the things one likes doing. We walk more, we cycle more. But you remember in the old days when serving at tennis, the first serve always was a thunderbolt, the next dead slow to get it in. Now the first serve is slow and the second fast out of desperation. My backhand is not functioning all that well, but to come to think of it, I don't think it ever did.

Sense of smell:

Very good shape thank-you, good for another 20 years. Love the smell of eucalyptus particularly when putting falling branches through the mulcher. Why do females and even males wear such appalling perfume in restaurants and picture theatres, when the simple smells are the finest on this earth? Any female could carry me right off if she had freshly ground coffee or a few leaves of basil behind each ear.

Advantages:

The Government takes a kindly view and issues you with a special geriatric card. You get cheap travel. It is possible, all around the world, to get into art galleries half price. Movie theatres offer special rates and recently there was even a geriatric week when geriatrics got in free. But I tell you what, it is downright infuriating when you ask the girl at the counter whether she would like proof of age and she gives you a long tired look: "No Sir, that won't be necessary, thank-you."

But there is another big advantage, an intensity of pleasure. How can one put it? You know when you have a specially good bottle of wine you savour particularly the last glass? In the same way life's simple pleasures become more important, the daily companionship of one's wife, the wonderful explosion of laughter from the kookaburras, announcing the dawn and the sunset; the sound of the cricket ball on the bat from the cricket ground over yonder, the morning beating of the bounds around the garden, checking to see whether the peace rose has created another artist's miracle, or watching those astonishing New Holland honey eaters pushing their needle beaks into every flower; how diligently they gather breakfast.

Or how about the ecstatic joyful arrival of all the grandchildren, then being able to send them home when you don't need them after 6 p.m. Bliss.

Rally Please to the Society Against Progress

As you may be aware this column is the headquarters for the Society Against Progress.

S.A.P. believes that nothing ever gets better, only worse. S.A.P.s look back with nostalgia to the days when the dollar was a splendid unchangeable thing not subject to daily absurd variations, to the days when there were two postal deliveries a day, and again on Saturday morning.

When you did not have to write a cheque to have an article delivered. Yes, your postage went up again yesterday. When the air was breathable and there was still a park or two along Batman Avenue.

Every so often S.A.P. likes to give a deterioration report. Last week your S.A.P. observer went shopping during the school holidays. In Bourke Street what with buskers, and characters flogging gadgets, the crowd was so intense one wondered whether this was a pre-election uprising.

You had to fight your way into the big store because right at the entrance they had a jazz band, pumping out music. To make matters worse there was a perfume promotion. Languid looking blondes were wandering around with guns squirting smell almost at random.

I took quick evasion action and jumped on the escalator. I ask you to believe the scene that was on the first floor. There were television sets everywhere. Indeed in one area close to the ceiling there were six of them in a row.

Now these TV sets were thumping out rock music. While I was there a gentleman with a guitar and a face that appeared to be painted an extraordinary color was making gymnastic leaps while he attempted to play his instrument. Meanwhile in front of him, a young female with short hair and a leather skirt about the width of a pair of shoelaces was indulging in the most remarkable writhing movements.

I thought it might be quieter down in the basement but here they had males and females with microphones who stood beside red and blue flashing lights. These flashing lights were precisely like those used by the police and ambulance. When first I saw the blue blinking light I had a feeling of security. At last a constable had arrived to restore law and order.

But, no, a salesman with full amplification was shouting: "Get your French sun glasses, only $15 each. Never again will you get an opportunity like this. Buy seven of them. Have a different style of glasses to wear for every day of the week."

In the midst of all this one couldn't help but note the difficulty one had in actually trying to purchase something. There was an amazing number of people employed to encourage excitement but few indeed to lead one to the article that was required.

The modern theory of shopping is "seek and ye shall find". Seeking for one item can take anything up to half an hour. Indeed in some stores and supermarkets you can virtually die of starvation before you find your quarry. You would think they would have a sort of Melway or handy chart to advise where you can find each item.

At one stage I was so desperate I went into a trance and a vision came to mind of how stores used to be. At the entrance there was an elegant gentleman, impeccably dressed in a morning suit. He would greet you, then direct you to the appropriate department.

The atmosphere was quiet. Piped music inside stores, mercifully, had not been invented. There was a barrier between you and the goods. This was known as a "counter." Ah, but in front of the counter there was always a seat or a stool. You sat down and a sales person, gentleman or lady, asked what you required and brought it to you.

A wonderfully convenient system it was. Then having bought your article they asked, respectfully, to which address you would like it delivered. Home delivery in those blissful days was automatic and free.

Under the "Seek and Ye Can Find" system you hunt down your quarry, try to guess what size you would be in centimetres, then you take it to a sales island, where you might find someone with a cash register.

I bought two singlets, then a belt, both splendidly wrapped. But at each island they insisted on putting these items in a huge plastic bag. Apparently it is compulsory that everything purchased must go in these bags.

One noticed further, incredibly, that they had areas called "WRAP BAR". My wife explained one went to a Wrap Bat when one wanted something beautifully gift wrapped.

Surely it would be more useful if the Wrap Bar unwrapped things for you, quietly disposed of the mountain of plastic bags that you don't want. No wonder we are having the Greenhouse Effect and the world is going to ruin. It is the hundred billion plastic bags that have to be burned every day.

My next shopping item was a compact disc. I thought it would be nice if we could play some gentle harp music while we were having dinner. However, the record shops are the most unnerving of all. They believe they attract customers through the volume of their sound and the hi-finess of their hi-fi.

Even before you approach the shop you can hear the rock reverberating down the street. Entering the shop is like swimming under water. You know that the human system can endure such overwhelming forces no longer than two minutes.

Find what you want, get in and get out quickly. I found a shop assistant, mouthed what I wanted hoping he could lip read. It was impossible for humans to conduct conversation and probably his hearing was destroyed back around 1978.

Alas, we did not establish communication. Gasping for silence I fled.

Now I wonder if there are many S.A.P. members who are enduring the same problems. Perhaps we could band together, and open a market. Now what would be the right name? I have looked up the opposite of 'Super' in my thesaurus and come with mini, bantam, dainty, diminutive, dwarfish, lilliputian, micro, minuscule, minute, pygmy, tiny and wee.

How do you think The Wee Market would go? We would have our morning suited greeter, no piped music, a counter between customers and goods, chairs, kindly sales people, and I think we would have one of those marvellous sales devices where tubes go zinging off on wires to a central cash lady.

We would make such a fortune inevitably Coles-Myer, David Jones and all, would want to take it over.

Mr Suzuki I'm Trying, Honestly.

Oh dear, we would like to be good, pure Suzuki people but the withdrawal pains are awful. It is not easy making an immediate switch back to the Stone Age.

Last week the Sunday Age printed the 10 golden rules for survival according to the greenie prophet, Dr David Suzuki. Unless we followed his golden rules the planet would be in big trouble.

1 Reject all disposable products; lighters, pens, razors. That's easy, I use an electric razor and I have always found the disposable ballpoint pen an invention of the devil, a loathsome illegible thing. So I am the last human in Melbourne that uses a dear, old fountain pen.

2 Buy longlasting clothes and avoid the trendy and fashionable. Going well. My problem is that my clothes are so long lasting and so untrendy they have gone the full cycle and become fashionable again.

3 Team up with neighbours, buy in bulk to avoid unnecessary packaging. Is he kidding? You just end up with bigger and more packages. In my mother's day everything at the local grocer was in bulk, flour, rice, sugar, and even soap. Biscuits she bought loose from marvellous big containers, the size of kerosene tins. Now even our meat comes wrapped in plastic and the super market doles out steak and chops in plastic boxes as if they were pills. But we are trying, really; young Lotte our poodle is deliriously happy because we have given up canned dog food.

4 Go for compost and reduce your garbage to one small bin a month. That will take a revolution. I think our council really likes garbage. It gave us one of these gigantic tombstone bins on wheels. You feel you have failed as a citizen if you don't fill it weekly. Yes, we have a compost bin, but last week the horse next door put his head over the fence and ate the entire contents. We tried burying all the chicken and meat bones. Result: the foxes came in and dug up the lot.

5 Recycle everything possible. O.K. The local church won't take our old newspapers or cardboard. Re-use all our jars, boxes, tins, paper and packaging. We started doing that and in two weeks we couldn't get the car into the garage and the place looked like Steptoe & Son, to say nothing of a threat from the rural fire brigade. But we are planning to do something decent and meaningful by returning to home brewing so that we can recycle all our bottles.

6 Refuse plastic bags when buying goods. We loathe the horrid things, but most of the super markets want you to use their bags otherwise you buck their carefully organised get-rid-of-customers-quickly system. Grandfather always shopped with his own Gladstone bag. If the dear old gentleman were here today our super market would want him out of the way. They would see him as a potential shoplifter, fast as you lift a box of detergent.

7 Make it a rule if you are travelling less than 10 blocks, walk. Leave the car at home, use public transport. I gave up public transport 30 years ago when a cantankerous union kept leaving me on railway platforms. I took to the bicycle and found it infinitely more reliable. Nothing has changed.

8 Don't use paper napkins, towels, tissues or nappies. Done. The return to cotton is lovely. It is a step forward not having the remnants of tissues in the washing machine that you forgot to take out of our pockets. But we have yet to find an alternative to the plastic coverings in the fridge and the microwave.

9 Choose goods which have little or no packaging. Is there anything that's not packaged? At our hardware all items are sealed in the hardest plastic known to science. There isn't an item that's not in a plastic box. Last week I bought a pair of secateurs and a torch with batteries. Both were sealed in plastic so hard it took me half an hour just to chisel them out of captivity.

10 Buy organic food. Probably could if I were prepared to get out the car and travel 20 kilometres, but that way I'd defeat the purpose by polluting the air in the process.

Tell your hardware store you want loose nails rather than boxed. He'd never do that. They sell you things in packages because that is the whole principle on which high speed cash and carry is based. And besides, how else can they always sell the customer four times as much as he needs.

Dear Dr Suzuki, I have scored only three out of 10, but I'm trying, honestly I am.

The Comforts of Being Locked Up

It is almost time to join some good religious order and give all one's property to the poor. I don't think I can stand it much longer.

Last week-end I went out to put something in the rubbish tin. I heard the gentle click of the front gate behind me and I knew I was done. I was locked out, me outside, keys inside, nobody at home. Almost everybody has been robbed in our street. The folk next door have a fence three metres high, which is permanently locked. You can only communicate with those inside, via one of those security phones. You press the button and eventually a disembowelled voice comes from inside, from afar off, as if you were trying to communicate with the Reserve Bank at 3 a.m.

The security at our place is also magnificent. We have bars on the windows. The side fence goes to three metres with nasty wire on top. The doors and gates are all deadlocked.

So there I was outside and I knew there wasn't a chance of getting back in. It was two hours before my wife came home. So what could a man do? Nothing. No money in pockets to go down to the pub for a drink. All I could do was sit on the footpath by the fence and meditate.

I was in my dirty jeans, joggers, and favorite old polo neck sweater. As people walked past they looked at me strangely, you could see what they were thinking. "What's he doing there? Horrid! Typical suspicious looking housebreaker. I wonder if I should call the police?"

Exactly the same thing happened several weeks ago to a son-in-law. He went out to the rubbish bin and the wind blew the front door shut. Trapped outside by the latest in magnificent double deadlocks, worth around $70 a time. He was in his dressing gown, bare feet, nothing on underneath. It was one of these double working households. His wife had already left for the office.

He had to walk a kilometre to our place seeking help, thinking all the time he would be picked up for being the local mystery rapist.

Two weeks ago I went to north-eastern Victoria and stayed with some friends. They kept their house as open as a tree.

When they went out they didn't lock anything. "Why bother, everyone's honest around here," they said.

Not in Melbourne. We have put fancy deadlocks on everything that opens and finally it is starting to get to me. The theory is that you must have deadlocks because the thieves come round with furniture vans and take not only your video, but the lot.

So you've got to have a key to get in and you've got to have a key to get out. "You don't have it deadlocked all the time," I say to my wife. "Not when we're inside."

"Yes you do," she says. "Some thief could break the glass, put his hand round, undo the lock and mug us all."

So every time we go out we have to find the keys. Or the postman's ringing on the front door with a registered parcel. We're not very well organised at our place. "HAS ANYONE SEEN THE DAMN KEYS?"

But first you have to find your glasses before you can find the damn keys. By the time you have sorted all this out the postman has gone and you have to go to the post office to get the parcel.

We haven't bought a burglar alarm yet, but that is the next stage of lunacy. Everyone over there in Toorak has one. You have to remember to turn the things on and turn them off. Very sophisticated they are. There are the types that just work when someone forces a window, but there are the fancy ones that work by sonar, or by breaking a beam of light, or if they are ultra fancy they pick up a rise in temperature caused by a human body.

In some streets you get a better sonic display than Big Ben, alarms going off all day and night. Meanwhile a friend of ours has a sign in his front window: "We have a burglar alarm, but don't worry. There's nothing left. This house has been robbed three times already."

Cars, now that's another thing. We have had cars stolen twice before. We bought a new one last year. We didn't think too much about dream upholstery, digital dash, fuel injection or any of that nonsense. Good locking we were after. So we bought a car with superb electronic thief-proof locks, one turn - kerlunk, all locked.

Well, we were down at the seaside, parked in the tea tree. Time 3 pm. I was putting things away after the picnic, keys on the carpet of the lovely hatchback. As soon as I closed the boot I knew what I had done. "Where are your keys?" I said to my wife. "They're in my handbag...uh...in the car."

We called the RACV. "No trouble," they said. "We do this all the time. Average time for getting into a car; 30 seconds."

Not with our car. After 45 minutes he said it was hopeless. The security was magnificent. "Your only hope is to get a locksmith."

It was 7 p.m. and after dark by the time the mobile locksmith arrived. He looked at our car under the tea tree, and leered: "What have you two been doing? Necking?"

He could just see my bunch of keys on the floor of the boot by shining his torch through the hatchback. He worked out the design, went back to his mobile workshop, scratched and filed for over an hour. He came back again and again to the lock, and just when we thought he was going to give up:

"Click," all the locks went free in a beautiful synchronised electronic motion.

"That will be $70 thank-you," said he.

And he told us what a marvellous business he had. It always started at around 8 a.m., people locked out of their offices. About 11 a.m. he got the domestic trade, housewives locked out of their houses, lost the keys at the super market, then the cars, then the folk coming home in the evening. And it was getting better all the time.

HAIL TO THE UMBRAGEOUS COAST...

Hail to the Umbrageous Coast

Don't you feel a trace of sadness that the era of sun worship is over.

Now when you see a superb sun-bronzed Australian, no longer do you think, "Ah, here is a member of the climate-blessed race, where else on earth could you get such abundant health?"

Your sun-bronzed Australian could be an old fashioned Digger, a stockman, a life saver at Bondi, or one of these triathlon characters roaring along the beach at Coolangatta.

Now instead of looking with envy at the beauty of that chestnut skin, you think he/she is one of the four out of five that is doomed to get skin cancer. If I look carefully I can see cancer spots, melanomas and all.

Remember how after the World War 2 we all went hatless? It wasn't just convenience. The theory was if only we could get enough sun it would bleach our hair, make us all a more lovely shade of blonde.

Remember too the start of the Christmas holidays, getting down to Anglesea, Lorne or Flinders with the shame of white legs under those shorts, or most shameful of all, a white back and a white chest? The first four days were devoted almost entirely to the careful cultivation of the mandatory brown skin.

Most of our old pleasures have now turned into sins. The loveliest of them seemed to be sunbathing. The innocence, the indulgence of lying face down on the sand, feeling the sun's rays on your back, this always seemed even better than getting into bed with an electric blanket. Total and marvellous indolence. Now it is a sin.

For health we go back to the English beauty, utterly white skin with pink cheeks and any display of flesh totally vulgar. See a topless girl on the beach, no longer a surge of passion, just a feeling of sympathy. What will the sun do to her delightful nipples?

But, wait, we can make use of this new fear of the sun. I have a plan which can restore Victoria's tourist fortunes. We have been warned that with the wrecking of the ozone layer eventually ultra violet rays could become so dangerous we might find it wise to sleep during the day and only go out at night.

You will have noticed that on the ABC TV news we now get a daily UV count, a graph which tells us of the menace of the sun's rays during the previous 24 hours. For example, the hours between 11 a.m. and 4 p.m. arch up on the graph a terrible puce color to show when the danger is extreme.

Until now anything to do with sunshine has been tourist bait. Queensland has exploited it with every means in its power, the Sunshine State, the Sunshine Coast and every second motel has a title sun, "Sunburst", "Sunray", "Casa del Sol,"...

I seem to remember even Alan Bond out west got his start with Sun City at Yanchep.

Sun was the cult. It has been the fashion for those rich people in Toorak, Hawthorn, Camberwell and Brighton to desert our cloud blessed city. As soon as the weather has become chilly in May their Mercedes and Jaguars have headed north like migratory birds seeking warmer climes to breed.

Now, don't you see, they will be merely heading into cancer country.

Take it from me, it is just a matter of time before they will have to build verandas over all those beaches on Queensland's Gold Coast. Perhaps we will even see the return of the 19th century bathing machine, the tiny house on wheels which you push into the water.

On your behalf I have been making a study of the Australia Year Book, looking up all the charts. Which is the worst, the most dangerous capital city? Answer: Perth.

Perth gets 108 utterly clear days, 47 cloudy days and mean average of 7.9 hours of sunshine. Darwin does better with an 8.4 hours average of sunshine, but then it gets 105 cloudy days. Brisbane, I think, is the most dangerous rival, 7.5 hours average of sunshine with only 34 cloudy days and 96.7 clear days in an entire year. Oh, very dangerous Brisbane.

Now you might ask which capital of all has the safest, the most blessed climate? Answer: Melbourne. I have looked at the statistics very carefully and I think Melbourne just edges out Hobart.

I am not quite sure what constitutes a clear day, but we get 48 and Hobart gets 22.1. We both get 132 cloudy days. We get 143 days of rain and Hobart gets 160. We get 18.2 fogs, Hobart gets 5.8. But here's the crunch. Hobart gets an average of 5.8 hours of sun daily, but Melbourne wins out as the most sunless capital with 5.7 hours.

Admittedly even on cloudy days you can be ultra violated to ruin, but surely some cloud blanket is helpful? Until now Melbourne has had a dubious record for weather. Not any more and we must make capital of it. Smart tourists will be looking for the cities, the beaches, with the least sun.

The problem is to find the right title, the sensitive catch phrase which will attract tourists to our Victorian beaches. The phrase has to allude instantly to their lovely sunless character.

The Umbrageous Coast? The Obfuscated Sands? No, such titles sound impressive but people would have to go to their dictionaries. The Shady Coast. Mmmm. Not bad. But shade can mean many things, ghosts for example. Shady might also suggest sin. That could make it attractive, but it could also suggest malpractice, which would be unattractive.

No, I think I have the answer. How about Pale Skins Paradise. I pass over the suggestion free of charge to the Victorian Tourism Authority.

We could even change our number plates from the Garden State to the Paleskin State, but I am getting discouraged, the Victorian Tourism people are singularly backward in taking up my suggestions. Too much sun probably.

In Bad Times You Cover Up

Undoubtedly you are aware of the cover-up theory of economics.

In good times skirts tend to go up and limbs are exposed to the view. In bad times skirts go down, and in shocking times they descend almost to the ankle.

Times indeed must be bad because I have seen some regrettable skirts in Collins Street this past week, girls with skirts so long and baggy they look like Mongolian refugees.

When times are bad nostalgia becomes all the go. We grab at the illusion that almost everything was better yesterday.

If you have been studying your female magazines you will have noticed that the inspiration for the new season bathing costumes has gone back to the nineteen thirties. Last summer not only did we have girls topless at Middle Park and St Kilda, but the bottomless look was, if not in, out.

Girls were displaying bare bums with what appeared to be a G-string.

Now for the coming season *avant garde* is to wear a costume just like we did when Claudette Colbert and Ginger Rogers were young girls, high at neck, modestly low at the hip. Glory be, some of the models for 1990 even have the old fashioned short sleeves and legs.

Just to give you a rough time table of what we used to wear in the water, up til World War 1 women went into the water virtually fully clothed. From 1919 to 1932 we favored the neck to knee. The year 1932 saw the backless costume. A Congregational Minister, the Reverend S.H. Cox, said that girls who wore these daring, disgusting, backless beach costumes were not the kind to uplift the moral tone of the community, nor when married, to teach morals to their children.

The bikini first came to Surfers Paradise in 1955 and from then on everything was downhill so to speak.

So you can see what will happen, if the economy gets any worse backless costumes will go and when interest rates pass 20 per cent presumably girls will be entering the water in full length skirts.

Now gentlemen, I want you to readjust your bi-focals. When you see a beautiful young girl on the beach this summer, topless, or even bottomless, I trust you will avert your gaze, blush even, and mutter to yourself:

"How unfashionable!"

Never Trust a Banker with a Christian Name

There is a bush song written by that great poet Anonymous which goes:

> *For the banks are all broken they say,*
> *And the merchants are all up a tree;*
> *When the bigwigs are brought to the bankruptcy court,*
> *What chance for a squatter like me?*

Actually the most disturbing thing is not much so the losing of money but what has happened to the fine old institution of banking. When I was leaving school it was the object of every mother to get her son into a bank.

If you knew someone high up in a bank, what bliss it was. "Could you please find a position for our Henry?" Yes, you got a position. Never crudely was it called a job.

Mother knew that once Henry was in the bank he would be trained according to the highest moral ideals. His manager would wear a three-piece suit even on days of 40 degrees. His hair would be correctly short back and sides. His care with money, his meanness, would be the perfect example for young Henry.

When any customer went to the bank for a loan, the money was not just handed out. Customer indeed! He or she was a penitent, one who had to confess. The customer had to grovel, to plead and, before signatures were placed on paper, the bank manager gave a lecture on the importance of money. Customer went away feeling guilty for having borrowed.

T.S. Eliot was an example of the majesty of banking. He started his career very correctly as a bank clerk. When he told his manager he was leaving there was shock all around the building. The manager asked what he proposed to do.

Eliot said he intended to make a living as a poet.

The shock was even greater. "Pity," said the important man, "I saw in you possibilities as bank manager material."

Look what we have learned in the past week. We were told at one inquiry that the former management of Victoria's State Bank was like an "old boys club", even a way of life. They had their own bathrooms and toilets, expensive originals on the walls, chauffeurs for their cars and, more than anything, they looked forward to their overseas trips.

The same thing was true of South Australia's State Bank. We were told over there that the banks indulged in long lunches, wonderful trips, good living and, what impressed me more than anything, Max Schubert was wine advisor to the Board. Max Schubert, as you know, created the marvellous Grange Hermitage for Penfolds.

Then Tim Marcus Clark, managing director of the South Australian State Bank, retired with just on a million dollars severance pay after receiving an annual salary of $500,000.

Does that startle you? No, no, no, not the money, the reference to "Tim". When I was leaving school and young Henry was going into the bank, managers, I am sure, didn't even possess Christian names. Mister Clark it would have been and that would have been the end of it.

This familiarity goes on with bankers everywhere. Who was appointed as the new chairman of the suffering State Bank of South Australia? Nobby Clark. Nobby Clark was the former chief executive of the National Australia Bank. I have noticed for a year or so that whenever this particular Clark turned up in the financial pages he was always "Nobby". It almost made me close my account with the National.

It is easy to trace the deterioration in banking. In the old days banks were always built like monuments or war memorials, lots of immense solid masonry with Corinthian or Doric columns. The windows were small to emphasise their impenetrable security. You spoke in hushed tones and crossed yourself when you went in. The bankers themselves wore hard collars, sombre ties and looked like funeral directors.

The idea was to awe the customer into submission and show that money did not come too easily.

Now there is no masonry at all. The buildings are like super markets, all glass, your corner Unsafeway Store. The top man is called Nobby or Tim and there are christian names for everybody.

At the teller's window you note that you are talking to Cheryl, Samantha, Wayne or Jason. Sometimes Jason doesn't even wear a tie and he sports an ear ring.

Even more disturbing is their liberality with money. You know these Easy Money machines. At our bank as soon as you pop in a card up comes a message on screen: ASK US NOW ABOUT AN EASY LOAN. You can get $40,000 dollars as fast as you bat a bank book.

The bank is all decorated with loan possibilities. They have pictures of speed boats, sports cars, holidays in Rome, Paris, Tahiti .... There are pictures all around the bank of warm, kindly, credit managers, who will help you on your way: Nevile, Scott and Patricia.

One bank down the road recently had little brochures: NO NEED TO BLUSH IF YOUR CHEQUE ISN'T FLUSH... Need a car loan? A personal holiday? Apply here. Personal loans $2000 to $99,000.

Unquestionably the whole banking system has to revert. I won't feel confident again until managers have haircuts, until managers wear waistcoats, until managers and staff abandon Christian names. I don't mind if there is a sign at the Teller's window: "Your attendant is T.S. Eliot." I don't want to know more than that.

Our local branch some weeks back was decorated with balloons to celebrate the joyous nature of their lending. Little cypress funereal shrubs would have been more appropriate.

In the meantime what profession would you advise for your son or daughter? You would never contemplate anything as racy and as risky as banking. Unquestionably you would seek something safe, like a bookmaker's apprentice, or even better, a good position working amongst one-armed bandits or baccarat tables.

Young Henry might rise to a really wonderful secure position like manager of a Tabaret.

COLUMNS OF IMMENSE SOCIAL IMPORTANCE...

12

Columns of Immense Social Importance

Our Dream Time Bill of Rights

You will have noticed that among other sweet discussions going on in Canberra they have been talking about a Bill of Rights.

Indeed it has been going on for years; Labor, Liberal and Democrats can't agree on what our rights should be.

Sir Robert Menzies used to say our rights were designated under common law and there was no need to go further. Yet to my mind the present discussions have been absurd; they don't even come close. It is all very well to talk about freedom of speech, one-person one vote, freedom of religion and that sort of thing. They should get down to even deeper, fundamental rights, protection from things that finally send us all out of our minds.

I would like to see a Bill of Rights which touches on domestic issues.

For example we would start with television. We would make it the right of human beings to have at look at no more than two repeats a day; not the current 26. We would it make our right that we have to look at commercials only for the first eight or 10 minutes in the hour. This system is the law in a number of countries and it makes a nice clean break so that you can make a cup of coffee. It should also be a fundamental right that there be at least one watchable program on Friday and Saturday nights. It has not happened to date. Why should they preserve the ultimate turgidity for the week-end?

What's more, we could include a rule that would return cricket telecasts to days of greater refinement. We would have cameras take pictures of events as they happen, not this constant turning back of the reel, giving us six replays every time a cricketer makes a decent shot.

And while we are thinking of advertising it should be the right of human beings that we don't have to look at advertising wherever we go. We will order there be no outside hoardings, no ads on the exterior of every public building, no disfiguring ads on the backs of seats, no shrieking messages on every corner of sporting grounds.

Our Bill of Rights will give us freedom of our letter boxes. No longer will we be besieged by every store, hardware merchant, insurance salesman, or strange Gold Coast lotteries. This will leave space again for the Myer, David Jones and Bankcard bills.

Our Bill of Rights will place severe restrictions on the two stroke motor. Our ear drums will have sacred rights against persecution and torture via chain saws, motor cycles, and rock noises from car radios.

Our Bill of Rights will help suffering humans in supermarkets. No longer will unfortunate husbands and even wives have to wander for two hours trying to find the mustard, the Earl Grey Tea or the self-raising flour. Supermarkets like to keep you confused so that you will indulge in impulse buying and spend more. My Bill of Rights will insist that every supermarket have a large illuminated directory board showing precisely where you can find every item.

And have you noticed the spreading curse of providing sweet music on the telephone when they put you on hold? You ring Board of Works, Telecom, or one of these big companies. A recorded message tells you that are you are going into a queue. Then they play musical gunk. This makes you part of their captive audience. The longer you wait the more maddening it becomes. If we have to wait why can't we be left alone with our thoughts. Is that so awful? Oh yes, silence should be part of the Bill of Rights.

Then there would be rights for people eating in restaurants. You know how the French have an *appellation controllee*, where they have to state the origin of the wine. Under our bill, if the restaurant has had their fish or their chicken in an ice box for six months, and just whacked it into the micro wave when they saw you coming through the door, then they will have to say so.

If they are not giving you real coffee but infamous soup made out of powder then surely it is the right of all humans to know about it. This fact must be stated on the menu. And would it not be right that all wines on the list have a mark up of no more than 25 per cent on retail prices?

There should be a few human rights for parents. Daughters should vacate the bathroom after 15 minutes, hair washing should be restricted to 10. Sons should be required to do three hours a week gardening and when they borrow the family car it should be back by midnight.

The rights of minorities should be protected, particularly those not obsessed by football. No newspaper should contain more than 10 per cent football in any given day and football replays should be restricted to one hour on any one channel. A less kindly liberationist would ban them altogether.

Finally, do you agree it should be a right that politicians sound at least half civilised, that they cease behaving as if they were conducting an eternal bar-room brawl and act as if they were working for the good of the nation?

How to Educate a Human

After being a barbarian for most of my life I am fascinated by the great education debate.

Last week a Senate Education Committee produced a highly critical report which suggested that many Australian universities were producing narrow-minded, uncreative, unskilled barbarians.

Oh dear, these suffering graduates were poor communicators, unanalytical, dull, and unfamiliar in any disciplined society. The education battle has raged in the letters column ever since.

Barbarians indeed. Of course, it has always been that way. I think I went through the education system without managing to learn anything that was useful. I had a friend who once remarked: "My dear father impoverished himself sending me to boarding school. I often wonder what I learned that has helped me since.

"Now if only he had booked me into the Southern Cross or the Hotel Australia it would have cost him less and I would have learned infinitely more."

This is a slight exaggeration. But we should not entirely blame our universities for the current lack of education. When I went to school I learned Latin and I learned Greek. I spent eight years studying French but finally when I arrived in Paris startled Parisians listened to me amazed. They wondered if I were speaking Icelandic.

I studied four different species of mathematics, which didn't help in the slightest in understanding an income tax return or working my way through a company prospectus.

I had a marvellous run down on all the kings of Europe and a complete list of the battles in which the Brits were triumphant. I learned that all the red bits on the map belonged to King George, but other peoples' histories were really quite unimportant. Asia, now where was that?

I would like to devise a new program for schools. There would be a course titled "Practical Materialism". You would learn all about the Stock Exchange, how to buy and sell shares, how to solve the mysteries of imputation, how not to get diddled investing in fly-by-night firms. Oh yes, there would be a chapter on company history, the theory and practice of beligerent take-overs, and a revealing study on the theory and working of building societies. We could even offer a lectureship to one of our failed corporate cowboys.

Indeed our VCE course would have to include a subject titled Advanced Form Filling: how to unravel income tax forms, medibank forms, driving licence forms, pension forms, passport forms, tax lotto ...

We did learn to do the fox trot, the waltz and the tango when we were at school, but that was the end concerning social graces. Food and drink is such a vital part of our lives, there would be the Social Graces course. We would learn the subtleties of Italian, Chinese, and French cuisine, how to read a menu, how to tip a waiter.

We would learn about alcohol, what it does to you and how to use it. We would study the grape, the difference between chardonnay and riesling, traminer and sauvignon blanc, shiraz and cabernet and naturally we would provide a thorough working knowledge on all the great wines districts. We don't want our graduates to be terrified of a wine list.

Our course will make the students familiar with all the modern Australian writers, playwrights, artists, poets, musicians and film-makers but our non barbarians will also make superb husbands and wives.

There will be a special course on how to fix washing machines, dishwashers, ailing videos, and lawn mowers. Handy-Mannery will be a VCE subject with the chance of taking honors at the University. It is my belief the cost of fixing things will become so enormous in the next decade none of us will be able to afford a handy man. This is the new era of communication, then perhaps we should have a course on how to understand the instruction booklets for some of these extraordinary gadgets we are buying and can't fix.

The automobile is unquestionably the most dangerous drug discovered in the 20th century. Therefore it will be a major subject; driving, handling and social consequences. I have never had the slightest understanding of the mysteries that go under the bonnet. We might even have a lecturer who was a former RACV repair man. He could teach us how to overcome all those embarrassing moments, when the internal combustion engine misbehaves.

Now sex would also be a major subject. We went through school learning nothing about human reproduction. Practical work would be a little tricky, but we should learn how the body works, about human behavior, about AIDS, about transmitted diseases, yes, and a few hints on how live with a partner for the rest of your life.

Religion? I am glad you asked that. Certainly we should continue with Christian education in schools, but let's broaden it to give instruction on the other great religions with also some practical work on racial tolerance. We could learn, too, why so often love of God causes so much bloodshed.

I would want a course on Government, how Parliament works; Federal, State, local. I mean, if we can really learn how politics works, who knows, we might do a service for Bob Hawke. We might learn how to love and trust politicians. We could certainly find out why we need so many of them.

As for the study of English I do believe we taught this much better 30 or 40 years ago. Perhaps it is not too late to resurrect the English language. If can't teach them how to write a letter we might be able to instruct how to send a lovely fax.

Yes, it would be interesting also to have a course in semantics, then we could discover how they find such extraordinary lines as "Multi Function Polis".

We Can Have a Dinkum Aussie Theme Park

Aren't you fascinated with the news that the Japanese Ministry of International Trade and Industry is planning to

CAN WE HAVE A DINKUM AUSSIE THEME PARK...

build an Australian Theme Park or even Aussie Multi Cultural Polis?

Probably it will be in Mishima or maybe Hokkaido and the theory is that it will give Japanese a deeper understanding of Australia and its people.

I wonder if I could have a hand in its planning? For a start, I would insist on a triple-fronted cream brick veneer on the classic quarter acre block, electric light pole right outside, liquidambar in front garden, a few beds with pansies, marigolds and azaleas.

Ah, but the key to the Australian character would be the backgarden. Its *piece de resistance* would be the Hills Hoist. The artist Donald Friend always used to insist that our only contribution to world culture was the rotary clothes hoist.

We would have a slightly leaking galvanised iron tank beside the kitchen, an outside dunny in the yard's right hand corner and in the left hand an incredible little cubby made out of packing cases, hunks of old iron and discarded bits of four by two. On the door would be the message: ADULTS KEEP OUT UNDER PAIN OF DEATH.

The silverbeet, cabbages and tomatoes, valiantly defying the weeds, would be on the left hand side and on the right we would have the one time woodshed filled with an amazing collection; the two-stroke power mower, the old pushmower now rusted solid, three bicycles, two skateboards, cricket bats, golf clubs, tennis rackets, the old refrigerator, the old wardrobe full of tools and Dad's motorbike which Mum won't let him ride.

Junior's go-kart, which he never wanted to throw out, would be there too. It was made out of a Marchants soft drink box, a hunk of timber off the back fence, and junior steered the pram wheels with a piece of rope.

In the centre of the lawn, little brick patio built all round, we will have Dad's joy; a splendid hand-made brick barbecue, chrome grill, little pegs on which to hang the tools, and a table area for the beer and meat. Recently it was converted to gas. Japanese, I think, would be fascinated by the Australian apartheid system where the female cooks inside and the male cooks outside.

If they moved into the kitchen I think the Japanese would be delighted by some great old Australian dishes; dim sims, pizza, flake and chips, the lamington, meat pies, Flo Bjelke-Petersen's pumpkin scones and, oh yes, hot crumpets dripping with butter then soaked in honey. What's more I would really like to show them a grand old favourite, the chocolate malted milk like they used to make at Hilliers in the city with a genuine, decent blob of ice cream mixed in.

There would have to be an Australian school classroom, but I would be really interested in giving them some Australian uniforms, particularly those antique uniforms worn by girls at polite schools in Malvern, Hawthorn and elsewhere. I reckon some of those uniforms beat the hell out of the kimono.

I would love to have a mock up of Bay 13. Indeed, now that the MCG is about to pull it down, this might be the chance to preserve it for all time. We could send the Japanese the real thing, a priceless piece of our heritage. We could have sessions, say, at 11 a.m., a football session; Collingwood versus the Demons. We could give a loving portrait of typical football fans when only two or three points separated the teams.

However, I think I would prefer a sample of the 4.30 p.m. cricket session. We could depict the Christmas Test against the Brits, that lovely time; the shadows are lengthening on a Saturday afternoon, Dennis Lillee is bowling, you can hear the gentle noise of Foster's Lager cans rolling down the concrete steps and the fans are kindly suggesting that English blood be spilt.

That's right, we would need to illustrate the Australian character, our wonderfully honed attitude to leisure, which would be such an interesting curiosity to the Japanese. We would show our ingenuity, how we find holidays in honor of horse races and agricultural shows and if we plan to celebrate the birthday of a monarch or a day of immense national importance, always we have it on a Monday in order to enhance a weekend.

Indeed we know how to nurture holidays, we give a pay loading for not working, and four to six weeks is a reasonable thing as opposed to two weeks which reigns in most other places. Yes, and we would like to help the Japanese character. They need our nice streak of independence. Could we have a booth manned perhaps by Norm Gallagher and a few chaps from the various transport unions on how to time and tune a good strike?

Then imagine how intrigued the Japanese would be by our financial system. I wonder if we could find some of those old TV commercials from the Pyramid Building Society or the Estate Mortgage lot? You know those ones, pledging eternal retirement bliss and interest rates of anything up to 18 per cent. I mean in a country where you would be lucky to get four per cent that sort of stuff would have them agog on their tatami mats.

We could have a collection or artifacts discarded by Messrs Skase, Bond, Elliott and Herscu; Falcon jets, 737s, yachts that would have been the envy of Aristotle Onassis, stately homes in England, the South of France and even Toorak.

But my ace item would be a gigantic supermarket. I think I would call it the Koala Privatisation Mart. It would have absolutely everything that was going for sale that week. We would have Telecom, Qantas, Aust Post, TAA, the ABC, Melbourne's Gas & Fuel Corporation, State Government Insurance, and why not Parliament House, Canberra? We don't need it. We've got two.

Indeed, I like to show off our politics, a screening of Question Time in Parliament. And we could let them see the true compassion of our M.P.s. It wouldn't be hard to give them pictures of both Bob Hawke and Wilson Tuckey in tears.

I tell you, my theme park would be so interesting, so lovable, we would have a million Japanese down here on Nippon Qantas in the first two months.

Printophobia - There's No Known Cure

At 7 pm during the week-end we cracked.

We turned off the news. "Don't they ever broadcast anything that is even faintly bright? Do we have to keep on living with disaster?" said my wife.

It was true. It had been a very disagreeable week. Medical reports on the state of the dollar continued to worsen. The Games were in disarray, the Commonwealth was falling apart, our wheat market was in ruins and our relations with the United States were in such a bad state it seemed we might even have to withdraw Greg Norman. What's more, we managed to turn the weather into a disaster, making it the worst for 40 years.

Actually I have always suffered from a disease called Printophobia. This is a fear of large print and banner headlines. Nothing good ever came out of a large headline. My printophobia was originally caused by newspapers like London's *Daily Mirror* which always carried headlines with letters larger than cigarette packets.

You know for a fact the bigger the print the more horrid the news. I can pick up a newspaper and go right round the front page reading the peripheral stories avoiding the shock horror in the big print. So at times I have arrived at the office in a state of happy innocence. Then an editor has said something like this.

"Terrible about the Queen."

"I didn't see anything about the Queen in the paper."

"You're joking?"

"What's happened?"

"Geez mate, it was the front page lead. What did you do this morning, use the paper for fish and chips?"

"Aw, you can't read everything. What's happened?"

Long sigh. "I'll tell you. The Queen is fed up with Prince Phillip and she's run off with the President of Nigeria. Mrs Thatcher's livid, and it has been condemned both by the Archbishop of Canterbury and the Roman Catholic Bishop of London. Except Bill Hayden thinks it might be good for the Commonwealth."

That's a somewhat bizarre example, but in these bad days I always approach the newspaper gingerly, in a somewhat odd manner. I begin on the back page. You get terrible news there too, but it is not quite so serious.

I check to see whether Dean Jones has made another century, whether Ian Botham has been forgiven yet, whether an Australian tennis player has magnificently survived into the second round, and which football teams we are exporting to friendly consenting States.

Next I look at the comic strips, take in the cartoons, particularly window box jobs like Tandberg and my old mate Jeff. I check to see whether there are any marvellously absurd letters to the editor then maybe I am sufficiently sanitized to face up to some hard news.

However, we get three newspapers so one has to be selective. I don't read any horror stories about footballers knees or coaches that have been taken out and shot. I steer clear of crime, bank robberies, murders and rapes. I skim prognostications by economists at Westpac, National Australia Bank, or various universities. My faith in their predictions on interest rates and the future of the economy died back around 1976.

Police court stories I rarely touch, Inside stories about the royal family, what they are wearing, how often they fall off their horses, palace romps and such, can be quickly avoided.

Then there are stories that suffer from the agony of over exposure, like Norm Gallagher's revival of the BLF, the state of the waterfront and the almost daily popularity ratings of Hawke, Hewson, Kirner and Keating. Surely we need to know how much we like them only once every six months.

I can skip tales about rock stars, Molly Meldrum, George Crawford, Susan Renouf, the wickedness or purity of Neville Wran, the loves of Jacqui Onassis and tales about all the various vessels that will be performing in the America's Cup.

One has to continue reading lugubrious stories about Murdoch, Bond, Bell Resources, and all the various State Banks. There is a morbid fascination in the news of the razor activity in Canberra and the eternal disaster of the balance of payments.

But I don't know how to solve my printophobia. There have been many attempts to produce newspapers that carry only happy news. Such an attempt was made in the United States as recently as last year. It lasted only six months.

The truth is that human beings adore horrid news. They like horrid news particularly if it is happening to other people. Ask any editor. News about vile events sell much better than those about sweetness and happiness.

The time that puts editors in a state of terror is Christmas and the silly season. In the profession editors look back upon their favorite Christmases. They remember particularly with love and affection the Bogle murders. They were never solved and dragged on beautifully until Parliament and the courts were going again with their rich vein of awfulness.

Then there was the Christmas that Harold Holt was drowned at Portsea. Sales and public readership reached a record high that awful Yuletide.

If the dollar goes to 40 cents, if the Queen runs off with the president of Nigeria, if we break off relations with the

United States, if Greg Norman abandons golf to play ping pong, if the Collingwood Football Club moved to Townsville, ah now, that would make a super silly season.

COLUMNS ON THE MYSTERIES OF DIET...

13

Columns Which Deal With the Mysteries of Diet

The Deadly Sugar Addiction

You appreciate that sugar has had a very hard time lately.

So much so, that the industry has organised its own backlash. There is a television commercial which comes on almost nightly. You see a succulent liquid drop of sugar in the middle of your screen and a soprano voice coos: "Sugar, it's a natural part of life."

Last week there was a passionate defence of sugar by Rudi Michelson, assistant secretary of the Confectionery Manufacturers of Australia. He said the US Food and Drug Administration had found it did not interfere with body vitamins; did not play a unique role in obesity; was not an independent risk factor in heart disease and was not addictive.

All this was superbly comforting, except the part about being addictive. We have personal evidence to the contrary. At our house we have been sugarholics and chocoholics for more than 20 years.

In my case it started quite simply. I developed a love for fresh licorice. There is a shop in the city which features huge coils of gorgeous licorice which gives off the most divine smell. Irresistible. This developed into a devotion for black jelly beans.

One would keep licorice or jelly beans in the glove box of the car. Soon one was hooked beyond redemption.

Now for the sugar junkie; the difficult time comes immediately after a good meal. Suddenly the system seems to pant for sugar. They are very clever. All the Confectionery manufacturers hit the prime TV air space between seven and 7.30 p.m. You see gorgeous girls deep throating all sorts of Confectionery bars. Or they have lovely Edwardian country scenes depicting a boy and girl in dappled sunlight walking hand and hand into bucolic splendor and the message is that their love is made possible by a chocolate bar. Then they have a female university student, saucy delightful looking creature, slim waist, and we are told the only thing that is getting her through her studies is a Snicker bar.

After a couple of these messages, I'm gone. I am down to the Seven-Eleven for some Crunchie Bars, a Violet Crumble or I am particularly addicted to a thing called a Bounty, sugary coconut covered in chocolate.

Well, I am not alone in this. Addiction exists everywhere. You can't go into a restaurant now where they don't provide chocolates and sweets with coffee. I belong to a particularly monastic club. The latest lurk is this. Coffee is served in the smoking room. Here they provide chocolate coated scorched almonds, sugared ginger, stuff like that. It is fascinating the way company directors, senior physicians, members of the house of representatives and judges pounce upon them.

Yes, some of the judges who pass sentence daily in court are deeply addicted.

The problem is mounting. The rage all around our district is for shops that make hand made chocolates. Wonderful, they are. We have four of them within walking distance. We have friends who have given up home weaving, wood carving and beachside painting. Now they go in for chocolate making. They have their own special moulds and they sit up late at night devising new wondrous fillings.

So when they come to dinner, no longer do they bring around a bottle of Brown Bros Cabernet Shiraz, you get a bag of home made chocolates, beautifully got up in a white box tied with a pink ribbon. We addicts haven't a chance.

In the United States they take it very seriously indeed. They have a publication called *Chocolate News* to which I became a subscriber. It comes on chocolate paper and every issue is drenched with the smell of chocolate

I have learned a great deal from *Chocolate News*. Every issue they have a profile on some famous chocoholic, like Vincent Price or Woody Allen.

Chocolate News also pointed out that not only does chocolate contain caffeine but it has a mood elevating chemical called phenylethan. This is a pick-me-up. It gives a sense of euphoria. It is one of the reasons they gave soldiers chocolate bars before going into battle.

So when things are really bad and you are suffering from unrequited love or the Bankcard bill has just arrived, you go on a binge with a whopper bar of Cadburys or a kilo of caramel creams.

Chocolate also has a history for being an aphrodisiac. According to Chocolate News the Aztec ruler Montezuma used to fortify himself with 50 cups of chocolate before entering his harem. This explains the sensuous nature of some of the television commercials.

Oh yes, I have seen Monopoly sets made out of chocolate for $600 each. I have seen chocolate chess sets. You can eat your opponent upon victory. There is a place in California where you can buy chocolate business cards, $12.50 for a set of 12. There is a very convenient way of disposing of cards upon receiving them.

Chocolate News reports that you can go on a chocolate lovers tour of Europe; probably beats the hell out of the cathedral tour or the vineyard tour.

But meanwhile, what hope is there for us addicts. Do you think there should be sugar free areas in aeroplanes and restaurants? Do you think there should be a sugar-chocolate ban in the public service?

Oh, we have tried to stop, really we have. You know, like only half a Mars bar each tonight. We have been told too that an apple or an orange immediately after dinner is beneficial. Then immediately after eating the apple, go jogging or a long walk with the dog until the sugar desire disappears.

But the temptation is overpowering. I'm going to write to Dick Smith and ask him if he will start a campaign to get all Confectionery ads off television.

No Shame for Carnivores

Have you noticed, it is all over? The shame is gone. It is quite all right, at least for several weeks, to be carnivorous.

I know what happens at our place. We believe all the scientific statements and all the advertising campaigns. We always have.

We are spellbound by that TV ad depicting the boneless leg of lamb. Out comes a carving knife and zap, zap, zap, a fine hunk of lamb is all sliced up before you can "Baa". The thought comes to mind that through a miracle of genetics, the accommodating sheep industry has produced a lamb for carnivore humans that possesses no bones at all.

Then we get an advertisement which shows a pair of scales. On one side there is a hunk of chicken, on the other a hunk of beef. The scales magically tip proving somehow that the much maligned beef is lower in fat, lower in cholesterol, much more filled with energy and succulent goodness than the chicken.

But the one we like best is the flirty young hussy with the telephone hanging on her ear. That telephone never stops ringing with admirers. But it is no problem. She has this menu box full of short cut recipes. Fast as you can bat a steak knife she can whip up a marvellous ragout, noisette, kebab or whatever, full of macho, male nourishing, heart-perpetuating goodness.

Oh, we have been through all the phases. Remember 20 years ago it was the fashion to buy a deep freeze bigger than a bath tub. They were so big you kept them on the back veranda or in the garage. We couldn't afford one, but they were all the go out our way. The theory was you made fantastic savings by buying your meat in bulk, half a sheep or half an ox at the one time.

You can imagine the dedication with which our neighbors chomped their way resolutely through almost an entire animal. There was the occasional panic when we had black-outs or the deep freeze broke down and there were para-medic dashes with wing ribs, legs and various pieces of frozen sheep cadaver to other friends whose deep freezes were still healthy and throbbing. I often wonder what happened to all those deep freezes.

Then we had the full assault of *Time, Reader's Digest, Vogue, Women's Weekly, New Idea*; they all told us red meat would kill us. Naturally at our place we kept up with every campaign.

We were amongst the first to succumb to Pritikin. Everything went white, an eternity of white fish, white chicken, and all the oil-less salad, accompanied very carefully with the one glass of white wine.

Dinner parties were hell. I mean you had to ring round tactfully and find out who was Pritikin, who was vegetarian, who was vegan, who was quiche-prone, who was free range, who ate only natural unsprayed fruit. As for red meat, that was not done, terribly untrendy. You could almost pause for two minutes silence in deep sorrow for all the marvellous executive gas powered barbecues and beautiful enamelled Webers that were sitting out there untouched on exquisite patios, while mother sweated over her Chili Bean Casserole, Aubergine Parmesan, her Vegetable Pasty with the wholemeal pastry, her Spiced Lentil Flan or her home made Pasta Parmigiana.

Yes, we have been vegetarian, organic, macrobiotic, high fibre. We notice too that our local grocer even sells "wholemeal eggs". Presumably you get bits of grit even in the yokes.

But now I think it is all over. You are reasonably free. It is a trendy once more to be a traditional Australian carnivore and all the butchers are going berserk. There was a time when a skilled gourmet could go out to dinner and instantly pick the recipes. Mmmm, very nice; Elizabeth David. Like that; Constance Spry. Delicious; Beverly Sutherland Smith. Mmmm, Peter Russell-Clarke, last Tuesday night on ABV2.

Now you pick your butcher. Mmm Mongolian Roast; Jim Toorak. Ahh Sourabaya Satay; Alf, Vaucluse. That meat sauce on the pasta - wait a minute - Bruno in Carlton.

Our local butchers are delighted with the new mood, but they admit they are done, ruined, if everything is not prepared, ready to go. Jim, for example, says one time he sold acres of stewing steak. Not any more, it all has to be cut ready to go.

His pepper steak is all peppered, his schnitzel is all schnitzed, his stroganoff is strogged ready to heat, his Mongolian Lamb, if not straight from Mongolia, looks like it, and his Hungarian goulash looks superbly Magyar.

Reiner, who hails from Germany, is always racking his brain for new recipes. His marinades are inspired. He has marinated spare ribs, he has lamb spare ribs, he has marinated beef with a black bean sauce, his pork is utterly fatless, he has Chinese Chicken, he has sweet and sour, and he has chicken olives, meats delicious stuffed and wrapped in bacon.

Reiner says a butcher these times is a chef, a creative cook, everything. He says you wouldn't believe the work involved, the day starts at 4.30 a.m. with he and his wife, cutting, slicing, preparing marinating and they finish, cleaning the shop at 7 p.m. They also have to work on Saturdays.

He says you still sell old fashioned joints at the week-ends, but during the week with husbands and wives all working, the prepared meats outsell the others 10 to one.

So we are eating meat again this week. Tonight we might have the boneless lamb seasoned with the apricot, sultana and honey mix or the Javanese lamb satay with the crushed nuts peanut sauce.

I think we had better get into it quickly, because there is sure to be a terrible backlash from all this. Any time from now we will be told that the only thing that doesn't kill you are dried, free range, fibre-rich, salt-free, un-sugared, organic, un-sprayed prunes with fat reduced yoghurt.

The Confessions of a Coffeeholic

Isn't it time some of us thought of taking legal action the medical profession?

I mean look at these experts; for countless decades they have been describing coffee as a poison, a lethal brew that will cause heart attacks and strokes.

Now the Harvard School of Public Health has put 45,589 men through long extensive tests and found not the slightest link between coffee and heart disease.

Oh wait a minute, there was just one problem. They found a slightly higher incidence of heart attacks and strokes among people who drank four or more cups of decaffeinated coffee a day.

I am - let's face it - a coffeeholic. The coffee bean is very nearly the most beautiful thing God created. It is the divine elixir that lubricates the mind, inspires the tongue, relieves fatigue, sends the olfactory senses into a state of bliss and gives the excuse to dally and commune with friends.

The smell of good coffee, just ground, is the perfect aroma, the aphrodisiac which can draw you in from the street. I have often wondered why women use those absurd and expensive scents like Chanel which they buy from France. It would be far more enticing if they placed just a pinch of fresh coffee behind the ear.

These remarks do not apply to instant coffee and regrettably 80 per cent of all the coffee consumed in Australia is instant. It has no aroma at all and tastes like it.

But let's get back to the real subject; constantly the doctors have warned against coffee. Sanctimoniously, health shops have refused to sell it. Instead they have sold those vile, probably extremely damaging, herbal teas.

As I have gone through life drinking my fourth, fifth, sixth cup of black coffee for the day, receiving warnings from loved ones, there has been constant stress. In restaurants there has been the lovely idea, the bottomless cup. Many a lovely waitress has returned again and again: "Can I fill your cup Sir?" Thank-you very much. But there has been this worry, this constant fear of impending death.

Surely that is worth damages before any wise, respectable court.

For more than five centuries coffee has suffered from bad P.R. In 1511 Kair Bey, the Governor of Mecca, banned all coffee drinking. One night when he was in the mosque for evening prayer, he spotted a group preparing for an all-night devotion. They were drinking coffee. It was too much for the Governor - this sort of thing might lead men and women to all sorts of dangerous behavior.

There were constant attempts throughout Egypt, Turkey, Yemen and Arabian cities to ban this black liquor which gave such happiness. In 1656 the Ottoman Grand Vizir Koprili prohibited coffee because it caused the citizens to meet too much and talk too much. For a first offence a coffee drinker received a terrible beating. If he or she persisted in drinking coffee they were sewn into a leather bag and thrown into the Bosphorus.

There was a similar problem in England when coffee came under attack from the Puritans. Coffee houses were patronised only by men. In 1674 the women of London took up a petition against coffee.

It said, not only did coffee render men impotent it caused them "to trifle away their time, scald their chops, and spend money all for a little base, black, thick, nasty, bitter, stinking, nauseous puddle water."

The women could have been right. I have always had a suspicion about English coffee. At the end of the 16th century coffee was banned in Rome. The priests would not touch it. They thought this black drink an invention of the devil. The Muslims forbad the use of wine (sanctified by Christ) and imbibed this insidious coffee as a substitute.

A cup of coffee was presented to Pope Clement VIII, who thought it necessary to taste this villainy so that he could make a papal decree. But upon tasting it, he was stunned. He said: "This is delicious. Why should we leave this drink to Satan? Christian power is greater than that of Satan. We will take it for our own." Coffee has been drunk in Italy with remarkable enthusiasm ever since. But the idea of it being a poison has always persisted. People have had to fight back. Sir James Mackintosh, a Scottish philosopher, asserted in 1800 that the powers of a man's mind were generally proportional to the amount of coffee he drank. Voltaire drank 50 cups a day, and Balzac could hardly write a line without his coffee. He used to go to bed at 6 pm, sleep until midnight, then write non-stop for 12 hours drinking coffee all the time. The ultimate remark about the dangers of coffee is attributed both to Voltaire and another philosopher, Fontanelle. When asked whether coffee was a poison Voltaire/Fontanelle said: "I think it must be. I am 85 years old and not dead yet." Perhaps coffee wasn't very good for Voltaire, he passed on at 84. Fontanelle lived on to be a 100.

But really, you should study some of the experiments on coffee. In 1981 there was the remarkable case of Dr Thomas F.X. Collins, a Government scientist in the U.S. He started feeding caffeine to 300 pregnant rats. He gave his rats the equivalent of 12 to 24 strong cups of coffee a day. The result: a high proportion of his mother rats gave birth to baby rats with deformed toes and "some delay in skeletal development."

But were rats ever meant to drink coffee? Give them concentrated carrot juice, yoghurt and muesli the result could have been just the same.

However, now that we have received such wonderful news from the blessed scientists at Harvard, I think we should celebrate with Alexander Pope's ode to coffee:

> As long as Mocha's happy tree shall grow,
> While berries crackle or while mills shall go,
> While smoking streams from silver spouts shall glide,
> Or China's earth receive the sable tide,
> While coffee shall to British nymphs be dear,
> While fragrant streams the bended head shall cheer,
> Or grateful bitters shall delight the taste,
> So long her honors, name and praise shall last.

Where Can We Go for Happy Bowel?

Frankly I don't think I can take any more. I am almost ready to slip back to potato chips

You will have noticed last week's hideous news. The latest survey of our national diet found that unprocessed bran was a toxic threat. It contained higher than acceptable amounts of chemical residues.

Oh yes, the scientists found that unprocessed bran contained seven milligrams per kilo of organophosphorus pesticide fenithrothion. That was far higher than any other food analysed.

WHERE CAN YOU GO FOR HAPPY BOWEL ?

I have never personally before met OPF, but I am shocked beyond measure. Bran to serious health food nuts - and I am one - is holy. It is way up there in the sanctified range beyond yoghurt, prunes, rose hips, and even lecithin.

Begging your pardon at breakfast, but two years ago I had to make visits to a specialist regarding a bowel complaint. When one started in journalism it was not permitted to mention such matters as Farmer Giles, but now we are in the world of realism and four out of five humans clearly have met Farmer Giles.

Well, this specialist who had wisely chosen a fruitful profession, gave his prescription. "Fibre is the answer," said he, "and the best of all fibre is raw bran. Drink at least six glasses of water a day and put bran on your fruit at breakfast. Have your daily dose of bran and never will you return to me again."

Oh yes, it worked. Gone for ever were such breakfast delights as sausages, bacon and eggs, toast with lashings of marmalade. The way to glory was bran.

Unprocessed bran, of course, is pretty ghastly, but you have a feeling of nobility and heroic pride, as you sprinkle it across your sliced bananas and apple. It is doing great things down there.

I have a very good friend from California called Marvin. Now Marvin, who has also met the Farmer, wherever he goes on earth, takes a plastic bag full of unprocessed bran. He just eats it out of the bag with a spoon. Even in very smart hotels he will bring out his B.Y.O. bag of bran and pour it into a bowl.

Thereupon (shudder) he eats it even without milk. How can I break this awful news to Marvin. The very mention that it contains organophosphorus, whatever it is, will be like speaking against mother and apple pie, worse even than any suggestion that President Reagan might not have been telling the whole truth about supplying arms to the Iranians.

To be fair to bran, I did tune in to a dietician on the ABC, who said, sure, bran contained pesticide residues like everything else, but it was O.K. as long as you had only a few spoonfuls a day. Don't eat it by the cup load.

But as far I'm concerned I wondering whether we should cut back on the research grants. When are they going to stop. Two weeks ago Choice magazine found unacceptably high levels of bacteria in 11 out of 14 samples of pate purchased from supermarkets. In two of them they found samples of staphylococcus aureus, which sounds even worse than the aforementioned organophosphorus.

In the column writing business one attends an appalling round of press conferences, book launchings, show biz arrivals and at 99 out of 100 they serve little biscuits smothered in pate no doubt laden with staphylococcus aureus. My insides must be appalling.

But where are you to turn? The Japanese and the Americans have been sending back our beef because of pesticide residues. We have been warned about sugar and salt. We have been told to lay off dairy foods because of cholesterol.

We can't eat fats. So we switch to polyunsaturated fats, but there is a new theory every day. There was a story from a Dr Kent Erikson, assistant professor of human anatomy at Davis in California who claimed that while fats did not directly cause cancer, high polysaturated fat like safflower oil, coconut oil and such, could increase the risk of skin, colon and breast cancer for people with family history of the diseases.

He had been feeding polyunsaturated fat to mice. Mice have much to put up with from humans. However, these theories appear to change almost weekly.

Where are you to go? You have to be wary of some fish because of mercury. You can get cadmium and nitrate in potatoes, cauliflower and tomatoes. And what about coffee; the most delectable drug created for mankind is under constant attack for caffeine. So too is tea. Good grief, there was even a suggestion in the food columns several months back that tea had close to the maximum permitted concentration of lead and there was a presence of aflatoxin in peanuts and peanut butter.

Now the National Health and Medical Research Council has approved the idea of adding a dose of thiamine to beer and cask wine on the theory that this will check Wernicke korsakoss S syndrome - debilitating short term memory loss.

But do they really want this to happen? Think of the excuse: "It's all right, dear, for me to have another glass. I am just curing my Wernicke korsakoss S syndrome."

The truth is there is little left that you can eat or drink, but it is the bran that is worrying the hell out of me. Will I have to fall back on prunes?

That's a fate worse than death.

Manic Cholesterol

Time Magazine, you may have noticed, last week had a cover story, titled "Cholesterol Mania".

MAY have noticed! Ye Gods, they took full page advertisements all over the place, depicting a poor male in a state of abject terror looking at his exposed heart, trying to keep alive feeding his stomach with fat free cabbage, pumpkin, apple, carrot and turnip.

It is not the first time they have done this. About five years ago they had a cover story on sugar. It was so scary about sugar it took our family nearly nine months to get over it. For weeks we went without Mars Bars, Kit Kats and for a frightful year we even had porridge without sugar.

Time, of course, is following in a great tradition. It was *Reader's Digest* that built its enormous circulation through disease. *Reader's Digest* back in the fifties and sixties was ingenious. It could come up with a new disease almost every issue.

I can remember so well that marvellous fruitful period. Pre-1950 we used to get just ordinary stuff like the common cold and influenza. But *Reader's Digest* discovered a whole range of interesting Viruses, Virus A, B, C, D and Virus X. There was URTI, Upper Respiratory Tract Infection, to say nothing of the Asian Flu, the Hong Kong Flu, and the Spanish flu.

There was much prestige to be had in getting a new disease announced in the latest issue of the Digest. What's more, it had much more effect if you could tell the boss at the office you were the first to get the disease, clearly explained on page 48 of this week's mag.

Soon all the other journals cottoned on to the idea. The *Women's Weekly* was always a very strong disease, diet, illness paper. *Woman's Day* liked them too. Disease sometimes was a circulation builder that could rival Princess Diana, Fergie and all the various creatures in Monaco.

The *Bulletin* recently had a run down on all the trendy diseases, and coronary bypass was absolutely the go. However, to be up with the best, it should be at least a triple or a quadruple.

The trouble at our place is we are so susceptible. I believe everything they tell me, so that I am in a perpetual state of fear. We have been through it all in our dreadful attempts to keep alive.

One of the first was the horrid Canadian 5BX. Do you remember, they gave you five minutes to go through an agonising series of exercises? Day by day they would get progressively harder until your five minutes was so frenzied you couldn't face going to the office.

We went through all the crazes as ordered by the various journals. We grew our own bean shoots because we were told they would give eternal life. You know, have little trays of tiny beans, put them in trays of water, so that they would catch the sun through the kitchen window, have them sprout and you eat the resulting grass in your sandwiches.

Yoghurt, said one of the weeklies, was essential for the interaction of digestive juices, the only thing for true survival. So as instructed we went through the business of cooking up gallons of milk and making our own. We used to have the car parked in the back yard, because that was the perfect warm place, the yoghurt jellied itself there on the dash board.

I have forgotten which magazine it was that announced on its cover that salt was certain death. For six months we went through this ghastly period where we were buying only salt free butter; we were allowed no Vegemite. All our bread was salt free, no salt in cakes or cooking. Our super healthy salt free, yoghurt-charged, mung bean inspired, friends, told us: "Look very soon you won't even notice it. You will never think salt again."

I remembered that when I gave up smoking it took only 15 years to get over the longing for tobacco. It was the same with salt. Not a thing had taste any more.

What irritates me about the new cholesterol mania is that we have been there before. We went through all this at least seven years ago. Remember when the American magazines, Mr Pritikin and others, first invented cholesterol. It was so hard to spell.

I had the idea that surely it had something to do with chlorine. It was vile enough for that. So one tended to spell it cholesterol.

We went through the whole anti-cholesterol bit. Never will one forget those awkward guilt-ridden moments in restaurants, you know, when they serve the delicious hot rolls, or when the garlic bread comes in. "You are not going to put butter on it, ARE YOU?"

Or when the marvellous baked potato, arrived sitting there by the steak. "You can substitute yoghurt for butter." Oh, the misery of it. Fat always seemed so beautiful, one of the finest things invented by God. We had a grandparent who was a big deal in the ham business. In my youth always there was a superb ham on the sideboard.

It was a family tradition that as you walked by, pull out the carving knife and nick off a slice. The ham had to be generous with a gorgeous border of fat an inch and a half thick. My father said, very correctly, the fat was absolutely the best part.

Cholesterol Mania No 1 killed all that. We had Christmases with every millimetre of ham fat ruthlessly peeled off. Anorexic steaks we had, as lean as tram tickets, and cheese, of course, was not even to be mentioned.

Well, we had just managed to get over this. This year we have been having eggs again for breakfast with even slices of old fashioned ham with a happy border of white fat and God bless the cheese maker, we have been enjoying Australian cheeses that beat anything else on earth.

Now *Time* does this to us. Admittedly they give the case for and against, saying that the cholesterol thing is unproven and they did find a specialist who likes meats, eggs, butter, cheese and proposes to keep on eating them regardless.

But it has got me terrified again. I pulled back yesterday when I was just about to have a second helping of delicious King Island brie.

Could one make a plea? Let's have an amnesty. Could we, say, have a year without any magazine bringing on a new disease, or a new health scare? I don't mind if the *Women's Weekly* sticks to the shortcomings and marriages of the Royal Family. The *Bulletin* can persecute us further with its public opinion polls and Time can return to the terrors of the Middle East.

But would they kindly leave my heart alone? It is in enough trouble already.

Caulie - The Perfect Flower

There has always been a deep streak of vulgarity in my nature.

You know, a sort of terror of not being noticed. There was only one way to overcome this: grow the biggest plants and vegetables in the entire street:

The theory was that people would wander past and say: "My, aren't they fantastic."

So I grew dahlias, not the miserable little dwarfs, but the giant variety with heads as big as rubbish tin lids. I would stake them so that would nod over the front fence for every neighbor to admire.

They all had names - Vivien Leigh, Pop Harris, Sammy Davis jnr.

It gave me a lot of satisfaction to be able to put Vivien Leigh in the same bed as Sammy Davis jnr.

We don't grow dahlias so much any more, but we are deep into vegetables. They are a passion really. The trouble is we believe everything we read.

Remember the Canadian 5BX plan. We did that. We were almost the first to get into jogging. We were right in the vanguard of eating Percy Cerutty's raw oatmeal and dried apricots.

Nathan Pritikin, the Egg Diet, Beverly Hills diet, did all those. We believed *Time* magazine when it told us to give up salt. Was it the *Reader's Digest* or *Women's Weekly* that told us to lay off sugar? Anyway we followed their instructions.

Fibre? We were on to that. We ate enough fibre to start a rope factory.

This vegetable thing , though, has sort of crept up on us. Almost everyone we know is vegetarian or going that way.

We had an American student with us for a year. She was a vegetarian.

Every time I put a chop on my plate she would glare. We used to like a wing rib of beef. This was pure Hereford homicide. I felt as cruel as a South African cop.

Dinner parties are becoming immensely complicated.

In the old days you would invite all the Catholics on Wednesdays, then perhaps get in the Protestants on Fridays. In the sixties one was careful never to mix ALP hard-liners with DLP lovers.

In the 70s you had to watch the affluent middle class. It could be dynamite if you let loose your Western District-top-end-of-Collins Street conservatives among your Range Rover keep-uranium-in-the-ground ALP trendies.

Now, my God, the worry is with the Liberals. Can you invite 'wets' and 'drys' to the same dinner table?

But our problem goes deeper. Do you have all vegetarian dinner parties, or do you have to cook two whole dinners on the one night and offer them a choice. Quiche or Kebabs? Beef or beans? Liver or lettuce?

It goes even further than that. We have some mates who have gone vegan. This means they are so serious they don't eat fish. They wouldn't touch an anchovy in a fit. They don't eat eggs or dairy foods.

Heaven's above, you can't even give them a cheese dip before lunch or caramel custard for dessert. You have to think before you put a dollop of cream in the avocado soup.

Fred and Mary claim they don't drink milk any more because it produces mucus, and mucus is allied with flu and colds. Honestly, you can't even mix vegans with normal vegetarians...

But clearly being vegetarian is the thing of the moment, so we turned the garden over to vegetables. Oh I tell you, it hasn't been easy.

The place was infested with rabbits so I had to build a rabbit-proof fence. $160.

The soil was miserably impoverished, so I had buy lime, blood and bone, organic soil improver; we made six excursions to the beach to gather seaweed. $80.

Snails , white butterflies, pests abounded. Derris dust, snail killer, insect sprays. $22.

We couldn't be on the spot all the time, so I had to buy sprinklers and a time clock device. $110.

The local water board spies were on to it immediately. Excess water rates. $125.

But it was pure bliss when the red runners, the lettuce, the squash, the tomatoes, the corn, the silverbeet, the red cabbage, the peas, all began to arrive.

The particular dream was the cauliflower. It is my belief that the cauliflower is the most beautiful flower God ever created. Drenched with white sauce or just made into a dish on its own with a little cheese, unquestionably you can get a sense of the divine order of things.

But just between you and me some of my vegetables have not quite reached the degree of vulgarity that I was looking for. The lettuce did not have the massive Phar Lap hearts that I had expected, some of the cabbage didn't heart at all.

There were spaghetti squash, which should have been bigger than league footballs, but only made the minor grade. And as for cauliflowers, they had a kinda grey look.

I did a little cost analysis and discovered that those caulies might have been worth around $5 each. If we had bought everything at the local market we would have saved $200.

But my wife said sweetly: "But darling they tasted so much better and they were all organic."

YULETIDE COLUMNS ...

14

Yuletide Columns

Yuletide All Over

Our Christmas was always utterly according to the script, practically written by Noel Coward.

It didn't matter if it was a bushfire fireban 104 fahrenheit classic, north wind and all, we still had hot turkey, hot pork, hot plum pudding with brandy sauce.

My mother, of course, boiled up all the shillings and put them in the pudding. She was smart, she had prior knowledge where the shillings were located. The smaller you were the better your chance of good silver booty.

My father always delivered the presents to the ends of our beds at 1 a.m. on Christmas morn, naively thinking we were asleep, presents were opened at 1.05 a.m.

This week we thought we would ask some well known people who were not born here to probe their memories and tell of their Christmases long ago.

Our first contact was Professor Julius Sumner Miller, you know the wonderful scientist who does the Cadbury ads on television? He wasn't easy to find. We called him in California.

"Christmas for us," he said, "was very simple. My mother came from Lithuania and my father from Latvia. We lived on a small farm and made a hand to mouth living.

"At Christmas we would cut a tree in the wood and decorate it with rings of paper, stuck together with flour and water paste. And we made stars out of colored paper to put on the top.

"My best present? One year my father made me a sled, the blacksmith made the rails. Before that we used to sled down the snow on our bellies using a barrel stave. If you were a bit broad in the behind you had to use two staves."

The Professor wasn't too pleased with the modern Christmas. "Pitiful! Shameful!" he said. "There's a helluva lot of lack of spirit in it."

Sir Arvi Parbo, chairman and managing director of Western Mining, chairman of Alcoa, thought back to Christmas in Estonia: "It was always very cold sometimes even minus 30 centigrade. It was dark until 10.30 a.m. then dark by three in the afternoon.

"We always had a Christmas tree, a real one cut a few days before. We would have straw on the wooden floor where we would sit and the big ceremony would start about 6 p.m.

"We would sing Christmas songs and we had a Father Christmas. Father would be the best candidate for that job, but when we were seven or more and a bit cynical, sometimes a neighbor would take it on to trick us.

"Each child would be called forward one by one. And this was quite a business - it took hours. You always had to recite something for Father Christmas, a few verses. And he would talk, ask you whether you had been a good boy.

"Christmas was all for the children. Late in the evening the adults would sit down to dinner. The children would be too excited. Dinner would be pork, lots of pork, heavy fatty food in that cold climate, lots of potatoes and sauerkraut, Christmas cake. We drank lemonade the adults, vodka, brandy and ale, nearly always brewed at home.

"A lovely time. You know, you make me feel very nostalgic."

Joe Galani, the Saba furniture man went back over 24 years to Lebanon: "Our Christmas had more atmosphere. We were in Beirut, there was snow; pine trees and reindeer were real to us.

"Christmas was family, very big family thing. We didn't receive toys, we received money. And clothes. On Christmas morn we got our new clothes, new shoes, new socks, new shorts, shirt, the whole outfit. Then it was the tradition to go round and call on all members of our family, uncle, aunty, knock, knock.

"They would give us a couple of dollar. But Christmas wasn't just on the 25th. It go for four days to a week, 24 hours a day. You call, and always dinner would be on, celebration. Food? Lamb, we are very big on lamb. Traditional Lebanese food, lots of nibble this and that, arak, whisky, lot of family.

Wolf Blass, the famous Barossa wine maker, went back to the town of Stadtlim in East Germany: "The biggest shock I ever had was when I first went to England in 1957. Christmas was just one helluva party. In Germany it was a serious family affair.

"We started looking forward to Christmas on St Nicholas Day, around November 7. Then you would get warned - if you were a good boy he'd bring you some goodies, if you were bad you'd get a smack on the bottom.

"On Christmas Day we had to get out of the house while preparations were being made. They put real candles on the Christmas tree. Dangerous business. Always there had to be a bucket of water handy in case they set the place alight. Every family got together. I mean the whole town was dead quiet, absolutely dead after seven, no taxi, no transport, nobody walking around.

"We would put on very best clothes and before we got our presents we had to sing. No way you'd get out of singing Christmas songs. Christmas dinner, a goose, potato, red cabbage. In Germany at Christmas it is always a goose.

"Presents. Girls, lots of dollies, dollies galore, cubby houses. Every German boy, always an electric train and he doesn't get a chance to play with it because Dad always does."

And Wolf thought back. He never really got a good go at that electric train.

Eric Jensen, Danish consul in Melbourne: "In Denmark it is not just celebrated on the one day. There is the four weeks leading up to Christmas. It is the tradition for the children to have the picture calendar. There is a window for each day, so you open up a new little picture every morning until Christmas. The excitement builds.

"And in the European style everything happens on Christmas Eve. As you know the Danes are pretty good at eating. Very big dinner. First there is a rice dish with an almond in it. The person who gets the almond gets a special prize.

"The main dish is goose or duck and after the eating is all over it is time to go to the tree. Of course, the children almost die with frustration wanting to get the dinner over. They have to walk round the tree, sing songs and so the presents are opened.

"Next morning you go to church and it is a very quiet day."

Franco Cozzo, the Footscray furniture importer, thought back to Christmas in Sicily: "Very, very special family time, when all the family get together.

"My mother have a special pasta, special lasagne, special dry ham, smoked, bravo. Church in the morning. Twelve to one we open the presents Christmas tree with big illumination.

"Everybody talk to each other, everybody kiss each other, everybody make peace. You upset with somebody, you enemy with somebody, this is the time to be friendly again.

"Presents? Sometimes I get little cars, things like that. But usually clothes, new shoes. Girls get new dresses.

"Dinner all the family get together, parents, grandparents, sister, mother, father. It a great day."

Then we spoke to Gupta Surinder, tourist promotion manager in the India Tourist Office. He told us he was a Hindu and back home in Delhi his family didn't celebrate Christmas, but you wouldn't believe how many did. Eight to 10 per cent of the population were Christian and after all, St Thomas, the apostle, died on the coast of Goa.

In Delhi they conducted Christmas in the traditional British style with turkey, bread sauce, potatoes, followed by plum pudding.

And that's what we will be doing. And I don't care if the temperature hits 50 degrees celsius.

Defy the Turkey Plot

There has been an ominous move afoot this Christmas - a plot against the turkey.

Some of our friends have openly announced they will be eating chicken. Yes, boring, wimpish, tasteless, battery produced chicken. Chicken that never once has walked outside into a decent open paddock.

Some are going for duck. Duck, greasy little objects nine times out of 10. Particularly in restaurants, they are a miserable disappointment. Others are having roasts, hunks of beef surrounded by potatoes cooked in fat.

But the biggest shock came in this newspaper last week, an unashamed assault on the turkey by that Sydney, *bon viveur*, Leo Schofield. He said it was unhealthy to eat too much turkey at midday in summer. He thought the taste was unexceptional, boring, and he had the nerve to add:

"Besides, I dread the leftovers, those obscene thighs, that gross carcass sitting in the fridge for weeks after the poor bird has been despatched."

DEFY THE TURKEY PLOT...

So do you know what he's going to eat? - Fish! Snapper, prawns oysters and small green lobsters.

Unhealthy to eat too much at Christmas in high summer? he says. Of course, it's unhealthy. You must have one day in the year when you can be decently, voluptuously, unhealthy with a clear conscience.

Now look here, I adore turkey. You can eat fish any time. I'd like to have turkey in February, April, July and September, but you can never gear up our dear ladies to get out there and make the grand effort. On Christmas Day they are spurred by a beautiful tradition.

Turkey became popular in England, because the bird comes to its prime in midwinter. But alas, nobody thinks about it here in midwinter, but I'm very happy to have two Christmases a year as long as Myer and David Jones keep out of it.

As an enthusiastic carver, turkey gives one the ultimate pleasure and challenge. The bigger and more obscene the better. I love that superb moment when the nut brown turkey is placed on the Christmas table, that splendid chest, those cathedral like dimensions, that wonderful nave filled with exquisite stuffing.

"Not stuffing," I can hear my mother saying. "It is seasoning, darling."

So one would caress the razor sharp carving knife across the ample breast taking off delicious long thin slices. Then one would sever a leg and drumstick. You would take slices off those too, giving everyone a generous mix of white and dark meat.

Take off the wing and then pick out a favorite, a cute grandchild and offer the pope's nose. My father always used to swear the absolute *piece de resistance* was the pope's nose or *nez du pape*.

Dammit, I'm in mouth watering tears of anticipation as I write this. It's not just the turkey, it's the marvellous things that go with it, the cranberry sauce, the delicious bread sauce, the way mother used to make it.

Then, golly, the left-overs are the best part. I go for the sandwiches, sliced French bread, succulent turkey, the bits you get out of all the little nooks and caves; more bread sauce, more cranberry, lettuce, a little pepper. Blow your mind.

Finally, when all the bones and architecture of the turkey cathedral are exposed, it is time for the curry. We do it the old fashioned way; turkey, remains of the delectable sausage stuffing, sliced banana, apple, some good stock, lots of quality fruit chutney - the most gorgeous curry you have ever tasted.

You must realise tradition has bitten deep in our family. My grandfather was manager of Farmer's Ham and Bacon. Ham has never tasted quite the same since. In my early childhood I could remember always there was a ham on the sideboard. Not one of these effete deboned canned things you see now, but a huge majestic leg of ham.

So every time you passed the sideboard you grabbed the carving knife and nicked yourself a slice. Bliss.

Therefore at Christmas always there would be the turkey allied with the majestic ham. The plum puddings, at least half a dozen of them, would be assembled and lovingly put in their bags, come late November and boiled for seven hours. Christmas cakes would be made then too and father would lose all his best brandy.

Sixpences and shillings would all go into the puddings. When, absurdly, we went metric in the early sixties, the silver content went out of our coins. I guess that was the beginning of all our troubles. So my mother had to resort to subterfuge. No longer did the coins go into the cake, she would sneak two bob pieces under each lucky child's slice.

Of course, the Christmas pudding, regardless of temperature outside, would be carried in blazing. It still is.

Heat the brandy first in a saucepan, set it alight and for a moment you would think it was a terrorist invasion.

All pretty unhealthy, I guess, but worth it. And I remember almost every Christmas, going into a half coma and about 3.30 p.m. or 4 p.m. and saying: "I'm stuffed."

My mother then would say, "You are not stuffed, dear. You are replete."

It is vital to preserve old traditions. Once they are gone you are left with nothing. It is said that Dr Stanley Livingstone, even when he was in remotest Africa, two months walk from the nearest white man, still dressed for dinner. An Englishman had to remain an Englishman.

I think our record for a Christmas dinner was 103 degrees fahrenheit, in the shade, cooked on an Aga anthracite burning stove. The kitchen was very cosy. But bravely, like Dr Livingstone, my mother carried on.

One year we did make an experiment. We were ruthless. We had cold chicken, cold pickled pork, some cold riesling, followed by some pudding like home-churned ice cream.

It was all a hideous mistake. To be honest, when it was over, I didn't feel replete.

Why Did Christ Do Everything in One Year?

As a child I was always puzzled by the Christian calendar. How did they whiz through Christ's life in no time at all.

Here he was born on Christmas Day, next minute you were suffering through Lent and he was dead by April. How long did he live? I didn't know, but it seemed to me he was at least 30.

So it should be 30 years before he was born again. Christmas we find is very hard on the nerves, unbelievably hard on one's Bankcard, Mastercard, cheque book. It would be lovely if we took it gently, and indeed it would be a marvellous climax if we did have it every 30 years.

As it is, Good Heavens, it seems only a few minutes since we had the last one. Actually Christmas really is like sailing a yacht around the world on your own, through storm heat and tempest...

It's lovely when you finally get there.

And oddly enough, when people say Christmas is too commercial, I don't mind that. The Christmas carols in the super markets beat the hell out of the garbage they usually play. The windows in Myer are very nearly the best thing that happens all the year round and I was enchanted by the real live choir singing in Georges. It was almost worth the awful prices they charge.

Could one, as an old hand with many Christmas campaign medals, offer a few thoughts?

You know you have left your shopping too late when all the shop assistants are down the back having their party.

I know it is a very hard time to be a turkey. But I am very grateful for what turkeys do for mankind, ah, peoplekind. Don't go for this modern lark of cold meat and salad for Christmas dinner. My rule is if you don't get hot turkey, cranberry sauce, and plum pudding on Christmas Day you don't get it any other day either.

Have you noticed they are selling legless turkeys this year? It's like offering a Monroe or a Bardot with a 24-24-24 figure.

At our place we gather all the children, all the grandchildren together and have a Christmas breakfast. We sit around the Christmas tree and open the presents together. It is the one time of the year when we really revel in a mess. The most beautiful mess, you will ever see is all the junk on the living room after they have opened their presents. It's nice to leave it there as decoration all day.

Inevitably, somebody loses some present then later you have to go out, sift through the garbage to find the piece of toy, which was under the living room chair all the time.

And apart from being the happiest time it is always the saddest. The let down can come, say, at four or five in the afternoon. Memories flood back of those people who are not present, the wonderful people with whom you once shared Christmas.

Then the older you get the more complex it becomes in bringing everyone together. When your children have grown up and are married there is the subtle diplomacy, do the children come to you or do they go to the in-laws. Mother cooks the dinner just the same and you know what invariably happens; lucky children get two Christmas dinners.

The parents prayer, that the kids won't receive too many build-it kits too complicated for your tired brain to handle; that they won't receive too many shrieking video games; that the toys will last three days without breaking down and there won't be too many gadgets that require batteries.

The hardest thing? Fitting the toys back into the boxes they arrived in.

And another hard thing. Remembering which present came from which aunty, which grandmother and getting them to say thank-you.

Some time, perhaps around 8 p.m. tomorrow, you will make two noble resolutions. (a) You will carefully fold up all the Christmas wrapping and save it for next year. (b) You will avoid all the last minute shopping for Christmas 1991. Instead of paying last minute absurd prices you will buy early, you will even get your 1991 presents at the January sales. (c) You will be absolutely brilliant with your Christmas cards. Instead of going broke with airmail prices you will send out your overseas cards in mid-October.

You won't, of course. In 1991 you will be in exactly the same muddle as this year.

If there are any electric trains or rail vehicles in the Christmas stockings, fondle them kindly. They are sure to be infinitely more reliable than the Melbourne public transport system.

You think you are having a hard time. The worst job would be working in a department store later this week taking back all those presents people didn't want on Christmas Day.

Have a Happy time.